Small Christian Communities and the Parish

Small Christian Communities and the Parish

An Ecclesiological Analysis of the North American Experience

John Paul Vandenakker

Sheed & Ward

Sheed & Ward™ is a service of The National Catholic Reporter Publishing Company.

Library of Congress Card Catalog Number: 94-69588

ISBN: 1-55612-709-X

Published by: Sheed & Ward
              115 E. Armour Blvd.
              P.O. Box 419492
              Kansas City, MO 64141

To order, call: (800) 333-7373

Contents

Chapter Two
Vatican II and the Parish

PART TWO: SMALL CHRISTIAN COMMUNITIES

Chapter Four
The Emergence of Small Christian Communities

PART THREE: ECCLESIOLOGICAL ANALYSIS

Chapter Six
Small Christian Community and the Magisterium

Chapter Seven
An Evaluation of the Ecclesiality of North American
Parish-Based SCCs

Acknowledgements

This dissertation was prepared under the supervision of Professor William Henn, O.F.M. Cap. His invaluable insights, scholarly supervision, and gracious encouragement are greatly appreciated. I would like to record my heartfelt gratitude for his unfailing patience and wise counsel during the entire course of my work at the Pontifical Gregorian University.

My special thanks to the priests, sisters, and staff of the Pontifical Canadian College, particularly to the Rector, Reverend Marcel Lagacé, P.S.S., and the Vice-Rector, Reverend Guy Piquette, P.S.S., for helping make my stay in Rome a pleasant and productive one.

As well, I would like to thank the entire diocesan church of Ottawa, Ontario, Canada, and especially Archbishop Marcel Gervais, who has supported my research and enabled me to complete this present study. To the church of Ottawa I owe my sincere gratitude.

Finally, I would like to thank both of my "families" back home in Ottawa: my community, the Companions of the Cross, in particular Reverend Bob Bedard, mentor and friend; and my natural family, in particular my parents Henk and Diny Vandenakker. Both these communities have shown me much love and have helped to instruct me in the ways of faith. May the Lord bless them and everyone who is involved with the work of fostering genuine Christian community in all of its manifold forms in the church today.

Abbreviations

1. Conciliar and Papal Documents

AA - *Apostolicam Actuositatem*: Vatican II, Decree on the Apostolate of the Laity

AG - *Ad Gentes*: Vatican II, Decree on the Church's Missionary Activity

AS - *Acta Synodalis Sacrosancti Concilii Oecumenici Vaticani II* Vatican City, 1970 ff.

ChL - *Christifideles Laici*: John Paul II, Apostolic Exhortation on the Vocation and Mission of the Lay Faithful in the Church and in the World

CT - *Catechesi Tradendae*: John Paul II, Apostolic Exhortation on Catechesis in Our Time

EN - *Evangelii Nuntiandi*: Paul VI, Apostolic Exhortation on Evangelization in the Modern World

FC - *Familiaris Consortio*: John Paul II, Apostolic Exhortation on Role of the Family in the Modern World

GS - *Gaudium et Spes*: Vatican II, Pastoral Constitution on the Church in the Modern World

LG - *Lumen Gentium*: Vatican II, Dogmatic Constitution on the Church

OE - *Orientalium Ecclesiarum*: Vatican II, Decree on the Eastern Catholic Churches

PO - *Presbyterorum Ordinis*: Vatican II, Decree on the Ministry and Life of Priests

RM - *Redemptoris Missio*: John Paul II, Encyclical Letter on the Permanent Validity of the Church's Missionary Mandate

SC - *Sacrosanctum Concilium*: Vatican II, Constitution on the Sacred Liturgy

UR - *Unitatis Redintegratio*: Vatican II, Decree on Ecumenism

2. Other Abbreviations

AAS - *Acta Apostolica Sedis*

AFER - *African Ecclesial Review*, Eldoret (Kenya)

AMECEA - Association of Member Episcopal Conferences of Eastern Africa

BCC - Basic Christian Community

BEC - Basic Ecclesial Community

CCCB - Canadian Conference of Catholic Bishops

CDF - Congregation for the Doctrine of the Faith

CEB - *Comunidade Ecclesiale de Base*: Basic Ecclesial Community

CELAM - *Consejo Episcopal Latinoamericano*: Episcopal Conference of Latin American Bishops

CEV - *Communauté Ecclesiale Vivante*: Living Ecclesial Community

CIC - *Codex Iuris Canonici*: The Code of Canon Law

DS - Denzinger-Schönmetzer, *Enchiridion Symbolorum, Definitionism, Declarationum*, 34th edition, Herder, 1967.

ICC - Intentional Christian Community

NAFSCC - North American Forum for Small Christian Communities

NAPRC - National Alliance of Parishes Restructuring Into Communities

NCCB - National Conference of Catholic Bishops (U.S.A.)

NFPC - National Federation of Priests' Councils

NRSV - New Revised Standard Version of the Bible (with Apocrypha), Oxford University Press, 1989.

PG - *Patrologiae Cursus Completus, Series Graeca*, ed. J.P. Migne, Paris, 1857 ff.

RCIA - Rite of Christian Initiation of Adults

SCC - Small Christian Community

SINE - Systematic Integral New Evangelization

Introduction

A. Background

In preparation for the 1987 Synod on the Laity, the U.S. National Conference of Catholic Bishops (NCCB) consulted over 200,000 people in an effort to find out what some of the major concerns of the laity were in the United States. Archbishop John May of St. Louis, then president of the NCCB, presented the fruit of this consultation in his official address to the Synod. In this address he observed that when people talk about where God is present in their lives, "the primary place they identify is the family. Next is the parish."[1] He went on to state that "parishes represent the first and often the most crucial experience individuals have of the church. The diocesan and the universal church is realized for most Catholics in the parish."[2]

In reflecting on various aspects of U.S. parish life, Archbishop May noted that many of the lay people who participated in the consultation drew attention to the growing proliferation of "small communities" in the parish as being a very positive development. Many saw such small communities as being a vital means for helping them to deepen their faith and enabling them to realize the mission of the church in the world. He comments:

> These communities provide the ongoing formation of the laity in prayer, Scripture study, life sharing and out-reach to the needs of society. Our laity seek this community experience within, or at least along with, their regular parish experience. Since most of our parishes, especially in cities, are large, such small groups are more and more necessary for productive Catholic life.[3]

In his conclusion, Archbishop May proposed three questions to the Synod for further discussion. One of these dealt with small communities. He asked about how best to help nurture in these small communities a true sense

---

[1] Archbishop John May, "Parishes in the Laity's Life," *Origins* 17/20 (1987), p. 354.
[2] *Ibid.*
[3] *Ibid.*, p. 355.

of the diocesan and universal church.[4] The reason for this question had to do with a concern which some bishops had expressed regarding the need for better integration of these small communities into the life of the parish and the local church.

While the Synod did indeed take up this question and many other matters in its discussions, and addressed many of these issues in its final report, there still remains a great need for ongoing theological reflection in this whole area. In a nutshell, the aim of this thesis is to explore the "ecclesiality" of one particular type of small community which has been recently impacting on the life and mission of the North American parish church: the small Christian community or SCC.[5]

B. Nature and Scope of Thesis

Small Christian communities (SCCs) are an ecclesiological phenomenon of major theological, pastoral, and institutional import.[6] They have sprung up literally around the world in the postconciliar church. They have proven to be, for the most part, an effective means of both personal and ecclesial renewal. They have been hailed as "a new way of being church."[7] As such, many people see them as representing a new paradigm for local ecclesial organization.

But this new paradigm or way of being church has not been without its problems. Some SCCs exhibit a strong tendency to promote their own autonomy within the church at large. This has led to accusations that certain SCCs are trying to operate as a kind of "parallel church."[8] While this kind of thinking prevails in a small sector of the SCC movement, it has never been indicative of the majority. Most SCCs desire to be part and

---

[4] *Ibid.*, p. 356.

[5] The term "ecclesiality" can be simply defined as the quality of belonging to, and expressing something of the nature of, what it means to be the church. A more detailed explanation of the meaning of ecclesiality, as it applies to SCCs in particular, will be the focus of chapter seven, part I, sections A and B.

[6] This phenomenon goes by many different names in various regions of the world (i.e. basic Christian community, basic ecclesial community, living ecclesial community, and so forth). These different names are explained in greater detail in chapter four, part I, under the heading of "The Many Faces and Names of Small Christian Communities." The term *small Christian community* (SCC) is what is most commonly used in North America at this time, and thus it is the term which predominates in this thesis. However, in the interests of accuracy, other terms such as BCCs, BECs, CEBs, and so forth, will be also used when appropriate.

[7] See the proceedings of the Seventh Ordinary Meeting of the Permanent Council of the National Conference of Brazilian Bishops, *As Comunidades Eclesiais de Base na Igreja do Brazil* (San Paolo: Ed. Paulinas, 1982), Doc. # 25, p. 5.

[8] Cf. Jeanne Gallo, *Basic Ecclesial Communities: A New Form of Organizational Response to the World Today* (Boston University: Doctoral Dissertation, 1989), p. 440.

parcel of the local/universal church. Because of this they have been welcomed and promoted by numerous bishops and episcopal conferences worldwide. Paul VI referred to them as "a great hope for the universal Church" and John Paul II has called them "a sign of vitality within the Church, an instrument of formation and evangelization, and a solid starting point for a new society based on a 'civilization of love'."[9]

Therefore, the question of their pastoral legitimacy, provided they fully adhere to the church, is no longer an issue. Neither is the fear that they are just a passing fad. Yet other issues pertaining to the task of how to understand better the ecclesiological implications of their role in the parish and local church still remain to be further clarified.[10] This is to be expected from a phenomenon which has made its appearance in the church only relatively recently and is still in the process of evolving. It also makes any attempt at evaluating their ecclesiological significance a real challenge.

Further complicating matters is the fact that SCCs, while sharing certain fundamental characteristics, also give evidence of great diversity. There is even a problem distinguishing between *small groups* in general, and those calling themselves specifically *small Christian communities*. SCCs see themselves as not being simply a prayer group, a Scripture study group, or a support group. What differentiates SCCs from the wider category of small groups and small group programs is not so much their function, but their self-perception of "being church." To what extent this thinking is legitimate will also be addressed in this thesis. This then is just one of the issues needing further theological clarification.

Many studies have been done on the Latin American, African, Asian, and even European manifestations of SCCs. However, there has yet to appear a comprehensive study of North American SCCs.[11] A good portion of the originality of this thesis involves a systematic presentation and exploration of the North American experience of parish-based SCCs. Before listing the particular programs/organizations which represent the major initiatives in this field (and which have thus been chosen for further study), it is first necessary to explain what is meant by restricting the scope of this thesis to "parish-based" SCCs.

The general dynamic of small groups has been utilized successfully by many lay movements and associations in the church today. For instance Cursillo *Fourth Day Reunion* groups, Charismatic Renewal *Share* groups,

---

[9] Cf. Paul VI, *Evangelii Nuntiandi* #58, and John Paul II, *Redemptoris Missio* #51.

[10] For instance Karl Rahner predicted SCCs would play a major role in the church of the future. But he also noted that the links between SCCs and the wider church would need ongoing juridical and theological clarification. Cf. Rahner, *The Shape of the Church to Come* (New York: Seabury Press, 1974), pp. 108-118.

[11] For the purpose of this thesis "North America" designates the United States and Canada.

Christian Life Communities, and so forth, each in their own way also promote a more personally focused experience of Christian community and discipleship which mirrors that of an SCC. Some of these movements have even established full-fledged residential communities. A fundamental difference however is that many of these types of lay communities are focused primarily on the life and organization of their particular *movement* or *association*, whereas SCCs are more clearly connected to a particular parish setting. This is not to imply that these lay movements and associations are somehow ecclesially deficient, or that they do not contribute in their own way to parish renewal. It is only meant to differentiate them from those SCC programs/organizations which focus specifically on the parish.[12]

Why concentrate then on "parish-based" SCCs? It is because in the opinion of many of their proponents, the goal of parish-based SCCs is not simply to be a worthwhile "small group," but to fundamentally reconstitute what it means for ordinary Catholics to participate in, and belong to, a parish assembly of believing Christians. They are claiming to challenge and alter the way and means by which the parish carries out its vocation and mission in the church. Hence the reason for speaking in revolutionary terms about "a new way of being church."

This is the why there is a need for greater theological analysis of the ecclesiological issues and concerns which these kinds of SCCs are claiming to raise. For instance, what exactly are the elements of "being church" which they see SCCs as helping to mediate in the parish community? What is the ecclesiological significance of their role? Are they deserving of some kind of recognition or status as a newly identifiable "unit" of the church because of this role? What does it mean to speak of the parish as being a "community of communities"? These are just some of the important questions and issues which are being discussed today by SCC groups and other commentators in the field.

Many of these questions are rooted in the more fundamental issue of what it means to be the parish and to be a part of the local diocesan church. Therefore, there is a need to thoroughly examine and evaluate the ecclesiality of SCCs in the light of Vatican II's understanding of the nature of the church. As well, the institution of the parish needs further scrutiny so as to better situate and evaluate the claims SCCs are making as to its regeneration. Without some awareness of the historical and cultural factors which helped shape the institution of the parish down through the ages, and

[12] The differences between lay movement/association communities and those of parish-based SCCs will be explored more fully in chapter four, part III, section B, under the heading of "A Typological Classification of North American SCCs."

in its North American setting, a proper appreciation of the impact SCCs are said to be having in this region of the world cannot be properly appreciated.[13]

By reflecting on the experience of SCCs, especially in their North American setting, it is hoped that new insight into these matters may be attained. While the North American experience of SCCs has much in common with what is found in other regions of the world, it has also developed its own particular approach and has generated its own theological reflection as well. This is only natural given the different historical and cultural factors which have helped shape the church in this region. What is particularly noteworthy and of significance to the study at hand is the importance of the parish institution to the sustenance of North American Catholicism.[14]

This in turn has helped give rise to an impressive degree of vitality and creativity in parish-based experiments with SCCs. For unlike certain other regions of the world where SCCs have been mandated and coordinated by the hierarchy as part of an overall pastoral plan (such as the African AMECEA countries), no such general strategy exists for North America (with the exception of the NCCB's official plan for Hispanic ministry). Thus, there is no central supervising or coordinating body in place to help steer the course of SCC development. Instead, in true frontier-like fashion, a multitude of SCC programs and organizations have emerged attempting to pioneer the concept. This gives rise to the necessity of choosing not one but several programs/organizations in order to arrive at a representative picture of SCC development in North America.

The seven SCC programs/organizations which will be studied for this purpose are as follows:

---

[13] The "lowly parish" has often been neglected by theologians as a subject unworthy of serious ecclesiological reflection until relatively recently. Cf. Sabbas Kilian, *Theological Models for the Parish* (New York: Alba House, 1977), p. vii.

[14] Cardinal Luis Martínez Aponte of San Juan, Puerto Rico, observes:

> The immense vitality of the Church in the U.S. has depended largely on the strength of its parish life. Indeed, the parish is the heart of American Catholicism. The tradition of Latin America has not been the same due largely to the fact Catholicism is not a minority religion. In the U.S. it has been the parishes that traditionally held together, educated, and sustained the Catholic identity in a non-Catholic environment. Not having this particular concern, Latin Americans are generally less attached to the parish structure.

Cited by Allan Deck in *The Second Wave: Hispanic Ministry and the Evangelization of Cultures* (New York/Mahwah: Paulist Press, 1989), p. 58.

1) Hispanic Ministry Initiatives[15]

2) *RENEW*

3) National Alliance of Parishes Restructuring into Communities (NAPRC)

4) St. Boniface Parish Cell System

5) Systematic Integral New Evangelization (SINE)

6) Buena Vista

7) North American Forum for Small Christian Cmmunities (NAFSCC)

While the above list is not an exhaustive one vis-à-vis all of the current parish-based SCC initiatives which are under way, they do collectively account for most of the efforts in this area. Although they are predominately American in origin, most have a presence in Canada as well. This is the reason for referring to this study as being "North American" in scope.

C. Method of Exposition

Each of the above listed SCC programs/organizations has produced its own literature outlining its particular vision of SCCs and the parish.[16] While most of this literature is of a pastoral nature, explaining the practical features of how to implement an SCC process, there is also a good deal of theological reflection. This latter kind of theological reflection will form the focus of this dissertation. The approach taken will be to analyze and evaluate the major ecclesiological issues which these particular programs/organizations have themselves identified and commented upon.

The author of this thesis has engaged in much fieldwork to research the current state of affairs vis-à-vis SCC development in North America. Many of the leaders of these SCC programs/organizations have been personally contacted in order to ascertain first-hand their viewpoints on some of the major ecclesiological issues arising. This research will

---

[15] This is not the name of a specific program/organization but of a general category that will be surveyed.

[16] When each of these selected SCC programs/organizations is scrutinized in greater detail in chapter five, the pertinent texts and statements will be reviewed. The literature specific to each program/organization will be listed in summary fashion in a "sources" footnote which precedes each section of this particular chapter. The entire body of this literature is also to be found in a special section of the bibliography which lists these sources along with other books and articles devoted to the North American SCC experience (cf. *Bibliography, Part Two: Small Christian Communities, Section II*).

complement the written material that is available.[17]

The aim of this thesis then is not to defend SCCs but to understand them. It is an attempt at gaining greater conceptual clarity of the nature of the North American experience, and an appreciation of its ecclesiological basis. There still exists a surprising amount of ignorance as to the state of affairs in North America vis-à-vis SCC development. For instance, one author in a recent book stated that North American SCCs were primarily "Hispanic entities."[18] As we shall see, SCCs are actually much more broadly established in the North American church than this characterization would indicate. Other authors have commented on the difficulty in getting good information about SCCs in North America.[19] This is partly due to the variety but also to the somewhat different character which North American SCCs display when compared to their counterparts in other regions of the world. Thus, a secondary aim of this thesis is to help fill this information gap.

It is important to reiterate the ecclesiological nature of this thesis investigation. It is not intended to be a work of pastoral reflection. What is being explored is what one author in the field has referred to as the "theological substrate" which underlies the process and vision of SCC development.[20] Because SCCs already exist as pastoral realities in many North American parish settings, the theological task is one of reflecting on their ecclesiological significance in an *a posteriori* fashion. This seems entirely legitimate from a methodological point of view given the fact that there has been much demand lately for ecclesiology to be more "praxis oriented" and open to the questions of our time.[21] A more systematic explanation of how this dissertation aims to proceed in achieving its task will be enunciated in the next section which deals with the content and structure of the presentation.

D. Content and Structure of Thesis Presentation

The dissertation is divided into three parts consisting of seven chapters. Part one has as its focus the parish, part two, the small Christian

---

[17] The addresses of these North American SCC program/organization offices are listed in the appendix.

[18] Cf. James O'Halloran, *Signs of Hope: Developing Small Christian Communities* (Maryknoll, N.Y.: Orbis Books, 1991), p. 6.

[19] Cf. Editor's Note, "Base Communities in the Church," *Pro Vita Mundi Bulletin* 81 (1980), p. 2.

[20] Cf. Marcello de Carvalho Azvedo, *Basic Ecclesial Communities in Brazil: The Challenge of a New Way of Being Church* (Washington: Georgetown University Press, 1987), p. 4.

[21] This is according to Walter Kasper, *Theology and Church* (London: SCM Press, 1989), p. 5.

community, and part three, an ecclesiological analysis of some of the important issues concerning the nature and role of SCCs in the parish and in the local church. Part one, consisting of three chapters, is largely introductory in character, and the topics treated therein will be handled in more of a summary fashion. But it is also essential for framing the terms of the discussion and analysis of SCCs which follows.

Chapter one examines the emergence of the parish system as an institution of the diocesan church. It begins with a brief look at the development of the early church, with attention being given to the nature of the early Christian communities. The "house churches" of Paul's missionary activity are specially scrutinized because of the many references made to them in the SCC literature. They are frequently appealed to as a model of what SCCs are trying to emulate in the parish church of today. A correct understanding of what constituted the ecclesiality of these house churches will be helpful later on when dealing with the task of evaluating the ecclesiality of parish-based SCCs.

After this analysis of the early church, a brief sketch will be made of the historical emergence and evolution of the parish from post-apostolic times, through the reforms of the Council of Trent, and up to the eve of Vatican II. Attention will be given to the reasons why the parish system as we know it today came into being. Mention will also be made of the variety of forms which it took on in different ages and in different cultural settings.

Finally in this first chapter, attention will be given to various efforts at rethinking the nature of the church and the role of the parish which were prominent in this century before the advent of Vatican II. Of particular importance here is the question of the "theological" identity or status of the parish. This was a question much debated at the time, especially between some leading figures in the Liturgical movement and some noted canonists and other theologians. The canonists claimed the parish was simply a juridical/sociological entity which derives its theological status entirely by virtue of its subsisting in the church at large. The liturgists and other theologians were not denying the essential link the parish has with the wider church. But they were arguing that the local assembly has a certain claim to call itself "church" as well. In certain ways this debate foreshadows the discussions taking place today vis-à-vis the question of the ecclesiality of SCCs in their relation to the parish/local church. Thus, taking note of some of this debate will be helpful later on, as well as serving as an effective bridge into the next chapter dealing with Vatican II.

Chapter two briefly deals with the nature of the church in contemporary Roman Catholic teaching. Special consideration is given to Vatican II and to some later theological reflection regarding the nature of the church portrayed in the Council documents. Vatican II is of supreme importance of course because it expressed in its documents the ecclesiology of the church for today. So some attention must be given to the major themes and images of the church it presents (focusing on *Lumen Gentium* and *Gaudium et Spes*). Again, this will be done in summary fashion in an effort to present the salient features of this ecclesiology which impact most directly on our understanding of the parish and SCCs today. As well, because the new Code of Canon embodies in its legislation a conception of parish, it too will be studied and briefly commented upon. This is being done in an attempt to discover to what degree this legislation reflects the renewed ecclesiology of Vatican II as it pertains to the parish.

Chapter three focuses on the parish as it exists in its North American setting. It is divided into three sections. The first section presents a brief historical overview of the development of parish life in North America, followed by a contemporary portrait of parish life today. One study in particular will be drawn upon for this latter task: the 1986 Notre Dame University study of parish life. This study is the largest and most comprehensive of its kind. The analysis is largely of a sociological nature, but it provides an important foundation for subsequent theological reflection. It is helpful for providing us with an accurate picture of the current state of parish life.

This will be followed in section two of this chapter by a brief look at the problems and challenges posed to parish life today by the cultural forces inherent in modernity and secularization. A major upshot of these developments is a need many people have articulated for more community in their lives as a way of preserving and strengthening their faith. The parish as currently configured does not seem always to be able to meet peoples' needs in this area. This also explains in part the success which many new movements in the church have had in gaining participants, and the strategy employed by various recent programs geared towards parish renewal. Some commentary on this seems in order so as to situate where and how SCCs fit into the overall picture of efforts aimed at parish renewal.

Chapter four begins part two of the thesis. It deals with the emergence of SCCs. It begins with an explanation of the various names by which SCCs are known by around the world (i.e. BECs, ICCs, BCCs). Next, it delves into a brief description of the nature of SCCs in several of these other regions, focusing on Latin America and Africa. Due to the influence of Latin America in particular on SCC development in North America and around the world, some awareness of the history and state of affairs of SCCs in this region is crucial for an understanding of the North American experience. It is also valuable to have some standard of comparison to measure North American SCCs by, so as to be able subsequently to note the nature of their particular contribution to this global phenomenon. Finally, a typological classification of SCCs in North America is outlined (movement-based, private association, and parish-based) so as to make clear the nature of the parish-based variety.

Chapter five will concern itself with an investigation of the emergence, characteristics, and ecclesiological reflection of seven major programs/organizations which are dedicated to promoting parish-based SCCs in North America at the present time. These are: *RENEW*; Buena Vista; National Alliance of Parishes Restructuring into Communities (NAPRC); St. Boniface Parish Cell System; North American Forum for Small Christian Communities (NAFSCC); Systematic Integral New Evangelization (SINE); and various Hispanic Ministry initiatives. In order to round out this survey, passing mention will also be made of certain other programs which promote SCCs. Finally, this chapter will conclude with a listing of the general features and ecclesial self-perception of these parish-based SCC programs/organizations so as to arrive at some kind of portrait of the North American experience.

Chapter six, which begins part three of the thesis, will afford a relatively brief look at how the Magisterium has responded to SCCs. Several papal and synodal statements which mention them will be examined in order to gain an understanding of how these documents deal with the issue of their ecclesiality. Certain "criteria of SCC ecclesiality" can be identified in these documents and utilized in our subsequent assessment of the North American phenomenon. This magisterial reflection forms an important part of the larger effort which is under way to understand the role of SCCs in the church. It also sets the stage for the final chapter which follows.

Chapter seven brings everything from previous chapters together in a systematic attempt to clarify and address the ecclesiological questions and issues which North American SCCs are raising, and to examine the appropriateness of some of their positions. The first section will recapitulate how the issue of North American SCC ecclesiality should be understood, and attempt to synthesize the various papal criteria of ecclesiality which are applicable in this assessment. Next, the SCC programs/organizations which have been examined in chapter five will be evaluated in the light of these criteria. Having ascertained the nature of SCC ecclesiality, it will be possible then to assess the contribution SCCs are making to the vocation, mission, and theology of the parish church. Of particular interest here will be the question of how to explain the ecclesiological significance of the parish-SCC relationship, and answer the question of whether or not parish-based SCCs should be recognized as constituting a new and bona fide "unit" of the parish/local church. A general conclusion will follow.

Part One: The Parish

CHAPTER ONE

The Early Church
and the Emergence of the Parish

I. THE ORIGIN AND EARLY DEVELOPMENT OF THE CHURCH[1]

A. Christ, Kingdom, Spirit, and Church.

The proclamation of the Kingdom of God plays a central role in the Synoptic Gospel accounts of the public ministry of Jesus.[2] Everywhere he went, Jesus is described as expounding upon the nature of this Kingdom (or Reign) of God through his preaching, teaching, and the many "signs and wonders" he worked. To aid him in this ministry he chose twelve apostles. In addition to these twelve apostles there were numerous other followers of Jesus known as disciples.

A question that arises for Scripture scholars is how to characterize the situation of those people who accepted Jesus' message during the period of his public ministry. Were they already the "church" in some embryonic form? If so, why is it that in all four Gospels the word *ekklēsia* appears on the lips of Jesus only twice?[3]

---

[1] Principal sources for this section are: Raymond E. Brown, "Church in the New Testament," in *The Jerome Biblical Commentary*, eds. Raymond E. Brown, Joseph A. Fitzmeyer, and Roland E. Murphy (London: Geoffrey Chapman, 1989), pp. 1339-1346; Raymond E. Brown, *The Churches the Apostles Left Behind* (New York: Paulist Press, 1984); Frederick J. Cwiekowski, *The Beginnings of the Church* (New York/Mahwah: Paulist Press, 1988); Michael A. Fahey, "Church," in *Systematic Theology, Vol. II*, eds. Francis Schüssler Fiorenza and John P. Galvin (Philadelphia: Fortress Press, 1991), pp. 3-74; Paul S. Minear, *Images of Church in the New Testament* (Philadelphia: Westminster Press, 1960); The Pontifical Biblical Commission, *Unity and Diversity in the Church* (Vatican City: Libreria Editrice Vaticana, 1991); and Rudolph Schnackenburg, *God's Rule and Kingdom* (New York: Herder and Herder, 1965).

[2] See for example: Mt 4:23; Mk 1:14-15; and Lk 4:43-44.

[3] Since Mt 18:17 clearly refers to the local community, only once is Jesus remembered to have spoken about the church in the larger sense: "Upon this rock I will build my church" (Mt 16:18). However, as Michael Fahey notes, "modern exegesis has shown that it may well be possible, indeed even likely, that the promise of *Matthew* 16:18 occurred after the resurrection and was retrojected by the gospel writers into the public ministry of Jesus." Fahey, "Church," p. 17.

3

One explanation of this somewhat minimal textual support for the idea of church in the Gospels is that Jesus' major concern during his public ministry was focused on trying to renew the faith of Israel, not on founding a separate church or religion.[4] If renewal was his original intent, then given the fact that Judaism already had in place its own religious practices and organizational structures, it is understandable that Jesus would not have needed to concern himself with making plans to replace them outright for his own followers.[5]

But scholars also point to the care which Jesus took in training the apostles and other disciples as teachers and evangelizers as being an indication that he always intended his message to have a perduring value.[6] In a similar fashion at the Last Supper, when Jesus instructs his disciples to "do this in remembrance of me" (Lk 22:19), a desire is implied for this community of disciples to continue on meeting after he is gone. It may well be true that Jesus had originally hoped that all of Israel would receive his message. But this does not rule out the likely possibility that towards the end of his public ministry, seeing the opposition he was encountering and knowing his end was near, he would have also envisioned and planned for a community of some kind to carry on his mission after he was gone.[7]

However, given the scriptural indications we have regarding the question of Jesus and the church, Raymond E. Brown thinks that the older "blueprint supposition," in which Jesus is seen as having clearly planned and laid out the church and its structure in the course of his public ministry, has little or no textual support. Thus, Brown concludes that the historical Jesus was "singularly silent on foundational or structural issues" vis-à-vis the church which would eventually come to bear his name.[8] It is all the more remarkable, therefore, that this lack of formal organization did not seem to impede the church's eventual emergence and development.

Because of the focus of this present study, the historical and theological arguments relative to Jesus' founding of the church need not

---

[4] Cf. Brown, "Church in the New Testament," p. 1340.

[5] As evidence of his original focus on Israel, scholars cite Mt 10:5-6, wherein Jesus instructs the twelve apostles to "go nowhere among the Gentiles, and enter no town of the Samaritans, but go rather to the lost sheep of the house of Israel." It is only after this mission has been definitively rejected, and after his resurrection, that Jesus is portrayed in Mt 28:19 as instructing his apostles to include the Gentiles in this mission. "Go therefore and make disciples of all nations, baptizing them in the name of the Father and of the Son and of the Holy Spirit."

[6] Fahey, "Church," p. 17.

[7] *Ibid.,* p. 18.

[8] Brown, "Church in the New Testament," p. 1340.

detain us here.[9] What is important is the incontestable fact that soon after Christ's death/resurrection his followers quickly became very community or church-minded.[10] In the light of the resurrection they saw more clearly that Jesus was indeed the Christ, the Son of God. They experienced his salvific grace and abiding presence through the ministry of the Holy Spirit. Because of this fact, Pentecost is often times associated with the "birthday" of the church.[11]

Although the early Christians living in Jerusalem still observed the Mosaic Law and continued to worship at the Temple, they soon developed other practices peculiar to their community life outside of this context. For instance, within a short time baptism became a standard feature of "Christian" faith practice. As a visible action it helped to designate those who belonged to this new "Way." Other features of this emerging sense of Christian *koinōnia* (community or communion) attested to in the *Acts of the Apostles* included: shared prayer, the breaking of bread, the teaching of the apostles, and the voluntary sharing of goods.[12] The early Christians understood this work to be in continuity with the will of the risen Christ. They carried on this activity with the conviction that the Holy Spirit was guiding and helping them. The ongoing guidance of the church by the Spirit is an activity which Christians have come to believe continues in every age.[13]

B. The Early Christian Communities

1. Some Aspects of *Ekklēsia* and *Koinōnia*

Ekklēsia (ἐκκλησία) is the word which was used in the Greek translation of the Old Testament (Septuagint) to translate the Hebrew word *qāhāl* (קהל). *Qāhāl* designated the entire assembly of Israel, which understood itself to have been called into existence and sustained by God.

---

[9] As a matter of Christian faith and belief it is certainly appropriate to speak of Jesus as having founded the church, and to see the church as having always been part of God's eternal plan, emanating from the divine life of the Trinity (cf. *Lumen Gentium* 1-5). The International Theological Commission affirms that "the Church has consistently held to the assertion not only that Jesus Christ is the Church's foundation (DS, 774) but also that he himself willed to found a church and did effectively so found one." Michael Sharkey, ed. "Select Themes of Ecclesiology on the Occasion of the Eighth Anniversary of the Closing of the Second Vatican Council," in *International Theological Commission: Texts and Documents* (San Francisco: Ignatius Press, 1989), p. 268.

[10] Brown, "Church in the New Testament," p. 1340.

[11] Cf. Fahey, "Church," p. 17.

[12] Cf. *Acts* 2:42-47.

[13] Cf. Michael Schmaus, *The Church: Its Origin and Structure, Dogma Vol. IV* (London: Sheed and Ward, 1972), p. 43.

It had a particular reference to the original assembling of Israel in the desert after the first Exodus.[14] Although it came to have a religious meaning when used as a translation for *qāhāl*, in secular Greek usage the word *ekklēsia* simply denoted any gathering of a group of people. Despite its absence from much of the Gospels, it is a term with which the early Christians came to designate their communities, and is frequently found in the rest of the New Testament. Paul, for example, uses it some sixty times in his letters alone.[15]

There was much activity going on in the early church as the Christian faith began to spread outward from Jerusalem. Many new communities were founded. These new communities often reflected a variety of different ecclesiologies and practices, depending on where and how they came into being.[16] We know that churches existed in Jerusalem, Antioch, Corinth, Rome, as well as in the regions of Judea, Galatia and Macedonia. At first these communities were predominately Jewish-Christian in composition and outlook. But as soon as Gentiles began being converted and received into the churches, more of them displayed a mixture of Jewish/Gentile-Christian membership, with some rapidly becoming predominately Gentile-Christian in composition.

The way in which *ekklēsia* is used in the NT also reflects a diversity of meanings. Sometimes it designates a certain place (i.e. a particular house church), other times it refers to a collection of churches in a given region, and still at other times it is applied to the church which exists in the entire world.[17] These distinctions may suggest to some that there was an emerging understanding of the universal/local nature of the church in place at the time, but such a conception would be anachronistic. It would be more accurate to describe the relations among various Christian communities as representing a "communion in diversity" in the early church at large.[18] Hence, "none of them claimed to be on its own the entire Church of God, but the entire Church was really present in each one of them."[19]

Besides the term *ekklēsia* there are other images and metaphors used in the NT to describe the church. For example: the sheepfold (Jn 10:1-

---

[14] Cf. Deut 23:2.

[15] Cf. Robert Banks, *Paul's Idea of Community* (Grand Rapids, Michigan: Eerdmans, 1980), p. 33.

[16] For a detailed discussion of this see Raymond E. Brown, *The Churches the Apostles Left Behind*. In his "Church in the New Testament" article Brown makes the point that this range of ecclesiologies represents a diversity, not a dichotomy, in the NT views of the church. Cf. p. 1346.

[17] See for example Rom 16:5, Gal 1:1, and Acts 8:3 respectively.

[18] For an excellent treatment of this theme, see the 1991 Pontifical Biblical Commission document *Unity and Diversity in the Church*.

[19] *Ibid.*, p. 34.

10); the vine (Jn 15:1-6); God's field, God's building (1 Cor 3:9); God's temple (1 Cor 3:16); the heavenly Jerusalem (Gal 4:26); the bride (Eph 5:23-32); a holy nation (1 Pet 2:9); and the body of Christ (1 Cor 12:12-27). Each of these metaphors highlights a particular feature or aspect of being church.[20] Many of them are relational images, and underline the *koinōnia* that the early Christians experienced with Christ and with one another.

2. Taking Note of Structural Development

We know that one of the earliest crises in the church was precipitated by the growing influx of Gentiles into it. This in turn raised all sorts of questions for the early Christians as to their identity and ecclesial practice. For instance, should Gentile converts be required to be circumcised or not (in effect making them Jews and holding them fully accountable to the Mosaic Law)? The meeting of the first "Council" of the church in Jerusalem, depicted in *Acts* 15, was called to address some of these issues. It was eventually decided that Gentile converts need not be circumcised nor beholding to the full prescriptions of the Law.

What these and other NT references indicate is that a clear distinction or separation between Judaism and Christianity was not yet in place. To most other Jews and Pagans these so-called Christians were initially considered as a sect of Judaism. It was not until after the destruction of Jerusalem in AD 70, and with Jewish Christians gradually no longer welcome in Jewish synagogues and no longer in the majority within the rapidly expanding church at large, that "Christianity" began to be treated more as a separate religion by the world at large.[21]

The meeting of this first Council underscores the pastoral authority which the apostles exercised in the early church. It is important to note that throughout the apostolic and post-apostolic period, much in the way of formal church leadership and ministry was in a state of considerable development. For instance, *Acts* 6 describes the selection and commissioning of the first so-called "deacons" in the church. This was a response to tensions that were evident between the Hellenists and the Hebrews at the time, and reflected the growing need for the various groups to have their own administrators. Commenting on this development Raymond Brown remarks: "while it is difficult to know whether *Acts* is historical in all these details, surely administrative structure emerged as an answer to problems like divisions and increased numbers—a development

---

[20] For an examination of how these images contribute to our understanding of New Testament ecclesiology see Paul S. Minear, *Images of Church in the New Testament*.

[21] Cf. Brown, "Church in the New Testament," p. 1344. The period 65-100 also marked the "great transition" in the church from Jewish to Gentile dominance.

that in NT thought was no contradiction to seeing such structure as part of God's guidance through the Spirit for the church in response to prayer (6:6)."[22]

The need for ongoing pastoral leadership and effective ecclesial organization was even more acutely felt once the apostles began to disappear from the scene and false teachers were becoming more problematic. The remedy for this was a more regularized church order, which the post-Pauline Pastorals (i.e. *Timothy* and *Titus*) make a central concern. *Presbyteroi* (presbyters, elders) are to be appointed in every town and they are to function as the *episkopos* (bishop, overseer, supervisor). They were seen as helping to ensure and preserve apostolic teaching and authority in the church.[23]

By the time of Ignatius of Antioch (c. AD 110) we see a more clearly delineated threefold ministry of bishop-presbyters-deacons take root in many places. He insisted that there was to be only one bishop for any given locale, and only he or his appointee was to celebrate the eucharist and to baptize.[24] Ignatius was also the first person known to have used the term "catholic" in referring to the church.[25] As a result of these post-apostolic developments, some scholars have referred to this period in the history of the church as representing the emergence of "early Catholicism."[26]

However, none of these developments were exactly the same from place to place. In many early communities leadership and ministry had been exercised by the apostles, and by those known simply as "prophets and teachers."[27] This earlier charismatic-type of church structure and leadership gradually evolved into the later bishop-priest-deacon paradigm.[28] But some communities seem to have displayed an initial reluctance in accepting this

---

[22] *Ibid.*, p. 1340.

[23] Cf. *Titus* 1:5-9.

[24] Cf. *Letter to the Smyrneans #8*, (PG 5, p. 851.)

[25] For an explanation of what the term "catholic" meant for Ignatius see: Piero Rossano, "La Chiesa è cattolica," in *Mysterium Salutis IV/I*, eds. J. Feiner and M. Löhrer (Brescia: Queriniana, 1972), pp. 578-579.

[26] Cf. K.L. Schmidt, "*Ekklēsia*" in *Theological Dictionary of the New Testament*, Abridged One Volume Edition, eds. Gerhard Kittel and Gerhard Friedrich (Grand Rapids, Michigan: Eerdmans, 1985), p. 401.

[27] Cf. 1 Cor 12:28.

[28] For an account of how this order arose in the early church see: Eduard Schweizer, *Church Order in the New Testament* (London: SCM Press, 1961). Schweizer is of the opinion that the development of this more official and formalized ministry and leadership in the early church represents something of a "loss" of the charismatic dimension in church at this time.

newer style of church order.[29] A small minority were openly hostile to it.[30] But it is interesting to note that those communities which rejected this more institutionalized form of church order disappeared completely in the course of the second century, or else fell victim to Christian Gnostic sects. Reflecting on this course of events Edward Schillebeeckx observes:

> In historical terms, it emerges from this situation that a community without a good, matter-of-fact pastoral institutionalization of its ministry . . . runs the risk of losing for good the apostolicity and thus ultimately the Christian character of its origin, inspiration, and orientation. . . . Ministry is connected with a special concern for the preservation of the Christian identity of the community in constantly changing circumstances. . . . [Thus,] ministry without charisma becomes starved and threatens to turn into a power institution; charisma without any institutionalization threatens to be volatized into fanaticism and pure subjectivity, quickly becoming the plaything of opposing forces, to the detriment of the apostolic communities.[31]

It can be said then that the New Testament depicts the early Christians in the process of both "being" and "becoming" church. And despite the evolutionary character of this growth in the early church's self-understanding, it is important to realize that Christian faith and practice always had a definite ecclesial dimension. From its beginning Christianity was an ecclesial reality, not just a personal affair. Reflecting on the theological significance of this, Karl Rahner has said that the church, as an expression of community and relationships, is not an accidental part of God's plan. It has something to do with the essence of Christianity because the social or interpersonal dimension of man has something to do with the essence of what it means to be human. Thus, the "personal" experience of grace that all believers have and the "ecclesial" nature of the church are not

---

[29] See for example the community depicted in *The Didache, or Teaching of the Twelve Apostles.* In *The Apostolic Fathers,* Vol. I of the Loeb Classic Library series, ed. K. Lake (New York: G.P. Putnam, 1919), pp. 9-121.

[30] For example, the author of the apocryphal work entitled *The Apocalypse of Peter* warns fellow gnostics of the opposition they can expect from church authorities. Cf. Pheme Perkins, "Apocrypha; Dead Sea Scrolls; Other Jewish Literature," in *The New Jerome Biblical Commentary,* p. 1068,

[31] Edward Schillebeeckx, *Ministry: Leadership in the Community of Jesus Christ* (New York: Crossroad, 1981), p. 24

opposed to each other, rather, they mutually condition one another.[32]

The communitarian nature of the early church is aptly illustrated in the life and mission of the so-called "house churches." For this reason, it is worthwhile to reflect more directly on this particular experience. This will be done briefly in the section that follows. A further reason for focusing on the house church phenomenon has to do with the many references made to them in the literature dealing with small Christian communities. They are often mentioned as being an experience of church that SCCs wish to emulate. Therefore, some knowledge of them, especially their composition and social setting, will help later on in understanding the community dynamic which is operative in SCCs.

C. A Closer Look: The House Churches of the Pauline Mission[33]

1. Composition and Social Setting

If one wanted to gain further insight as to the nature of the early Christian house churches, there is no better place to start than with the house churches of the Pauline mission. The reason is twofold. First, they represent the simplest form of this phenomenon. Second, it is Paul who gives us the most information about them.[34]

Paul's letters mention house churches (*oikon ekklēsia*) by name on several occasions. For example, there is the reference to the couple Aquila and Prisca, "together with the church in their house" in 1 Cor 16:19. In *Philemon*, Paul greets his "fellow worker Philemon and Apphia our sister and Archippus our fellow soldier, and the church in your house." In *Romans* there is again mention of the church that meets in the house of Aquila and Prisca (16:3-5). Also mentioned by name in this same chapter are several other Christian households or families, including "those who belong to the family of Aristobulus" and those "who belong to the family of Narcissus" (16:10-11). It is interesting to note that these other households or families are not referred to as being "churches." It does not seem to be the case then

---

[32] For a more detailed discussion of Rahner's thought on the ecclesial nature of Christianity, see chapter seven of his *Foundations of Christian Faith* (London: Darton, Longman & Todd, 1978), pp. 322-401.

[33] Additional sources for this section include: Rafael Aguirre, "Early Christian House Churches," *Theology Digest* 32/2 (1985), pp. 151-155; Robert Banks, *Paul's Idea of Community: The Early House Churches in Their Historical Setting* (Grand Rapids, Michigan: Eerdmans, 1980); Raymond E. Brown, *Biblical Exegesis and Church Doctrine* (New York/Mahwah: Paulist Press, 1985); Hans-Josef Klauck, "The House Church as Way of life," *Theology Digest* 30/2 (1982), pp. 153-157; and Gerd Theissen, *The Social Setting of Pauline Christianity* (Philadelphia: Fortress Press, 1982).

[34] This twofold reason is according to Raymond E. Brown, *Biblical Exegesis and Church Doctrine*, p. 119.

that every Christian household was automatically considered to be also a church per se. Otherwise, why would not Paul have greeted them in the same manner he greeted Aquila and Prisca earlier?[35]

The house churches of the Pauline mission usually included more than just immediate family members or servants. They would include others from the area who would come and attach themselves to the community that met there. Since many of the first Christians were members of the lower class, they would have relied upon some of the more wealthier members for houses big enough in which to meet. Due to the restrictions imposed by the size of the largest meeting room in these houses, many Scripture scholars believe that these house churches numbered no more than thirty to forty persons.[36]

The house of Gaius in Corinth seems to be a case in point. Paul refers to Gaius as being, "host to me and the whole church" (Rom 16:23). The house of Gaius was presumably large enough for the whole body of Corinthian Christians to gather there.[37] These assemblies were for the Service of the Word and for the Lord's Supper. Paul denounces the factionalism that seems to have marred some of these gatherings in 1 Cor 11. This is why in the next chapter he articulates the need for unity in the church by comparing all of its members to parts of the same body (1 Cor 12).

We do not know whether the house of Gaius was the only one being used for these purposes in Corinth at this time. There were presumably others as well. This may be indirectly indicated by Paul's criticism of the different cliques that were in existence there (1 Cor 1:12). In an interesting observation, Hans-Josef Klauck notes that this may be the earliest recorded mention of some friction existing between the "local" church taken as a whole, and various individual house churches of a given area.[38]

---

[35] The significance of this interpretation of *Rom* 16 is open to debate. Some see it as indicating that the smallest ecclesial unit in the wider church of that time was more than simply a Christian family household. At a minimum, a typical house church seems to have involved a number of other individuals and families who would meet in someone's house for the purpose of church activities. This is not to deny the relevance of later theological reflection which sees the family as being a kind of "domestic church." But in terms of understanding what a basic ecclesial unit was in the early church, the distinction between household and house church is important to remember. This distinction will be helpful later on in this thesis when it comes time to assess the claims some small Christian communities are making about "being church" in the parish/diocese of today.

[36] Cf. Aguirre, "Early Christian House Churches," p. 154; Banks, *Paul's Idea of Community*, p. 42; and Klauck, "The House-Church as Way of Life," p. 154.

[37] "Most commentators think Gaius was designated to care for Christians in transit, but *ekklēsia* as 'church universal' is rare in Paul. Gaius' house may instead have been the meeting-place of the entire local church in Corinth. This reading is supported by 1 Cor 14:23, which presumes such a gathering." Klauck, "The House-Church as Way of Life," p. 154.

[38] *Ibid.*

In the *Acts of the Apostles* it is often recorded that Paul would begin his missionary activity in a given place by first visiting the local Jewish synagogue and explaining the message of Christ to the people in light of the Scriptures.[39] More often than not he would eventually encounter stiff opposition and would not be welcomed back. But at least a few converts were usually made. These Jewish converts, in addition to other Gentile ones, would form the nucleus of the new Christian community in the area. This Christian community would then begin to meet on a regular basis in someone's home. The house church thus became a base for liturgy, catechesis, fellowship, and further mission.[40] These types of activities were not much different from those undertaken at Jewish synagogues at the time. The use of a house as a center for the church was thus a practical necessity, but also a natural one, given the importance of the family and of religious practices centered on the home in both Graeco-Roman and Jewish society.[41]

The relatively small size of these house churches, as well as their household setting, promoted a more personally focused experience of catechesis and discipleship. It would not have been difficult for the Christians of these house churches to get to know and support one another in a very direct and personal manner. There also seems to have been the opportunity for members to exercise their own personal charisms more freely in such a setting.[42] This kind of close-knit community helped the early Christians live out a life-style which was different from their contemporary pagan surroundings. Edward Schillebeeckx has thus characterized these early churches as representing "exodus communities."[43]

It is helpful to see the concept of community operative in early Christianity in general, and Paul, in particular, against the social and religious setting of the day.[44] At this time we witness a growing

---

[39] Cf. *Acts* 13:13-42; 14:1; 17:1-3; 18:4-5; and 19:8.

[40] Robert Banks states that Paul's strategy of preaching the Gospel and establishing house churches wherein this faith could be nourished and supported in the context of Christian community was the outcome of a deliberate policy on his part. For Paul, "to embrace the Gospel, then, is to enter into community." Banks, *Paul's Idea of Community*, p. 33.

[41] Cf. Klauck, "The House-Church as Way of Life," p. 156.

[42] In 1 *Cor* 12-14 Paul describes a variety of charisms, services, activities and other forms of ministry that believers share in for the sake of building up the local body of the church. Not everyone is an apostle, prophet, or teacher. But everyone has a role to play in being the church. Paul is also concerned that the exercise of spiritual gifts not be undertaken in a disordered fashion in the assemblies.

[43] Cf. Edward Schillebeeckx, *Christ: The Experience of Jesus Christ as Lord* (New York: Crossroad, 1981), pp. 544-561.

[44] For a detailed treatment of this topic see Robert Banks, *Paul's Idea of Community: The House Churches in Their Historical Setting*; and Gerd Theissen, *The Social Setting of Pauline Christianity*.

proliferation of clubs and associations in the ancient world, many of which were relatively small in size. Some of these had a religious character (i.e. the mystery cults), some a philosophical character (i.e. the Stoics), and still others were of a more general social type. These newer forms of community and association arose due to a need that was being experienced in the ancient world by many people for a more personal point of reference and for a deeper experience of community. The novel feature of these groups was their basis in something other than the *polis* (city/nation) or the *oikos* (home/family). They bound people together from different backgrounds on a basis different than that of geography, race, or natural ties. Their principle was *koinōnia* (i.e. a voluntary sharing or partnership).[45]

The presence, then, of different voluntary religious and social organizations in the ancient world during this period means that, from one point of view, there was nothing particulary novel about the appearance of Christian communities gathered in a household setting. In retrospect they can be seen as part of the wider movement towards the spontaneous association of individuals in society and as paralleling the development of the religious fellowships that were growing in popularity within Judaism and Hellenism during this period.[46]

An investigation of Paul's understanding of *ekklēsia* reveals that it was both in continuity and discontinuity with prevailing aspirations for community which existed in the ancient world at the time. It was a voluntary association, with regular gatherings of like-minded people. This feature it shares with the synagogue and mystery cults of the time. It had its roots in, and in some ways took on the character of, the household unit. Although Judaism had a strong basis in the family, and likewise many pagans regarded the family very highly, neither group organized its religious life around the household to quite the same degree as the early Christians did.[47]

Furthermore, these small local churches were invested with a strong sense of having both a temporal and a supra-temporal significance. This is brought out in the eschatological dimension of the church that is found in later Pauline thought (cf. *Colossians* and *Ephesians*). Here the notion is developed that Christians are members simultaneously of both an earthly and a heavenly community, with Christ at the head of both. Thus, when all of these different aspects inherent in Paul's conception and practice of Christian community are taken together and compared with what was happening at the time in Jewish and pagan circles, Robert Banks concludes

---

[45] Cf. Banks, *The House Churches in Their Historical Setting*, p. 17.

[46] *Ibid.*, p. 22.

[47] *Ibid.*, p. 49.

that Paul's understanding was "conceptually richer and more socially relevant than others advanced in his day."[48]

2. Implications for the SCCs of Today

We will examine in greater detail later the ecclesiality and role of small Christian communities in the parish/local church of today. However, at this point it is beneficial to take preliminary note of observations which some Scripture scholars have made vis-à-vis the appropriateness of SCCs appealing to the house church as a model for reorganizing Christian community. As evidence of this appeal, which is widespread in the literature, attention is drawn by way of example to an official joint statement which was issued at a recent international symposium on the topic. Therein it is stated that small Christian community has its roots in "very early Christian history when Households of Faith were the usual expression of ecclesial existence, and reconstructs the experience to address needs and longings, discouragement and hope, in a very complex and swiftly changing world."[49]

Was the house church the usual expression of ecclesial existence in the apostolic era? Although we have focused only on the house churches of the Pauline mission, there is little doubt that similar types of house churches existed in other settings as well.[50] As we have seen, using someone's home as a basis for liturgy, catechesis and fellowship was a practical necessity in much of the early church. In this sense, the house church was indeed a common organizational structure at the time. But it was probably not the only such structure or locus of ecclesial activity. There are many references to *ekklesia* in the NT, used in a local sense, which are not preceded by the word *oikon*. Does this mean these churches did not meet in homes? Not necessarily. We simply do not know much about how the local Christian community in many areas organized their meetings and activities.

But not all early Christian communities were necessarily small. We do know that some communities, especially in particular cities (i.e.

---

[48] *Ibid.*, p. 50.

[49] International Consultation on Basic Christian Community, *Final Report* (Notre Dame University, Indiana: Institute for Pastoral and Social Ministry, Dec. 8-12, 1991), [Mimeograph], p. 1.

[50] Raymond Brown refers to the existence of Johannine and other non-Pauline "house churches." He also points out that depending on who founded these communities there could have been a variety of them co-existing in relative isolation from one another in such larger cities as Antioch or Ephesus (due to differing christologies and approaches to the question of the Law). Cf. Brown, *Biblical Exegesis and Church Doctrine*, pp. 123-126.

Jerusalem, Antioch, Rome), grew to be quite large.[51] How they organized their internal activities at this time is really a matter of speculation. Certainly the eucharist, in some form, was celebrated on a regular basis. Was it celebrated in only one particular setting in these cities? If it was also celebrated in household settings, were these households considered to be house churches?[52] What was the connection between various households? Was the fundamental "unit" of the church seen as being the household or the broader local community?

Many of these questions may be anachronistic or else cannot be fully answered. One thing which seems clear from the biblical evidence is that house churches and other types of early Christian communities did not exist as isolated islands. Even when a given locale may have had only a single house church, they had frequent contact with other communities and with the wider church by means of hosting travelling missionaries, exchanging letters, aiding in each others financial relief, and so on. They also looked for doctrinal guidance to the tradition of the apostles and to the leaders of "apostolic" communities.

What this means then is that one must be wary of oversimplifying the perceived ecclesial status of house churches in the early church. This is why Robert Banks, in noting the way that reflection on the early house churches has been spurring the development of cell groups (or SCCs) within the traditional church structures of today, observes that many of these groups may lack a proper appreciation of the wider ecclesial "foundation" upon which the NT house churches were established and nourished.[53] For similar reasons Hans-Josef Klauck, in his article about house churches, likewise cautions that "this model may not be transferred without adaptation to the modern era."[54]

Another caution which is sounded is a warning to avoid the tendency to idealize the community experience of the early Christians. It should be remembered that many of Paul's reflections on community came as a response to the problems these early Christians were experiencing in trying to be church. These problems occurred in spite of, or even because of, the close-knit nature of the community. So although these smaller

---

[51] For instance in *Acts* the church in Jerusalem is depicted as growing rapidly in the apostolic era. Cf. *Acts* 2:47; 6:1,7.

[52] *Acts* 2:46 describes the Christians in Jerusalem as spending much time together in the Temple, yet also "breaking bread" in their own homes. Given the fact that the Jewish Passover meal and some other Jewish liturgical celebrations were centered in the home, would not the household have been a natural setting for Christian liturgical activity of this kind in the early church?

[53] Banks, *Paul's Idea of Community*, p. 41.

[54] Klauck, "The House-Church as Way of Life," p. 157.

communities seemed to lend themselves to a more participatory form of church membership, this did not diminish the necessary role of formal leadership in these communities. In fact, as we shall see in our next section dealing with the emergence of the parish, the local church in post-apostolic times came to have a strong episcopal identity. This development was seen as helping to preserve and ensure Christian *koinōnia* in the local church.

To be fair, most advocates of SCCs recognize and readily agree with these cautions. They do not want to glamorize small Christian community. Neither are they trying to argue, within a Catholic context at least, for a more "Congregational" approach to ecclesiology. They generally approve of and welcome the pastoral role exercised by bishops and priests in the local church. (Much of this will be made evident later.) What advocates of SCCs see in the phenomenon of NT house churches is a more personally focused and pastorally effective experience of Christian community. This is said to be a direct consequence of its small size and how it allowed for all members to be able to utilize their own personal charisms in the building up of the local ecclesial body. This style of close-knit community, coupled with the experience of discipleship it engenders, is what SCCs are seeking to emulate and help restore to the church of today.

II. THE HISTORICAL DEVELOPMENT OF THE PARISH[55]

In order to understand the present-day form of parish church community, it is worthwhile to summarize its history. This will be done by means of presenting a brief synopsis of the major developments which have impacted on the emergence and institutionalization of the parish. An appreciation of how it evolved, the shape it took in different cultures and eras, and how it was understood theologically, will help shed light on its vocation and mission in the local church. This information will be particularly helpful later in comprehending how today's small Christian communities see themselves functioning within the parish system.

A. The Etymology of "Parish"

A brief look at how the word "parish" originated and came to be understood in the church furnishes us with a good introduction to the development of the institution itself. Etymologically speaking, "parish" is

---

[55] Principal sources for this section are: Alex Blöchlinger, *The Modern Parish Community* (New York: P. J. Kenedy, 1965); W. Croce, "The History of the Parish," in *The Parish: From Theology to Practice*, ed. Hugo Rahner (Westminster, Maryland: The Newman Press, 1958), pp. 23-35; Casiano Floristan, *The Parish: Eucharistic Community* (London: Sheed and Ward, 1965); and Sabbas Kilian, *Theological Models for the Parish* (New York: Alba House, 1977).

derived from the Greek word *paroikía* ($\pi\alpha\rho o\iota\kappa\acute{\iota}\alpha$).[56] In Hellenistic usage, the verb *paroikéin* denoted the act of living beside or near. A *pároikos* was therefore a neighbor.[57] But it also came to be used as a synonym for someone who was a foreigner living in the land who had no rights to citizenship. When used in the OT (Septuagint) it had this latter connotation. Thus, Abraham is described as having been a foreigner (*pároikos*) during his sojourn in Egypt (Gen 12:10). A group of foreigners, such as Jacob's sons in Egypt, were designated a *paroikía*.

In the New Testament the term is used in this OT fashion. We are told, for example, that Christians are really "aliens and exiles" in this world (1 Pet 2:11). Not only individual believers but the community as a whole, as *ekklēsia*, is a type of *paroikía*. It is *ekklēsia* relative to God, but *paroikía* relative to the world. This is because the Christian has no citizenship papers for earth, since his permanent homeland is heaven (Heb 13:14).

It is important to realize that the meaning of this term in the NT is profoundly theological. Reference is being made to the state of the church in the world, which is likened to a colony of resident aliens. Its meaning then is theologically much richer than simply being an organizational designation for a part of the church. Thus, Casiano Floristan, in reflecting on this biblical meaning of *paroikía*, sees it as not only having been a crucial aspect of how the early Christians saw themselves as church, but as still being normative for our understanding of what parish is suppose to represent today.[58]

For a time in the early church the term *paroikía* was used interchangeably with *ekklēsia* as a designation for the Christian community in general. Gradually the term *paroikía* narrowed in scope as it began to be applied as a designation for individual communities.[59] But it still carried much of its biblical meaning. It was a very appropriate image for a persecuted minority sect struggling to survive in the Roman Empire. However, once the church ceased to be a persecuted minority and was granted legal recognition by the Emperor Constantine, and soon after made the official religion of the Empire towards the end of the fourth century, the situation of the church changed drastically. It had to adjust to this new reality. In this process of accomodation it was influenced by many existing Roman legal and organizational practices.

---

[56] Cf. K.L. and M.L. Schmidt, "*Pároikos/Paroikía/Paroikéō*" in *Theological Dictionary of the New Testament*, pp. 788-790.

[57] Note that *par-oikos* literally refers to someone who lives next to or beside a person's home/household (*oikos*).

[58] Cf. Floristan, *The Parish: Eucharistic Community*, p. 42.

[59] Cf. Blöchlinger, *The Modern Parish Community*, p. 25.

The Latin version of the word for parish became *paroecia*.[60] Alongside the term *paroecia*, the Roman administrative term *diocesis* was adopted into the language of the Western church. *Diocesis* had a juridical connotation in that its original reference was to the territory of a Roman civil province. In ecclesiastical usage, it came to designate the area under the jurisdiction of a bishop. From the fourth century onwards, *paroecia* and *diocesis* were used interchangeably for awhile. This led to a certain amount of confusion and to an eventual mutation in meaning. Gradually the term *diocesis* came to refer exclusively to the wider territory under a bishop, and *paroecia* to the specific communities under the care of priests which comprised this territory.[61] This development had the advantage of clarifying certain organizational features of the church. But in the process its meaning became more technical and juridical. Alex Blöchlinger laments that because of this, the original theological sense of parish became largely obscured. "From meaning the people and the community, the term came to mean almost exclusively the territory."[62]

B. An Historical Synopsis

1. From Post-Apostolic Times to the Fall of the Roman Empire

It is not an easy matter to trace the development of the early church from its post-apostolic setting. We have already commented on the diversity of these early Christian communities.[63] We have also noted that a more regularized church order which arose at this time was only gradually taking root. Furthermore, while our primary concern here is to outline the organizational shape the church came to take, with a particular eye on the parish institution, important developments in other areas of church life such as doctrine, liturgy, spirituality, and so forth, were also proceeding apace. We will not be focusing on these other developments, but it should be understood that all of these manifold aspects of church life, which always mutually condition one another, together constitute the life of the organism we call the church.

Christianity first took root in the cities and towns of the Roman Empire, and so it was initially an urban phenomenon. With the development of a more regularized church order each city and town with a Christian community came to be headed by a bishop. He was assisted by presbyters and deacons who usually lived with him. But the bishop was considered to

---

[60] This was rendered *parochia* in later Latin usage.

[61] Cf. Blöchlinger, *The Modern Parish Community*, pp. 28-29.

[62] *Ibid.*, p. 29.

[63] See part I, section B § 2, above.

be the overall pastor of the local community.[64] Initially, he alone is said to have presided over the celebration of the eucharist. The presbyters, deacons, and other local Christians would gather with him to participate in the celebration. The area under the care of the bishop was considered to be a single and undivided ecclesial unit. The idea of a diocese comprised of individual parishes did not yet exist. Thus, the fundamental identity of the local church was that of being an "episcopal" community.[65]

With the spread of Christianity into the countryside, and with growth taking place in the larger cities, it became increasingly difficult for all the Christians of a given locale to assemble together with the bishop for eucharist. In trying to deal with the situation in the countryside, the East adopted the solution of ordaining a multitude of rural bishops known as *chorepiscopi.*[66] In the regions of North Africa and elsewhere in the West, many rural bishops were likewise ordained to meet the need. In the East, these rural bishops were often subordinated to the bishop of the nearest city, who came to exercise a certain primacy in the area as a whole. But the practice of ordaining *chorepiscopi* began to disappear once a more developed notion of priesthood and parish came into practice.

In the larger cities there was a similar problem in having the entire community assemble in one place with the bishop. There were no large buildings which were used for the assemblies as of yet. Thus, in Rome, for example, Christians would gather in many private homes, which came to be known as "titular" churches because they were originally named after the owner of the house. These titular churches can be seen as being descendants of the early house churches in Rome.[67] The practice arose whereby the presbyters who lived with the bishop would go out to these titular churches and preside over the celebration of the eucharist in his name. As a sign of unity, a piece of the host consecrated by the bishop at the place he presided (the so-called *fermentum*) was carried by various deacons and acolytes to the various titular churches and was placed by the presbyter in the chalice during the eucharist there. In this way the local church in Rome helped retain the character of an episcopal community.[68]

It would be anachronistic to view these titular churches in Rome as somehow functioning as parishes in the modern sense. One reason for this is that they were not organized along any kind of formal territorial lines. Nevertheless, they were important centers for pastoral work. They continued

---

[64] Cf. Floristan, *The Parish: Eucharistic Community*, p. 46.

[65] Cf. Croce, "The History of the Parish," p. 9.

[66] Cf. Kilian, *Theological Models for the Parish*, p. 4.

[67] Cf. Croce, "History of the Parish," p. 10.

[68] Cf. Blöchlinger, *The Modern Parish Community*, p. 46.

to be so even with the advent of the great basilicas, which functioned mainly as places for worship. Thus, it is possible to see these titular churches, along with the rural communities of the first few centuries, as being forerunners of the diocesan parish system.[69]

It is important to realize from this historical survey that the parish as a pastoral reality existed before the parish as a formal ecclesial institution. What gave rise to the parish church was the need for the faithful to be able to participate more meaningfully in the life of the local church. As W. Croce observes, the significance of this development is that it indicates that "very early we find a certain decentralization in favor of pastoral care and the apostolate."[70] As we shall see later, this is the same kind of principle many proponents of small Christian communities invoke to justify their ecclesial role in the parish/diocesan church of today.

It was not until the fourth century that the practice of permanently stationing priests in distant villages of a diocese was introduced. This marks the beginning of the parish system in the modern sense of the term. This decentralization did not detract from the bishop's role as pastor of the diocesan church, nor from the faithful's perception of being an integral part of it. The bishop would make visits to these village churches, hold provincial synods, appoint pastors, mandate repair and construction of new buildings, and so forth. From the very beginning then, these outlying communities were under the direct pastoral care of the bishop, with the priests being fully accountable to him. This helped to keep intact the idea of diocesan church being a unified ecclesial entity.[71]

2. The Medieval Period

With the onset of the barbarian invasions and migrations in the fifth century, the old Roman Empire faded away. With its demise went much in the way of established political and social order in the Empire. This was to have a major impact on church organization and custom in the medieval period. Initially the barbarians destroyed many existing church buildings. However, relatively soon afterwards many of these largely Germanic tribes were converted to Christianity and many new churches were built. However, a problematic new development arose in that it was no longer the bishop alone, but also the king, the nobility, and the rich landowners who began to establish private churches, chapels, and oratories on their properties.

These kinds of feudal private churches became known as *Eigenkirche*.[72] In virtue of the so-called "private" nature of these

---

[69] *Ibid.*, p. 48.

[70] Croce, "History of the Parish," p. 11.

[71] *Ibid.*, p. 12.

Eigenkirche, direct supervision of these newer churches slipped out of the control of the bishop. The landowner arrogated to himself the right to administer it. He could sell it, give it away, or trade it as he desired. It was the landowner who also kept most of the tithes from the parish. In fact, many churches were built to create new sources of income. The landowner would also appoint his own choice for priest to be the pastor. Some of these priests were little better than mere hirelings who could be released and replaced like any other serf. It is not hard to imagine why this state of affairs soon became very detrimental to the pastoral care of people and to the unity of the church.[73]

The Church tried to overturn these practices, but the nature of the feudal system was such that many of them became too deeply entrenched. There were as well a whole host of other political and social forces at work at the time that militated against the suppression of *Eigenkirche.* The best the Church could do was build more churches on lands it directly controlled, decree that the faithful had to be baptized in its own "baptismal" churches, and lobby for more say in who got appointed to parishes outside its immediate jurisdiction. Attempts at reform, such as the Gregorian reform of the eleventh century, managed to eventually suppress the lay ownership and administration of churches. But as compensation many of the landowners (both lay and religious) were given the right to a certain percentage of the parish revenue. Thus, was born the medieval benefice system, a development which did not improve the pastoral welfare of the church.[74]

Not all of the abuses that crept into the church at this time, then, were the result of outside forces. The church must take its fair share of the blame for the increasingly miserable state of apostolic life in its parishes. One great abuse which was allowed to go unchecked for the longest while was the turning of parishes and dioceses into "benefices." This resulted in many patronage appointments. On the parish level, it resulted in the incorporation of parishes into single, larger entities, and militated against the establishment of more parishes in areas where the population was increasing. This was due to the fact that the larger the parish, the more income it brought in for the landowner, and the fewer the costs involved in paying for new buildings and more clergy.[75] It is little wonder that many voices began to be heard calling for radical reform. But many of these reforms would have to wait until after the Council of Trent.

---

[72] *Ibid.,* p. 13.

[73] *Ibid.,* p. 14.

[74] Cf. Blöchlinger, *The Modern Parish Community,* p. 66.

[75] Cf. Croce, "History of the Parish," p. 17.

The situation was not all bad during this era. The work of the new mendicant orders, such as the Franciscans and Dominicans, did much to help renew the faith and experience of church for many people. They established many oratories and new parishes. But their success brought a jealous reaction on the part of many secular clergy. Disputes arose as to parish boundaries and loss of income. Legislation was enacted stipulating that the faithful were welcome to attend missions and other services hosted by these orders, but had at the same time to fulfil their Sunday obligation in their local parish church. But even this measure did not end all the bickering. These disputes were to last for almost three centuries.[76] One result of these disputes was to further confuse the state of affairs that existed vis-à-vis parishes in the local church.

In reflecting on the significance of these medieval developments, it is worthwhile to quote some of Alex Blöchlinger's incisive observations at length. Many people hail this period of *Christendom* as being one of the great epochs in the history of the church. But what is sometimes forgotten is the manner in which many of the church's institutions became undermined as a result of its fusion with much of the secular culture of the day. Thus:

> The institution of the parish was so changed that it became itself almost a foreign body within the church. In the extreme forms we have the paradox that the *paroikía*, which should represent the church's exile in this world, became a place where the world had made itself at home in the church. . . . The parish community became less important than the profitable land of the parish property; the office was separated from ordination and was overshadowed by the benefice. . . . Because neither church nor parish could disassociate themselves from their worldly surroundings, the parish became untrue to its mission. Nevertheless, the authentic spark was never quite extinguished; though even today the foreign elements which largely gave the parish its enduring form are in some measure still present.[77]

3. Trent and the "Parish Principle"

The modern reorganization of the parish system came about gradually in the wake of the Council of Trent (1545-63). This council mandated many changes affecting the life and organization of the church.

---

[76] Cf. Floristan, *The Parish: Eucharistic Community*, p. 55.

[77] Blöchlinger, *The Modern Parish Community*, p. 78.

One of its principal aims was to renew and consolidate the role and ministry of bishops.[78] It was stressed once again that the bishop is the pastor of his diocese, and has as his primary responsibility the spiritual welfare of the people. To carry out this task effectively he was required to live in his diocese. An end was put to the practice of individual bishops sometimes being in charge of multiple dioceses. He was also to pay careful attention to the training of his clergy and establish seminaries for this purpose.

After the bishop, the parish priest was also responsible for the *cura animarum* ("care of souls"). He too was to live in his parish and engage in preaching and other apostolic activities on his parishioners' behalf. In order for the pastor to fulfil these duties the parish must be of a reasonable size and have clearly defined boundaries.[79] Dioceses were to be reorganized to ensure this was the case. An exception to the rule of clearly defined boundaries was made for so-called "personal" parishes. These included various types of military chaplaincies, parishes for national minorities, and parishes for those belonging to different rites.

The practice mandated by Trent by which the inhabitants of a defined territory were juridically attached to a parish, and compelled to receive the sacraments from their proper pastor, became known as the "parish principle."[80] This principle was to pass virtually intact into the 1918 Code of Canon law. It is important to realize that this principle did not derive from explicit theological considerations, but mainly from practical ones. Although this principle appears somewhat heavy-handed by today's standards, it was seen at the time as a means of ensuring that the laity got proper pastoral care. Thus, the somewhat juridical approach that was taken to the reform of the parish was designed to help clarify a confused state of affairs.[81]

The missing dimension in these reforms was the absence of any real biblical theology of church and appreciation of the role of the laity. The idea of a parish being a community in the biblical sense was not a feature of Trent's decrees. The main focus vis-à-vis the parish was on clarifying its boundaries and describing the duties of the pastor. The church at this time was largely understood in terms of being a visibly constituted "society" which was hierarchically ordered. Much of this language was invoked in reaction to certain Reformation ideas of the church. But the impact of this

---

[78] Cf. Floristan, *The Parish: Eucharistic Community*, p. 59.

[79] Cf. Croce, "The History of the Parish," p. 20.

[80] The pertinent passage conveying this parish principle can be found in H.J. Schroeder, *Canons and Decrees of the Council of Trent* (St. Louis, Missouri: B. Herder, 1960), Chapter 13, Session 24, p. 204.

[81] Cf. Kilian, *Theological Models for the Parish*, p. 5.

thinking, and of the clericalization of ministry in general, was to instill in the laity an evermore passive understanding of their role in the church.[82] The organizational status quo established by Trent was to hold sway in the church for a considerable period of time. It was not really until the twentieth century that the ecclesiological deficiencies inherent in Trent's treatment of the parish began to be seriously questioned.[83] Before turning to look at this renewal in ecclesiology that occurred, and the effect it had on understanding the significance of the parish, a final note must first be made of the social impact of the Industrial Revolution on this institution.

4. The Impact of the Industrial Revolution

The big cities and newly created industrial centers spawned by the Industrial Revolution attracted to them masses of workers who became often times socially dislocated and out of contact with the church.[84] In the countryside, where most people had always lived, the centre of village life had been the parish church. Its inhabitants had been baptized in its font, married before its altar, and buried in its graveyard. In these villages the parish priest knew his people and his parishioners knew him. Even in the established neighborhoods of cities before the onset of the Industrial Revolution, a similarly close-knit sense of community spirit existed.

But much of this changed with the population explosion and demographical shift from countryside to city which the Industrial Revolution helped create. While in the country the parish was still able, at least outwardly, to meet pastoral needs, in towns and industrial areas such pastoral care became increasingly difficult to effectively minister. Everywhere, urban parishes were growing beyond the capacities envisioned by the original demarcation of their boundaries.[85] In spite of the

---

[82] Cf. Blöchlinger, *The Modern Parish Community*, p. 92.

[83] Cf. Kilian, *Theological Models for the Parish*, p. 8.

[84] Cf. Blöchlinger, *The Modern Parish Community*, p. 100.

[85] Milan provides a telling example of this phenomenon. Dr. Hienrich Swoboda, a pioneer in religious sociology, compiled the following statistics on certain Milanese parishes:

Parish	Numbers in:			Number of places in church
	1800	1850	1900	
Francesca	1,600	3,600	43,000	2,500
Calvairate	2,600	2,720	20,000	4,500
S. Rocco	1,300	1,920	20,000	600
S. Gottardo	4,200	5,600	22,000	3,000
S. Pietro in Sala	2,000	5,120	32,000	1,000
Ss. Trinità	3,000	10,000	35,000	3,200

(Cited in Blöchlinger, *The Modern Parish Community*, p. 104.)

considerable changes that were wrought in the towns and cities as a result, there was no change in the basic structure of the parish. This is why Floristan states that, vis-à-vis the state of the parish in the 19th century, "never in all the history of the Church was the parish pastoral problem more critical than at the end of this century."[86] The Industrial Revolution was not the sole cause of the problems the church faced in trying to minister to people in this era. One must also factor into the equation the cumulative effects of the Enlightenment, the French Revolution, and other profound cultural, political, and philosophical changes which contributed in their own way to a growing erosion of faith and practice.[87] The culture of the modern era that was dawning was characterized by a "secular" mindset. The medieval synthesis of faith and culture had long since ruptured.

With the absence of a biblical sense of community in place, parish piety at this time was becoming excessively individualistic. It is not much of an exaggeration to say that the faith, instead of being celebrated communally, was being administered individually. The vitality of the parish was at low ebb.[88] But the communal spirit was not lost altogether. Into the void arose a host of new Catholic associations and sodalities which helped keep alive a more evangelical sense of community and a more active means of participating in the life of faith.

This in itself was not really new. Fraternities of one kind or another had flourished since the Middle Ages. But the success of these groups begged the question as to why this type of experience was not being actively inculcated in the parish as a whole. In large measure this was due both to a lack of renewed ecclesiology and pastoral vision, as well as to basic sociological constraints resulting from the sheer size of many urban and suburban parishes.

III. THE PARISH IN 20TH CENTURY PRECONCILIAR THEOLOGICAL REFLECTION

In the wake of the Council of Trent the conception of church as a *societas perfecta* (visible/complete entity) became a dominant feature of Roman Catholic ecclesiology. This stress was intended to counter certain Reformation claims about the nature of the church, and also to defend its independence from the state. The sources for this "society" analogy were not

---

[86] Floristan, *The Parish: Eucharistic Community*, p. 65.

[87] The impact of these other developments on modernity and secularization, which have been just as significant as those of
industrialization and massive urbanization, will be examined later when the North American situation vis à vis the church and faith practice is briefly examined in chapter three, part II.

[88] Cf. Blöchlinger, *The Modern Parish Community*, p. 66.

drawn from biblical texts but from the civil realm, and the terminology which was used to express and defend this image was highly juridical. One result of this emphasis was that the pneumatological dimension inherent in being the church was neglected in the official ecclesiology of this period.[89]

It was thanks to the articulation of a more "spiritual" understanding of church by such people as Johann Möhler, the Tübingen school, and others in the 19th century, that helped bring more balance and renewal to Roman Catholic ecclesiology.[90] Their work in re-emphasizing the idea of church as being the "Mystical Body of Christ," together with Emile Mersch's later contribution to this line of thought, was eventually to receive official approbation in Pius XII's 1943 encyclical *Mystici Corporis*.[91]

Other efforts begun around the turn of the century in scriptural, patristic, and liturgical studies, also contributed greatly to a renewed appreciation of the nature of the early church. The Lay Apostolate movement of this time gave rise to a new era of lay involvement in the church. All of these influences were to make themselves felt on the way the parish was being looked at in theory and practice.

A. The "Ecclesiola" Debate[92]

Of special interest for the parish is a discussion which first arose in the 1920s, especially among proponents of the Liturgical Movement, as to the theological nature of the parish community. This was largely a "new" question for its time. Discussion about it was to engender a subsequent debate on this matter among a wider audience of theologians and canonists. This debate casts much light on the changes in ecclesiological thought that were occurring then. It also represents the first modern efforts to articulate a "theology of parish."

In a 1925 article on the nature of the parish, Athanasius Wintersig called into question the theological adequacy of expressing its reality in exclusively juridical-sociological terms, as had been the custom. He maintained that the parish should be seen from a theological perspective as being an integral part of the Body of Christ. The parish is not church in and of itself, but is nonetheless, "an integral cell which reflects and unites in a

---

[89] Cf. Fahey, "Church," p. 32.

[90] Möhler's *Die Einheit in der Kirche oder das Prinzip des Katholizismus*, originally published in 1825, has become a classic text in ecclesiology.

[91] Cf. Emile Mersch, *The Whole Christ: The Historical Development of the Doctrine of the Body of Christ* (Milwaukee: Bruce, 1938).

[92] Details of this debate are taken largely from the following sources: Blöchlinger, *The Modern Parish Community*, pp. 120-132; Floristan, *The Parish: Eucharistic Community*, pp. 91-98; and Kilian, *Theological Models of the Parish*, pp. 21-24.

microorganism the life of all the Body of Christ, which is the Church."[93] Wintersig further grounds this idea in the nature of parish eucharist. As a consequence, the parish is of vital importance because it is there that the church becomes "concrete" for the Christian.

Following Wintersig's explanation of parish as being a "cell" of the church, other liturgists such as Pius Parsch were to give expression to the related concept of parish as representing "the church in miniature."[94] Further reflection on this idea would lead Maurice Schurr to state that the parish is as much a supernatural reality as the wider church. It is in effect a "little church" within the wider church, an *"Ecclesiola in Ecclesia."*[95]

The first negative reaction to this *"ecclesiola"* thesis came from the noted canonist Oswald von Nell-Breuning. He considered it to be "extremely dangerous."[96] But his opposition was not so much theological, as canonical. Basing himself on the conception of parish found in the 1918 Code of Canon Law, he declared it was inappropriate to describe it in terms of being a "community" since the Code had not used this terminology. The parish is simply a means of organizing pastoral care in the church. Its origin is of a *de jure humano* nature, and not *de jure divino*. As such, its basic identity is that of an administrative unit of the diocese, and so is not a proper object of theology.

The general reaction to von Nell-Breuning's critique was very negative. It was seen as being unilaterally juridical. This in itself was significant because it pointed to the success that the liturgical thinkers had already achieved in changing people's awareness of the parish. In the words of J. Homeyer, it indicated that "the awareness of the parish as a community in faith, worship, and love had really found its way back into Catholic Consciousness."[97]

Despite the rejection of von Nell-Breuning's juridically-based critique of the *ecclesiola* thesis, there were others who took exception to it on theological grounds. For instance, L. Siemar forcefully declared that, "a diocese, and much less a parish, is not the Christ that mysteriously survives,

---

[93] A. Wintersig, "Pfarrei und Mysterium," *Jahrbuch für Liturgie-Wisenschaft* 5 (1925), pp.136-143. French Translation: "Le réalisme mystique de la paroisse," *La Maison Dieu* 8 (1936), pp. 15-27. Quote taken from p. 16 of the French Translation.

[94] P. Parsch, "Die Pfarrei als Mysterium," in *Die Lebendige Pfarrgemeinde* (The Vienna Congress of 1933: Seelsorger-Sonderheft, 1934), p. 14.

[95] M. Schurr, "Die Uebernatürliche Wirklichkeit der Pfarrei," *Benediktinische Monatsschrift* 19 (1937), p. 89.

[96] O. von Nell-Breuning, "Pfarrgemeinde, Pfarrfamilie, Pfarrprinzip," *Trier Theologische Zeitschrift* 56 (1947), p. 258.

[97] J. Homeyer, "The Renewal of the Parish," in *The Parish: From Theology to Practice*, ed. Hugo Rahner (Westminster, Maryland: The Newman Press, 1958), p. 128.

since only in the overall Church does the Lord go on living mysteriously with full strength. Therefore, to consider the parish as *ecclesiola* is not only disconcerting but false."[98] What Siemar and others reacted to in the *ecclesiola* thesis was the thinking that what was true of the whole must be true of the parts. This fallacious reasoning was seen as dangerous by many theologians because it tended to accord a certain independence to the ecclesiality of the parish. It was not sufficiently balanced with the idea of parish deriving its fundamental identity from being a part of both the diocesan and universal church.

F.X. Arnold attempted a more balanced explanation. He nuanced the question by saying that whatever can be validly said of the diocese and universal church vis-à-vis their intrinsic ecclesial character, can also be applied to the parish *"per modem participationis."*[99] This is because the parish, as well as the larger church, participates in the fullness of the Spirit which Christ gave to the church. But Arnold was careful to add that the manner of this participation was always subordinate to, and dependent on, the wider church.

Thus, during the 1930s, 40s, and 50s, there were many significant contributions to this subject, especially among German theologians. It was generally recognized that further refinements would be needed to counter the well-meaning, but exaggerated position which the *ecclesiola* thesis represented. Nevertheless, this discussion helped forge the beginnings of a new and more comprehensive theology of parish. Two very important and influential contributors to this effort were to be Yves Congar and Karl Rahner.[100] We will turn momentarily and briefly examine their thoughts on the matter.

But before doing so, mention should be made of how many features of this *ecclesiola* debate are reflected in the discussion going on today vis-à-vis the ecclesiality of small Christian communities in the church. Even the same terminology of cells, church in miniature, little churches, and so forth, is sometimes invoked by the proponents of SCCs to describe their ecclesiality.[101] This is why an appreciation of the background wherein this

---

[98] L. Siemar, "Pfarrgemeinde und *Ecclesiola*," in *Die Neue Ordnung* 3 (1949), p. 44.

[99] F.X. Arnold, *Glaubensverkündigung und Glaubensgemeinschaft*, (Düsseldorf, Germany: 1955), p. 100.

[100] This is according to Sabbas Kilian, *Theological Models of the Parish*, pp. 24-35.

[101] For example, the idea of SCCs being "cells" of the parish is a central feature of the St. Boniface Parish Cell System. See the book by this name authored by Michael Eivers and Perry Vitale, (Pembroke Pines, Florida: St. Boniface Catholic Church, 1991). For references to the idea of SCCs being "little churches" and the "church in miniature", see pages vii and 74 respectively of Arthur R. Baranowski's *Creating Small Faith Communities* (Cincinnati, Ohio: St. Anthony Messenger Press, 1988).

terminology first emerged, as well as the ecclesiology involved, will be helpful later on in analyzing the theological claims being made by SCCs.

B. Efforts Towards a More Comprehensive Theology of Parish

1. Yves Congar

According to Avery Dulles, Yves Congar was the most influential Catholic ecclesiologist in the period between the Second World War and Vatican II.[102] Although he wrote on a wide range of ecclesiological topics, only a few of his more seminal thoughts on the parish are related here. As with many French theologians at the time, Congar paid special attention to the social dimensions inherent in being a parish community.[103] He invoked the idea of communion/community as being something which comes both from "above" and from "below." He compares the nature of parish community to that of family, something which corresponds to a basic structure of human life and arises from "below." The diocese he compares to the idea of *civitas*, which is a higher principle of social organization and civilization. It exists not in small units but only as a whole, and in this way can be understood to come from "above." Hence the parish has a predominately family structure, while the diocese a predominately *civitas* structure.[104] But Congar does not want this family-*civitas* analogy to be seen dualistically. He stresses that the church is simultaneously family and *civitas*.

To Congar's way of thinking the parish was born historically because of the pastoral convenience it afforded in attending to the spiritual and social needs of people.[105] Its fundamental role was that of a missionary community forming people in the Christian life. Despite the parish's important pastoral role, the diocese was seen from a theological and historical perspective as remaining the primary unit of the early church. Thus, the parish was not granted the same kind of ecclesiological status as

---

[102] Avery Dulles, "A Half Century of Ecclesiology," *Theological Studies* 50 (1989), p. 424.

[103] Other French pioneers in the realm of social analysis and the parish include: G. Michonneau, H. Godin, F. Boulard, Y. Daniel, and others. The fundamental thrust of their analysis indicated that the parish, especially in its urban setting, was not well adapted to being a community in the sociological sense. Thus their research and speculation helped make an important contribution to the overall theological-pastoral effort that was underway before Vatican II. Even today the question remains as to whether or not it is legitimate to refer to the parish as being "theologically" constituted a community, when in fact it does not sometimes meet the "social" requirements of being one.

[104] For Congar's discussion of this analogy see his article: "Mission de la paroisse," in *Structures sociale et pastorale paroissiale* (Paris: Union des Oevres Catholiques de France, 1949), pp. 48-68.

[105] *Ibid.*, p. 51.

was the diocese. Instead it has traditionally been seen more in terms of being a pastoral or social construct.

But given today's renewed ecclesiological awareness of what being the church entails, it seems that the parish should be accorded a greater theological weight. It is inadequate to refer to it solely in territorial or juridical terms. For the parish has the character of being not only a natural community, but a supernatural one as well. It thus shares in the supernatural character of the diocesan church, as do other groups on the local scene. Like the parish as a whole, these other groupings of lay people can also legitimately lay claim to the title of being Christian communities. The family itself has always been considered a Christian community in its own right and a fundamental cell of the church.

For these reasons Congar thinks it beneficial to describe the parish in terms of being "a community of communities."[106] Families and other small groups, built up naturally from below, constitute the primary experience of community in the parish. Together they give rise to the higher experience of communion which the parish represents as a whole. Congar is in a sense applying his family-*civitas* analogy of the nature of parish-diocesan community to the internal dynamic at work in the individual parish. He feels it is essential to understand the dynamics of Christian community in this way so as to recover a proper pastoral vision of parish. He states:

> Many of our contemporaries find that for them the Church's machinery, sometimes the very institution, is a barrier obscuring her deep and living mystery, which they can find, or find again, only from below, through little Church cells wherein the mystery is lived directly and with great simplicity. . . . A need is felt to seek, beneath the ready-made administrative machinery, the living reality of basic communities, the aspect in which the Church herself is, at the same time as an objective institution, a community to whose life all its members contribute.[107]

2. Karl Rahner

Karl Rahner probably examined the question of the possibility and conditions for a theology of parish more thoroughly than anyone else before

[106] Yves Congar, *Lay People in the Church*. First published in 1953, (London: Geoffrey Chapman, 1985 Revised Ed.), p. 341.
[107]*Ibid.*, pp. 339-340.

Vatican II.[108] For Rahner, it is not possible to articulate a theology of parish without first realizing that the church as a whole is the primary and original theological reality. The best manner in which to understand the nature of the church as a whole, is to see it in terms of being an "event." It is only within this context that it is correct to describe the parish as being an entity that "actualizes" the church event in a given place. Thus, the parish by its nature is a necessarily "local" event. It is in this setting that the church is made visible and comprehensible to the world. This concept is explicitly linked to the nature of eucharist, which itself is the event par excellence whereby the Body of Christ is made manifest. Furthermore, "placeness" is an essential characteristic of both eucharist and parish. This is because, "the eucharist can be celebrated only by a community which is gathered together in one and the same place. . . . All this means that the Church, in its innermost essence, is itself directed to a localized concretization."[109] Rahner goes on to add that this fact does not take away from the church being at the same time a fully "universal" reality.

Despite the fact that the parish is a vital realization of the church event, it is not the only manifestation. There are other types of Christian community in which people come together locally and celebrate the eucharist. These too actualize the church in their own way. But Rahner sees the parish as still being "the primary, normal, and original form of local community."[110] Thus, the "parish principle", in so far as it is rooted in the concept of territory, helps reflect the theological character of the local parish church. However, as a pastoral strategy, it is no longer viable as an exclusive means with which to organize pastoral ministry.[111]

Rahner's thoughts on the theological character of the parish met with a certain degree of criticism. But these criticisms, some of which misconstrue his position, need not fully concern us here. However, one objection is worth noting because it did cause Rahner to alter somewhat his later thinking on the parish. This had to do with his stress on the link between the eucharist and the local "placeness" of the parish community. In a later work, which reflects the changes wrought by Vatican II, Rahner places more stress on the role of the bishop, and also on the liturgical rather than on the territorial nature of local eucharistic celebrations. He also recognizes that the massive cultural changes which have occurred lessen the

[108] This is according to Blöchlinger, *The Modern Parish Community*, p. 140.

[109] Karl Rahner, "Theology of the Parish," in *The Parish: From Theology to Practice*, ed. Hugo Rahner (Westminster, Maryland: The Newman Press, 1958), pp. 28-29.

[110] *Ibid.*, p. 31.

[111] Cf. Karl Rahner, "Peaceful Reflections on the Parochial Principle," *Theological Investigations*, Vol. II (Baltimore: Helicon Press, 1963), pp. 283-318.

meaning of "locale" for many people.[112] Hence, he foresaw a need for structural changes to the parish in the future, to correspond better to the "Diaspora" situation the church finds itself in.[113] All the same, he still viewed the idea of territory, or more exactly "placeness," as being an important component of the theological character of parish.

C. Conclusion

To recapitulate, some of the important insights which can be gleaned from the discussion about the parish in 20th century theology prior to Vatican II can be summarized in the following points:

1) The parish derives its theological identity from being an integral part of the diocesan church, which itself is an integral part of the universal church.

2) The diocese, as an episcopal community, is the fundamental unit of the local church. It preceded the existence of the parish. The parish does not originate directly from any datum of Revelation. Rather, it was born historically as a pastoral convenience. Yet it also has a supernatural character.

3) The parish, as a concrete realization of church, does not have any ecclesial status independent of the diocese.

4) The theological reality and identity of the parish is intimately linked to its being a eucharistic community.

5) The parish is not an exclusive expression of church in a given locale. However, because of its historical importance, it can be considered a primary expression.

This investigation into some of the theological reflection on the parish which began in the first half of the 20th century helps to clarify certain features of the ecclesiality of the parish. It also serves as an effective bridge into the next chapter wherein Vatican II's conception of church, as it specifically relates to parish, is addressed. Although the work of theologians such as Congar and Rahner before the council contributed greatly to a renewed appreciation of the parish's theological character and pastoral role in the church, Vatican II's position will be needed in order to round out the state of the question.

---

[112] See Rahner's discussion of this point in his *Theology of Pastoral Action* (New York: Herder and Herder, 1968), pp. 103-104.

[113] Cf. Karl Rahner, "Structural Change in the Church of the Future," *Theological Investigations*, Vol. XX (London: Darton, Longman and Todd, 1981), pp. 115-132.

Even this will not represent the end of the matter. For in the years after the Council closer attention began to be paid to the concept of "local church." This continues to be a major area of investigation by ecclesiologists today. Thus, an analysis of how some of this postconciliar reflection impacts on the theology of parish will also be briefly noted. All of this reflection is needed in order to provide a proper theological context for analyzing the ecclesiality of small Christian communities in the church and in the North American parish of today. It is specifically needed in order to theologically situate and assess the claims being made as to their ecclesial status. Are SCCs merely pastoral constructs? Or do they deserve to be accorded greater ecclesiological weight in recognition of their role and function?

CHAPTER TWO

Vatican II and the Parish

I. THE NATURE OF THE CHURCH ACCORDING TO VATICAN II

A. The Major Ecclesiological Themes of Vatican II[1]

1. Interpreting the Signs of the Times

The Second Vatican Council (1962-1965) brought about a revolution in Catholic ecclesiology, a profound paradigm shift in the way we look at and understand the vocation and mission of the church.[2] In convening the Council Pope John XXIII spoke of the need for *aggiornamento*, a need to bring up to date and reformulate many of the traditional truths of the faith and structures of the church.[3] It was to be primarily a pastoral council, seeking to articulate and communicate a renewed vision of the church. In many ways it can be said that Vatican II as a whole sought to take into account the "signs of the times" (Mt 16:3) in

---

[1] Principal sources for this section are: Walter M. Abbott, ed., *The Documents of Vatican II* (New York: America Press, 1966); Giuseppe Albergio, Jean-Pierre Jossua, and John Komonchak, eds. *The Reception of Vatican II* (Washington, D.C.: Catholic University of America, 1987); Avery Dulles, *Models of the Church* (New York: Doubleday, 1987 Expanded Edition); Dulles, "Catholic Ecclesiology Since Vatican II," *Concilium* 188 (1986), pp. 3-13; Extraordinary 1985 Synod of Bishops, *A Message to the People of God* and *The Final Report* (Washington, D.C.: NCCB, 1986); Walter Kasper, *Theology and Church,* (London: SCM Press, 1989); Bonaventure Kloppenburg, *The Ecclesiology of Vatican II* (Chicago: Franciscan Herald Press, 1970); René Latourelle, ed., *Vatican II: Assessment and Perspectives, 3 Vols.* (New York/Mahwah: Paulist Press, 1988); Joseph Ratzinger, "The Ecclesiology of the Second Vatican Council," *Communio* 13 (1988), pp. 239-252; Gérard Philips, *L'Église et son mystère au IIe Concile du Vatican, 2 Vols.* (Paris: Desclée, 1967); Alberic Stacpoole, ed., *Vatican II: By Those Who Were There* (London: Geoffrey Chapman, 1986); and Herbert Vorgrimler, ed., *Commentary on the Documents of Vatican II, 5 vols.* (New York: Herder, 1967).

[2] This is according to Dulles, *Models of the Church*, p. 31.

[3] Pope John XXIII was careful to distinguish between the substance of the doctrine of faith and the way it is presented. It is not the case that this doctrine is somehow erroneous, but rather that it needs ongoing clarification and new expression if it is to remain alive and authentic. Cf. John XXIII's Opening Address to the Council (Oct. 11, 1962), reprinted in Abbott, *The Documents of Vatican II*, p. 715.

Given its nature and subject matter Vatican II has been referred to as being "without a doubt *the* council for ecclesiology."[5] This is why a brief account of some of its major ecclesiological themes is in order. This will help prepare us to situate theologically the manner in which the parish is treated in the council documents, as well as provide a point of departure and context for the discussions of the ecclesiality of small Christian communities in the church today.

The ecclesiology of Vatican II, in its main lines, is well known.[6] It is reflected in various ways in all of the council's sixteen documents. But the two most important documents for our purposes, which represent the two pillars of the Council's ecclesiology, are the Dogmatic Constitution on the Church (*Lumen Gentium*) and the Pastoral Constitution on the Church in the Modern World (*Gaudium et Spes*). A simplified way of describing the major thrust of these documents is to see the former one as dealing more with the nature of the church "*ad intra*," while the latter focuses on the "*ad extra*" nature of the church's relationship to the wider world.[7] Although both of these documents are vitally important for a comprehensive understanding of the council's ecclesiological concerns, more attention will be given to *Lumen Gentium*, for it has been called the "keynote" document of the Council.[8]

2. *Lumen Gentium* and *Gaudium et Spes*

The rejection of the initial draft of *Lumen Gentium* (LG) by the Council Fathers signalled more than anything else the desire which was felt at the time for a new approach to the expression of the church's ecclesiology. This initial draft had reflected the traditional *societas perfecta* image of church that had held sway since the days of Robert Bellarmine in the 16th century.[9] This image, even though it was now being linked to the

---

[5] This is according to Daniel Donovan, *The Church as Idea and Fact*, (Wilmington, Delaware: Michael Glazier, 1988), p. 31.

[6] See any of the major commentaries listed in note #1 above.

[7] It should be realized of course that *Lumen Gentium* is not wholly *ad intra* in focus, and neither is *Gaudium et Spes* wholly lacking in *ad intra* elements. This *ad intra/ad extra* rubric was seen at the time as being a helpful way of distinguishing between the major concerns of these two documents on the church. Cf. Gérard Philips, "History of the Constitution," in Vorgrimler, *Commentary on the Documents of Vatican II, Vol. I*, pp. 107-108.

[8] This is according to Richard McBrien, "Catholicism: the American Experience," in *American Catholics*, ed. Joseph Kelly (Wilmington, Delaware: Michael Glazier, 1989), p. 20.

[9] For a good discussion of the theology of church reflected in this initial draft see Yves Congar, "Moving Towards a Pilgrim Church," in *Vatican II: by those who were there*, pp. 129-152.

more spiritual concept of the Mystical Body of Christ, still communicated an overly hierarchical and institutional view of the church. This is not to say that the Council Fathers were rejecting the importance of institution and hierarchy. But they wished to see was more attention being given to other fundamental aspects of being church, and to have this expressed in terms and images that were less neo-scholastic and more biblical in nature.

After considerable work on the text the present structure of the document emerged.[10] It is divided into eight chapters. In examining the content and theme of these chapters, Gérard Philips states that "there are always two chapters in unquestionably logical connection."[11] Thus, the first two chapters deal with the origin and essence of the church both in its transcendent dimension and in its historical realization. Chapters three and four then describe the organic constitution of the church, elaborating on the respective roles of the ordained ministers and the laity. The next two chapters deal with the "finality" of the church which involves the call to holiness and sanctification of all people (with religious life seen as being a special expression of this call). The final two chapters deal with the pilgrim nature and eschatological goal of the church with special attention given to the Blessed Virgin Mary's role in salvation history (because of which she is seen to be an abiding image of the church "as it is to be perfected in the world to come"[12]).

Although all eight chapters form an integrated account of the nature of the church, it is not germane for the purpose of this thesis to attempt a detailed overview of each one of them. What will be highlighted instead are simply some of the more seminal ideas pertaining to the essence and structure of the church which are reflected in the first four chapters of LG in particular. This will be done in summary fashion. In the following section dealing with the reception and interpretation of the Council, various comments as to the significance of these images and ideas will be noted so as to round out our understanding of the ecclesiology of Vatican II.

Lumen Gentium begins with a consideration of the "mystery" of the church, describing it as a kind of "sacrament" that is both a sign and instrument of "communion" (LG 1). It is a mystery because it images the divine life of the Trinity, which in itself is the expression of communion par excellence (LG 2-4). The church is also an expression of the Kingdom of God[SRt]that Christ proclaimed, an embodiment of the Good News (LG 5).

---

[10] For an excellent account of how LG came to take on its present form see Philips, "History of the Constitution," in *Commentary on the Documents of Vatican II, Vol. I*, pp. 105-137.

[11] *Ibid.*, p. 131.

[12] Cf. LG 68.

The nature of the church is further conveyed by the various biblical metaphors of the sheepfold, the cultivated field, the building of God, the temple, the holy city, the Jerusalem from above, the spotless spouse, and especially the Body of Christ (LG 6-7).

As a consequence of the natural and supernatural dimensions inherent in being the Body of Christ, the church can be seen as being both a "visible society" and a "spiritual community." These are not two separate entities, but are rather "one complex reality" consisting of both these human and divine elements (LG 8). Furthermore, the sole church of Christ, which according to the ancient Creeds is professed to be "one, holy, catholic and apostolic," is said to "subsist in" the Catholic church (LG 8). In chapter two, the image of church as "the People of God" is elaborated on (LG 9). Herein it is stated that the entire people of God, both laity and clergy alike, and each in their own proper way, share in the priestly, prophetic, and kingly mission of Christ (LG 10-12). Thus, the church as a whole, guided by the Spirit, is endowed with a supernatural appreciation of the faith (*sensus fidei*). The people of God are also empowered with charisms from the Holy Spirit to help in the building up of the church in the world (LG 12).

As a result of Christ's grace working through it, the church becomes a "necessary means of salvation" (LG 14).[13] This means that other Christians too are in some way "joined" to the mystery of the church. The Catholic church, for her part, recognizes the validity of baptism and other sacraments in these other "Churches" and "ecclesiastical communities" (LG 15).[14] Even those who are not baptized Christians are also described as being "related" or oriented to the church in various ways (LG 16). Because there are people who have not yet heard the Good News, the church has the duty to evangelize and to help make disciples of all nations (LG 17).

Chapter three deals with the hierarchical nature of the church. In a previous draft of LG, this was to have preceded chapter two's discussion of the People of God. But this was changed so as to accent the fact that the church as "people" comes before any subsequent treatment of its hierarchical structure.[15] Here the leadership of the church is no longer portrayed in overly juridical terms. The Roman Pontiff, as successor to the ministry of Peter, is the "head" of the church, source and guardian of its unity and catholicity (LG 18). But the Pope is described as exercising his

---

[13] For a good discussion of what this statement implies see Francis Sullivan, *Salvation Outside the Church?* (New York/Mahwah: Paulist Press, 1992).

[14] These matters are fully addressed in the Decree on Ecumenism (*Unitatis redintegratio*) and also in the Declaration on the Relationship of the Church to Non-Christian Religions (*Nostra Aetate*).

[15] Cf. Philips, "History of the Constitution," p. 119.

primacy in union with the rest of the episcopal college (LG 19). The nature of this collegiality, as well as the nature of the leadership which bishops exercise in their local dioceses, is given much attention (LG 20-24). Likewise, the nature and exercise of the *magisterium* that both Pope and bishops participate in is elaborated.[16] The authority of this magisterial teaching, and the modalities inherent in its infallible character, are also outlined (LG 25).

The church is seen as being rooted in the Eucharist and as existing in every legitimate local congregation under its bishop (LG 26). The church also exists in the communion of all these local churches. It is thus both a local and a universal reality.[17] The ministry of priests is also referred to in this context as being derived from and dependent on their bishop. They represent the bishop in each "local assembly of the faithful" (LG 28). Together, the priests form a type of college (*presbyterium*) around their bishop. Mention too is made of the ministry of deacons, and a call is voiced for the restoration of the permanent diaconate in the church (LG 29).

Chapter four gives an eloquent description of the vocation and apostolate of the laity in the church and in the world. By virtue of their baptism all God's faithful are called to share in the work of the church, and to make use of their charisms accordingly (LG 30-31). Their role does not usurp the pastoral leadership of the ordained members of the church, but complements it (LG 32). Everyone in the church is to work together for the building up of the Body of Christ. Everyone shares in the mission of Christ (LG 33-35). The laity have a special role to play in witnessing to the gospel in the world (LG 36). Finally, pastors are called upon to aid the laity in their mission and to promote their role in the church (LG 37).

Unlike *Lumen Gentium*, which was a so-called "dogmatic" constitution, *Gaudium et Spes* came to be designated a "pastoral" constitution. This was because its aim was not so much doctrinal clarification but rather pastoral reflection on a wide range of issues affecting the church's relationship to the world.[18] Themes and issues addressed by

---

[16] A *Preliminary Explanatory Note* was affixed to the end of LG in order to clear up any possible confusion pertaining to the theological and juridical nature of episcopal collegiality. It is stressed that bishops exercise their ministry only in union with the Pope, who is the head of the church.

[17] A closer look at this concept of the local/universal character of the church in Vatican II, and in postconciliar ecclesiology, will follow later in this chapter (part B).

[18] This does not mean *Gaudium et Spes* is devoid of dogmatic content. It simply indicates that the genre of the document is of a different kind, which reflects its fundamental "pastoral" purpose. It was John Paul II, then a bishop delegate at Vatican II, who had suggested the adjective "pastoral" be used to designate this unprecedented kind of constitution. Cf. Richard P. McBrien, *Catholicism: Study Edition* (Minneapolis: Winston Press, 1981), p. 673.

Gaudium et Spes include: an analysis of the situation of man in the world today (Introduction); an excursus on Christian anthropology, including reference to the problem of atheism (part 1, chap 1); the necessity for respect of the human person and work on behalf of social justice (part 1, chap 2); the value of human activity and the autonomy of secular activities in their rightful sphere (part 1, chap 3); the role of the church in the modern world (part 1, chap 4); the nature of marriage and family in the modern world (part 2, chap 1); the relationship of faith to culture (part 2, chap 2); the relationship of faith to the economic and social order (chap 3); the relationship of faith to the political order (chap 4); and the problem of war and the need to foster peace and development (chap 5).

   Gaudium et Spes has had a considerable impact on the development of postconciliar ecclesiology.[19] This can be attributed to the "dialogue" stance it adopted in addressing the situation of man in the modern world. It sought to forge a more open and cooperative relationship so as to help collaborate with all people of good will in the promotion of basic human values. It was recognized that the spiritual work of evangelization did not preclude but rather necessitated attention being also paid to the promotion of people's welfare in all spheres of life. It expressed hope for the success of these endeavours in optimistic terms.[20] For these reasons *Gaudium et Spes* has had a continuing influence on the contemporary understanding of the "integral" nature of the church's mission in the world.[21]

3. The Interpretation and Reception of the Council

   It is difficult to understand why Vatican II, which was intent on increasing the missionary dynamism of the church, and which was initially greeted with great enthusiasm by Catholics, led instead to a period of much internal conflict, confusion, and malaise.[22] Two observations are worth mentioning by way of partially explaining the reasons for this initial state of

---

[19] Angel Antón goes so far as to claim that "no other document of Vatican II had an impact on the development of postconciliar ecclesiology as decisive as *Guadium et Spes*." Antón, "Postconciliar Ecclesiology," in *Vatican II: Assessment and Perspectives,* p. 431.

[20] *Ibid.,* p. 435.

[21] For a discussion of postconciliar reflection on the idea of church as sacrament of "integral salvation," see chapter seven of Francis Sullivan, *The Church We Believe In* (New York/Mahwah: Paulist Press, 1988).

[22] This is how Avery Dulles characterized the general situation of the church in the late 1970s, about a decade after the Council had ended. Cf. Dulles, *The Resilient Church: The Necessity and Limits of Adaptation* (Garden City, N.Y.: Doubleday, 1977), p. 11. More recently, both Walter Kasper and Joseph Ratzinger have also voiced similar appraisals. See: Kasper, *Theology and Church,* p. 150; and Ratzinger, *Principles of Catholic Theology* (San Francisco: Ignatius Press, 1987), pp. 367-393.

affairs. One has to do with the fact that the Council happened to coincide with a period of unprecedented social change in the world. Yves Congar has remarked: "Vatican II has been followed by socio-cultural change more extensive, radical and rapid and more cosmic in its proportions than any change at any other period in man's history."[23]

Another reason has to do with the dynamics involved in a council's "reception." It was Cardinal John Henry Newman, with a solid knowledge of the history of the church, who was led to remark a month after the closing of Vatican I that, "it is rare for a council not to be followed by great confusion."[24] Councils have generally taken a while to fully penetrate into the consciousness and life of the church and forge a new ecclesial equilibrium. This is why it is important to take some note of how Vatican II is being interpreted and received. Of special concern for our purposes is the interpretation of the council's ecclesiology.

The concept of *koinōnia* (communion) is widely recognized to be the central concept which is operative in the ecclesiology of Vatican II.[25] The fact of having focused the theology of the nature of the church on the recovery of this concept of *koinōnia* can be seen as representing the most important development of the Council.[26] This is not meant to imply that the idea of communion was non-existent in official preconciliar ecclesiology. It is only meant to underline the central role it plays at Vatican II and in much postconciliar ecclesiology. Other images of church, such as those of "sacrament" and "People of God," while equally significant, have been less successful in establishing themselves in both theological and popular discourse.[27]

In assessing what this new ecclesiology represents, many commentators have noted that upon closer examination, it can be seen that it did not make any sharp break with the official teaching of the recent past.

---

[23] Yves Congar, "A Last Look at the Council," in *Vatican II: by those who were there*, p. 351.

[24] J. H. Newman, Letter to O'Neill Daunt (Aug. 7, 1870), quoted by Yves Congar, "A Last Look at the Council," p. 349. A similar historical observation is made by Joseph Ratzinger in noting the reaction of Gregory Nazianzus to his invitation to attend another session of the Council of Constantinople (381). Gregory stated "I am convinced that every assembly of bishops is to be avoided, for I have never experienced a happy ending to a council; not even the abolition of abuses . . . , but only ambition or wrangling about what was taking place" (*Ep. #130*). Cited by Ratzinger, *Principles of Catholic Theology*, p. 368.

[25] This is the assessment made by the bishops at the 1985 Extraordinary Synod. Cf. *The Final Report*, p. 17.

[26] Cf. Antón, "Postconciliar Ecclesiology," p. 416.

[27] This assessment is made by Avery Dulles, *A Church to Believe In: Discipleship and the Dynamics of Freedom* (New York: Crossroad, 1982), pp. 4-6.

"The shift was one of emphasis more than substance, of rhetoric more than doctrine."[28] As Antonio Acerbi has pointed out, in *Lumen Gentium* there seems to be two basic ecclesiologies at work. The older, more traditional "juridical" understanding of the church is juxtaposed with that of the newer "communion" based vision.[29] These two ecclesiologies do not contradict one another, but they do coexist in certain tension in the document.

This explains, in part, the controversies which soon arose after the Council regarding the hermeneutics of its documents. So-called "progressives" wanted to give priority to the innovations inherent in Vatican II's ecclesiology. Other so-called "traditionalists" stressed the continuity of the council's ecclesiology with previous Catholic teaching.[30] This polarization of discussion also colored the way in which the postconciliar call for further "structural" changes was greeted. The progressives wanted more in the way of democratization and the practice of subsidiarity in matters of church leadership and ministry. The traditionalists urged caution and a respect for the necessary hierarchical and institutional dimensions of church leadership and structure.[31]

This discussion in large measure reflects the fact that *koinōnia* is realized not only in a natural, organic context, but also in the hierarchical or institutional dimension inherent in being church.[32] This finds a parallel in the description of the fundamental nature of the church as being both charismatic and institutional in composition. The two cannot be separated. The discussion seems to hinge on the question of which dimension, the hierarchical or the charismatic, should be given priority in the process of implementing Vatican II's mandate for ongoing renewal of church structures and practices.[33]

---

[28] Dulles, "A Half Century of Ecclesiology," p. 429.

[29] For a detailed analysis of this see Antonio Acerbi, *Due ecclesiologie: Ecclesiologia giuridica ed ecclesiologia di communione nella 'Lumen gentium'* (Bologna: Dehoniane, 1975).

[30] Cf. Dulles, "A Half Century of Ecclesiology," pp. 430-431.

[31] The International Theological Commission has recently reaffirmed the need in the church for clear pastoral structures. "As a visible community and social organism, the Church needs norms that express her fundamental structure and give greater definition to certain conditions of communal life in virtue of judgments of a prudential kind." Michael Sharkey, ed. "Select Themes of Ecclesiology on the Occasion of the Eighth Anniversary of the Closing of the Second Vatican Council," in *International Theological Commission: Texts and Documents* (San Francisco: Ignatius Press, 1987), p. 288.

[32] Gianfranco Ghirlanda states that "the Church is thus the communion, both spiritual and institutional, of all the baptized. . . . [Thus] the fundamental structure of the Church should be seen as both charismatic and institutional." Ghirlanda, "Universal Church, Particular Church, and Local Church at the Second Vatican Council and in the New Code of Canon Law," in *Vatican II: Assessment and Perspectives*, pp. 236-237.

[33] Cf. Dulles, *A Church to Believe In*, pp. 19-40.

Some of these changes were stipulated, such as the renewal of the liturgy, creation of parish councils and episcopal conferences, and so on. But these changes alone were not seen at the time as exhausting the process. However, in the absence of further explicit conciliar directives, it is sometimes difficult to determine what other changes can or should be wrought. Hence there is a an ongoing need for a faithful interpretation and application of conciliar principles so as to better serve the needs of the church of today. All of which constantly raises the issue of what aspects of the church's current organization and practice are mutable and which are immutable?[34]

Part of the problem can be traced to a certain amount of doctrinal ambiguity that is evident in some of the documents of the Council. This in turn is due to the fact that the Council opted not to formally define dogmas, as had happened in the past, but rather to elucidate the nature of the church in more of a pastoral vein.[35] For instance, the laity are portrayed as active participants in the threefold office of Christ, and as recipients of charisms from the Holy Spirit, but the full implications for the ministry of laity are not spelled out.[36] Some theologians have regarded this as indicative of a certain "lack of integration" between theory and practice in the council's ecclesiology.[37]

The question of how to "interpret" Vatican II has remained a continuing source of tension in the church ever since the Council ended. In one sense the 1985 Extraordinary Synod of Bishops can be seen as an attempt to address this question of interpretation and also some other related

---

[34] Cf. Antón, "Postconciliar Ecclesiology," pp. 420-421.

[35] Hermann Pottmeyer, reflecting on the difficulties in interpreting the documents of Vatican II, states that "the rules customarily applied in interpreting dogmatic texts . . . do not work here. The texts, even those that are doctrinal in character, lack the conceptual precision, the unambiguous definition of positions, the technical form, and the unity of literary genre to which Trent and Vatican I had accustomed us." Pottmeyer, "A New Phase in the Reception of Vatican II: Twenty Years of Interpretation of the Council," in *The Reception of Vatican II*, p. 27.

[36] Cf. Giovanni Magnani, "Does the So-Called Theology of the Laity Possess a Theological Status?" in *Vatican II: Assessment and Perspectives*, Vol I, pp. 595-624. Walter Kasper sees the increase in lay involvement and responsibility for the church as representing "perhaps the most valuable and most important contribution of the postconciliar period." But he also laments that "*corruptio optimi pessima!*. . . . There was, and is, hardly any aspect of conciliar doctrine which was, and is, so fundamentally misunderstood as this one." Kasper, *Theology and Church*, p. 162. As we shall see later, the issue of lay leadership and ministry in SCCs has a bearing on the question of SCC ecclesiality.

[37] See Joseph Komonchak's discussion of this point in "The Church: God's Gift and Our Task," *Origins* 16/42 (1987), pp. 735-741.

problems which have arisen in the postconciliar church.[38] The stated purpose of the Synod was to "celebrate, verify and promote" Vatican II.[39] It marks an important moment in the ongoing reception of the Council by the church. It is significant to note that in its official *Final Report* there was stress placed on the notion that the communion of the church constitutes primarily and essentially a divine mystery. This was affirmed in order to balance a certain trend in postconciliar ecclesiology that emphasized the sociological dimension of being church, sometimes in a reductionist manner. "We must not replace a false, one-sided, hierarchical notion of the Church with a new one-sided sociological concept."[40]

However, the 1985 Synod has by no means ended postconciliar discussion on the subject of Vatican II's ecclesiology. Some critics have seen in this Synod, and in other recent official pronouncements, what they describe as an "over emphasis" on church as mystery. In their eyes this amounts to an abuse of this idea and an improper attempt to relegate to secondary importance the necessarily concrete social dimensions inherent in being church. For instance Edward Schillebeeckx has denounced this manner of thinking for being "dualistic" and ultimately "fundamentalistic."[41]

Thus, the effort to work out the implications inherent in Vatican II's ecclesiology continues so that a proper integration of both supernatural and sociological elements can be properly realized. Joseph Komonchak expresses the need for this task very well:

> Because the genesis of the church is the genesis of a human community, it is proper and necessary to look for help from the human sciences of community. As theology is not the full science of the human, ecclesiology is not the full science of the church; and no serious study of the challenges facing the church or of the ways in which the church may be able to meet them can ignore the psychological, sociological, organizational, political or cultural sciences. . . . It is a profoundly Catholic instinct that one need not, indeed one must not, choose between a

[38] This is according to Russell Shaw who was the Press Secretary to the United States Bishops attending the Synod. His comments can be found in the "Introduction" to the NCCB publication of the Synod's *Message to the People of God* and *The Final Report*, pp. 2-3. The *Final Report* itself speaks of there being certain "shadows in the postconciliar period, in part due to an incomplete understanding and application of the council." *Ibid.*, p. 10.

[39] *The Final Report*, p. 9.

[40] *Ibid.*, p. 13.

[41] Cf. Edward Schillebeeckx, *Church: The Human Story of God*, (London: SCM Press, 1990), pp. 210-213.

supernatural and a sociological view of the church. No
reductionism, sociological or theological, will yield an
adequate theory or practice of the church.[42]

This is not meant to imply that the ecclesiology of Vatican II is
somehow deficient. But it helps to explain the reasons for these discussions
and why calls are still heard in some quarters for ongoing structural change
in the church (some of these are loudest within the small Christian
community movement). What is important to realize in all of this is that
Vatican II is not a "dead letter" in the church today.[43] It was an event in the
history of the church that is continuing to have an impact. This impact is
being felt in a variety of new theologies the Council can be said to have
helped spawn, and in other movements and initiatives that are attempting to
carry forward the Council's vision for the renewal of the church.[44]

The small Christian community phenomenon is a good case in
point. It really only came into existence after the Council had ended and was
an unforseen development. Because of this fact, there are no explicit
references to SCCs in any of the documents of Vatican II. But the two are
often described as being "causally connected."[45] This is because the new
ecclesiology of Vatican II acted as a catalyst for the development of SCCs.
Marcello de Carvalho Azevedo thinks it unlikely that they could have
emerged in the context of a preconciliar church.[46] This is all part and parcel
of how Vatican II continues to bear fruit in the life of the postconciliar
church, sometimes in ways that were not foreseen by the council Fathers at
the time. This explains too the challenge involved in evaluating their claim
to be a legitimate expression of the Council's ecclesiology. In order to help
understand more fully the nature of their claim, and the terminology they
invoke, it is necessary to look more closely for a moment at a the concept of
"local church."

---

[42] Komonchak, "The Church: God's Gift and Our Task," pp. 740-741.

[43] Cf. Antón, "Postconciliar Ecclesiology," p. 435.

[44] For a survey of postconciliar developments in ecclesiology, see the articles by Avery
Dulles, "A Half Century of Ecclesiology," and Angel Antón, "Postconciliar Ecclesiology," as
well as another Dulles article, "Catholic Ecclesiology Since Vatican II," *Concilium* 188 (1986),
pp. 3-16.

[45] See the 1991 International Consultation on Basic Christian Community (Notre Dame
University), *Final Statement*, p. 3.

[46] Cf. Azevedo, *Basic Ecclesial Communities in Brazil*, p. 32.

B. A Closer Look: The Concept of Local Church[47]

1. The Local/Universal Nature of the Church in Vatican II

The concept of *local church* was not a prominent feature of theological reflection before Vatican II. Emmanuel Lanne, after a survey of preconciliar ecclesiology, is led to conclude that, "of theology of the local Church as such, there was none."[48] This was because the traditional stress placed on the oneness, catholicity, and apostolicity of the church, centered to a great degree on the ministry of the Pope, promoted an understanding of the church as being essentially a universal reality. Vatican II still endorses this concept of the essential universality of the church, but it also seeks to make more explicit how the bishops in their local settings share in their own way in the apostolicity, catholicity, and communion of the one church.[49]

However, it would be a mistake to think that the Council, in mentioning the concept of local church, provides us with a fully developed theology of it. In actual fact there is in the Council documents neither a systematic exposition of this idea nor consistent terminology with which to discuss it.[50] Nevertheless, it is important to review what mention is made of the idea because these indications have come to form the basis of much postconciliar reflection on the topic.

In Vatican II the universal church remains the point of departure for any subsequent consideration of its local expressions. It is asserted in *Lumen Gentium* 23 that the universal church is realized in and through the variety of "particular" churches:

> The Roman Pontiff, as the successor of Peter, is the perpetual and visible source of the foundation of the unity both of the bishops and of the whole company of the faithful. The individual bishops are the visible source and foundation of unity in their own particular Churches, which are constituted after the model of the universal

---

[47] Additional sources for this section include: Henri de Lubac, *Les églises particulières dans l'Église universelle* (Paris: Aubier Montaigne, 1971); Joseph A. Komonchak, "The Local Realization of the Church," in *The Reception of Vatican II*, eds. Giuseppe Albergio et al. (Washington, D.C.: Catholic University of America, 1987), pp. 77-90; Emmanuel Lanne, "The Local Church: its Catholicity and its Apostolicity," *One in Christ* 3/6 (1970), pp. 287-313; Hervé Legrand, "Enjeux théologiques de la valorisation des Eglises locales," *Concilium* 71 (1972), pp. 49-58, and "La réalisation de l'église en un lieu," in *Initiation à la practique de la théologie*, Vol. III, eds. Bernard Lauret and Francois Refoulé (Paris: Cerf, 1983), pp. 146-180; and J. M.-R Tillard, *Eglise d'églises* (Paris: Cerf, 1987).

[48] Emmanuel Lanne, "The Local Church: its Catholicity and its Apostolicity," p. 297.

[49] *Ibid.*

[50] This according to Joseph A. Komonchak, "The Local Realization of the Church," p. 77.

Church; it is in these and formed out of them that the one
and unique Catholic Church exists.

In LG 26 it is further stipulated that, "this church of Christ is really
present in all legitimate local congregations of the faithful which, united
with their bishops, in the New Testament are also called churches."
Returning for a moment to LG 23, mention is made of the Eastern Churches
in the latter part of this section. These churches are described as being "local
Churches," having their own spiritual patrimony and liturgical disciplines.
Nevertheless, they too contribute to the "catholicity of the undivided
Church."[51]

These passages use different expressions to refer to what appears
to be a diocese (i.e. local church, particular church). The diocese is referred
to as a *particular* church in LG 23, but is termed a *local* entity in LG 26.
Local church is also used in LG 23 in more of an ecumenical context to
indicate the essential ecclesiality of various Eastern churches that possess
different rites. The new 1983 Code of Canon Law opted to speak of dioceses
in terms of being *particular churches* because this expression was used
more consistently in the documents and in more of an explicit manner. But
many theologians in the postconciliar period frequently speak of the diocese
as being an expression of *local church*. This is being pointed out here to
explain the reasons for the diversity in current usage.[52]

The idea of a diocese being a *particular church* wherein the
universality of the church is realized finds similar expression in *Christus
Dominus* 11:

A diocese is a section of the People of God entrusted to a
bishop to be guided by him with the assistance of his
clergy so that, loyal to its pastor and formed by him into
one community in the Holy Spirit through the Gospel and
the Eucharist, it constitutes one particular church in which
the one, holy, catholic and apostolic Church of Christ is
truly present and active.

The reference to the actualization of the church in the celebration
of the Eucharist that is alluded to in the above passage, is given its strongest

---

[51] It is interesting to note that the renewed emphasis on the idea of *local church* within
Roman Catholicism is actually quite close to Eastern Orthodox thought, where this form of
ecclesiology goes by the name of *eucharistic ecclesiology*. Cf. Fahey, "Church," p. 39.

[52] In this thesis the term *local church* will be used as a designation for the diocesan church.

expression in *Sacrosanctum Concilium* 41, wherein it is stated that "the principal manifestation of the Church" consists in the celebration of the Eucharist, especially in the cathedral church of the bishop. But because it is not possible for all the faithful to gather with the bishop the celebration of the Eucharist in parishes and in other groups by priests who represent the bishop are also seen as being most important, "for in some way they represent the visible Church constituted throughout the world" (SC 42).[53]

Since the universal church exists then in the communion of local churches, the fact of diversity and culture also enters into the understanding of local church. In numerous texts the Council showed a great sense of respect for particularity and diversity (i.e. SC 37-40; OE 2,5; UR 14, 16-18; LG 13). Careful to avoid syncretism and ethnocentrism, the church nevertheless encourages the genius and character of every culture. "Thus, new particular Churches, with their own traditions, will take their place in the communion of the Church" (*Ad Gentes* 22). The catholicity of the church does not necessitate a monolithic uniformity in local expression. This insight is the basis of much recent theological reflection on the meaning of *inculturation* or *contextualization* in the local church.[54]

Thus, Vatican II gave clearer expression to the universal/local character of the church. The local churches are not treated as simply parts or administrative districts of a universal confederation, but rather as expressions of the same supreme reality of the one church of Christ, present and actualized in a specific place. In light of this ecclesiological principle one can see that there will always exist a certain necessary tension between the requirements of unity and the need for genuine local expression. There have been, and no doubt will continue to be, sometimes exaggerated claims made as to what this principle entails or justifies on the local level. All the same, this recovery of a more balanced presentation of the universal/local character of the church truly represents, in the words of Hervé Legrand, "a considerable reorientation" in Roman Catholic ecclesiology.[55]

2. Postconciliar Reflection on the Concept of Local Church

Postconciliar theological reflection on the nature of local church has helped shed more light on the universal/local dynamic that is operative in being the church. The entire course of these deliberations will not be

[53] For a discussion of how the Eucharist is seen to be a means of actualizing the local church, see Adrien Nocent, "The Local Church as Realization of the Church of Christ and Subject of the Eucharist," in *The Reception of Vatican II*, pp. 215-229.

[54] Komonchak gives an overview of the scope of this theological reflection in the context of his article "The Local Realization of the Church," pp. 81-85.

[55] Cf. Hervé Legrand, "La réalisation de l'église en un lieu," p. 155.

treated in any great detail here.[56] However, it is important to make note of several features of these discussions because they figure into our later analysis of the ecclesial status and role of parishes and also of small Christian communities in the church.

One question which has received much attention has to do with ascertaining what elements or characteristics can be said to constitute the local character of the church.[57] The classic approach has been to start first with a definition or description of the universal church. This is done by listing various characteristics of its universality, notably the presence of Word, Spirit, Sacrament, Apostolic Ministry, and so forth. This approach leads to the conclusion that each time you find these features in operation, you have an expression of the universality of the church.

This approach is then likewise applied to the local church. The usual characteristics listed here include: a defined diocesan territory, under the care of a bishop, and so forth. But the problem with this kind of analogical approach is the tendency for the local qualities of being church to be seen in more of a socio-cultural sense than a theological one.[58] The concept of local church is therefore not accorded the same theological "weight" as that of universal church. Thus, the universality of the church is sometimes regarded as more important than the local expressions of it.[59]

However, the fact remains that without the local presence of Christian communities rooted in time and space, the universal church would not exist. To speak of "where" the church is realized is to recognize the fundamental ecclesiality of its local character, which is a concrete realization of its universality. This is not to claim that it has in itself all the elements needed to be church. The question most often raised about this state of affairs is which aspect of being church, the local or the universal, deserves recognition for having greater ontological priority. Usually the universal is accorded a certain "pre-eminence" because it is through it that one can speak of the church being a sacrament of salvation, a repository of infallibly held dogmas, and so forth.[60]

---

[56] For an overview of some of the contemporary theological reflection on this topic see Joseph Komonchak, "L'articulation entre Église locale et Église universelle selon quelques théologiens contemporains." Paper presented at the 2nd Salamanca Colloquium on *Local Churches and Catholicity*, April 1-7, 1991, pp. 1-53.

[57] *Ibid.*, pp. 23-40.

[58] *Ibid.*, p. 26.

[59] For a more in-depth elaboration of the theological significance of the socio-cultural values inherent in the local church, see Henri de Lubac, *Les églises particulières dans l'Église universelle*, pp. 43-45.

[60] Cf. Komonchak, "L'articulation entre Église locale et Église universelle selon quelques théologiens contemporains," p. 16.

But this pre-eminence has been challenged by some theologians. Leonardo Boff is notable in this regard because of the length he goes to in arguing for the generative priority of the local over the universal. His speculation on the nature of *comunidades eclesias de base* (CEBs) in Brazil, led him to assert that they possess in themselves all the necessary local and universal requirements for being "church."[61] The universal dimension is subsumed into the local in this way of thinking. This position strongly resembles a certain kind of Protestant "congregational" ecclesiology. At any rate, Boff's position was officially condemned by the Vatican.[62]

Other theologians think it is an error to try and decide which aspect should have priority, for the reason that it is ontologically impossible to conceptualize the existence of the universal church without the existence of the local church, and vice-versa.[63] Thus, it is not a matter of the universal church transcending the local church, rather it is realized or constituted in the very communion of the local churches. Again we see that it is not a question of either/or but of both/and. Each aspect is fundamental and has its own necessary role to play.

But a question still remains as how best to express the theological character of the local church. It is recognized that the local church contributes to the catholicity of the universal church by manifesting its own particular charisms in a given locale. The church is not exactly the same everywhere. This is part of its so-called human dimension. But surely this human dimension also forms an integral part of the divine plan. Furthermore, the local church by necessity manifests these charisms in social, cultural, and historical terms. What theological status do some of these latter elements have?

For theologians like Giuseppe Colombo, elements like Word, Eucharist, and Charisms, do not only originate from a universally held common heritage, but are also constantly being generated locally, reflecting in the process a rich theological plurality.[64] Thus, "unity in diversity" is a

---

[61] Leonardo Boff, *Ecclesiogenesis: The Base Communities Reinvent the Church* (Maryknoll, N.Y.: Orbis, 1986), pp. 10-22. We will examine Boff's argument in greater detail in chapter four, part II, section A § 3.

[62] Describing Boff's position Avery Dulles notes that "he seems to depreciate the institutional in relation to the charismatic, to exalt the local over the universal, and to advocate the priority of praxis over theory. Not surprisingly, some of his writings have come under criticism from the Congregation for the Doctrine of the Faith" (cf. Congregation for the Doctrine of the Faith, "Notification regarding L. Boff, *Church: Charism and Power*," *Origins* 14/42 (1985), pp. 683-687). Dulles, "A Half Century of Ecclesiology," p. 439.

[63] Cf. Tillard, *Eglise d'Eglises*, pp. 15-36.

[64] Cf. Giuseppe Colombo, "La teologia della Chiesa locale," in *La Chiesa locale* (Bologne: Dehoniane, 1969), pp. 32-38.

theological insight, not just a sociological one. There is a legitimate multiplicity in the local ways in which the church has taken root. This illustrates the need to take seriously the implications of inculturation and contextualization, for they have been an integral feature of the church's ecclesial character since Pentecost.[65] In this regard, the Holy See has an important role to play in preserving and promoting Catholic unity, and in helping local churches discern which aspects of its local expression of faith practice are truly authentic and which are not.

What this discussion reveals then is that the structural or organizational element of how church is realized on the local level is important from a theological perspective and not just a sociological one. This is why developments that are underway vis-à-vis small Christian communities are not simply a matter of restructuring the parish or local church, but also of expressing a particular charism or insight into the nature by which the local church is best realized. Related to this is the question of how best to characterize and express the ecclesiality of the small Christian community.[66] However, before turning our attention more directly to SCCs, an overview of how the parish is treated in Vatican II's documents is first in order.

C. The Parish in the Council Documents[67]

At first glance it is somewhat surprising to see how little specific mention there is of the parish in the Council's documents.[68] In itself, it is not

---

[65] Tillard states that as a result of this fact, inculturation should not be treated as some kind of exclusively "local" aspect of church existence, but seen as being intrinsically constitutive of its universality as well. Cf. Tillard, *Église d'églises*, p. 30.

[66] This question will be fully addressed in chapter seven, parts I and II.

[67] Additional sources for this section include: Franco Brambilla, "La parrochia nella Chiesa: Riflessione fondamentale," *Teologia* 13/1 (1988), pp. 18-44; Jim Castelli and Joseph Gremillion, *The Emerging Parish: The Notre Dame Study of Catholic Life Since Vatican II* (San Francisco: Harper and Row, 1987); Albert Houssiau, "L'approche théologique de la paroisse," *Revue Théologique de Louvain* 13 (1982), pp. 317-328; J. Lescrauwert, "Die Parochie in de Ecclesiologie van het Tweede Vaticaanse Concilie," in *De Parochie*, ed. A. Houssiau et al. (Brugge: Uitgeverij Tabor, 1988), pp. 37-49; and John Zizioulas, *Being as Communion: Studies in Personhood and the Church* (Crestwood, N.Y.: St. Vladimir's Seminary Press, 1985).

[68] The word *paroecia* (parish) is found on 22 occasions, the word *parochus* (parish priest) is found on 19, and the word *paroecialis* (parochial) is found on another 10. However, there are a variety of other expressions which are also used to designate the parish. These include: local assembly of the faithful (*congregatio localis fidelium*); assembly of the faithful (*congregatio fidelium*); local community (*communitas localis*); cell of the diocese (*cellula diocesis*); ecclesiastical family (*familia ecclesiastica*), and so forth. Cf. Philippe Delhaye et al., eds. *Concilium Vaticanum II: Concordance, index, listes de fréquence, tables comparatives* (Louvain: Cetedoc, 1974).

a major subject of reflection. This is partly a result of the broader ecclesiological focus of Vatican II. But it was certainly envisioned that the deliberations of the Council, especially in areas touching on liturgy, laity, and the role of bishops and priests, would have a considerable impact on parish life. This, indeed, has been the case. Vatican II has helped restore a more communal and collegial sense to what it means to belong to and participate in a parochial assembly of the local church.[69]

Of the various references to the parish in the conciliar documents there are seven texts in particular which deal more explicitly with the parishes' ecclesiological identity and character. These references warrant some further examination. They are found in: LG 26,28; PO 5,6,8; AA 10; and SC 42.[70] Some of these texts we have already seen in dealing with the Council's understanding of local church. But all of them bear further review so as to get as comprehensive an understanding as possible of the council's theology of parish.

In LG 26 reference is made to the "altar communities" of the bishop's church. "In these communities, though they may often be small and poor, or existing in the diaspora, Christ is present through whose power and influence the One, Holy, Catholic and Apostolic Church is constituted." LG 26 indicates that the parish is a fundamental component of the bishop's church, and hence shares in the ecclesiality of the universal church.[71]

In LG 28 we find mention made of the parish as being "a local assembly of the faithful" under the care of a priest who represents the bishop. Referring to the duties of the pastor, it is further stated that "those who, under the authority of the bishop, sanctify and govern that portion of the Lord's flock assigned to them render the universal church visible in their locality and contribute efficaciously towards building up the whole body of Christ." Of particular significance here is the idea of the parish rendering visible the church in a particular locale, and contributing to the building up

---

[69] Recent statistics indicate that there are over 210,000 parishes worldwide—plus an additional 158,000 mission stations and chapels that are served from neighboring parishes—for a total of over 368,000 "pastoral centers" serving some 825,000,000 Catholics. Cited by Jim Castelli and Joseph Gremillion, *The Emerging Parish: The Notre Dame Study of Catholic Life Since Vatican II* (San Francisco: Harper and Row, 1987), p. 1.

[70] This according to the research of Albert Houssiau, "L'approche théologique de la paroisse," *Revue Théologique de Louvain* 13 (1982), p. 317.

[71] "The ecclesial community, while always having a universal dimension, finds its most immediate and visible expression in the parish. It is here that the Church is seen locally." John Paul II, *Christifideles Laici* 26.

of the whole Body of Christ.[72]

In the Decree on the Ministry and Life of Priests (*Presbyterorum Ordinis*), there are noteworthy references to the parish in sections 5, 6, and 8. Beginning with PO 5 it is stated that, "the eucharistic celebration is the center of the assembly of the faithful over which the priest presides." The faithful are further described as being "fully incorporated in the Body of Christ by the reception of the Eucharist." Here again stress is placed on eucharist as being an activity which *makes* the church.[73] But priests are also to engage in other evangelical activities to promote the spiritual welfare of the people. Of significance in the mentioning of these other activities is the realization that, as important as eucharistic celebration is, it is not the only thing that happens in the parish. There are other important activities that contribute to the building up of the life of the community.[74]

PO 6 deals more specifically with the nature of the pastoral authority which has been delegated to priests by their bishops as a result of their presbyteral ordination. The priest is not only the presider of the eucharistic assembly but is also the overall pastoral leader of the parish community. Within this context it is further stated that:

> The pastor's task is not limited to individual care of the
> faithful. It extends by right also to the formation of a
> genuine Christian community. But if a community spirit
> is to be properly cultivated it must embrace not only the

---

[72] Reflecting on the importance of this passage in LG 28 for a theological understanding of the parish, Aloys Grillmeier says that the parish is thus "a microcosm of the diocese, indeed of the whole church...this is an indication of the theological significance of the parish in the Church as a whole, and provides a foundation on which other texts could build." Cf. Grillmeier, Commentary on LG 28, in *Commentary on the Documents of Vatican II*, Vol. I, p. 224.

[73] "Plainly and simply, the parish is founded on a theological reality because it is a Eucharistic community." John Paul II. *Christifideles Laici* 26.

[74] Some liturgists have complained of an over emphasis in ecclesiology on eucharist as being the primary means of realizing the church in the parish. For instance Daniel Callahan sees the quality of the relationships among parishioners and clergy as being more foundational to the engendering of authentic Christian community. Eucharist would be seen as helping to celebrate and solidify it. According to Callahan the eucharist therefore presupposes community more than it creates it. See Daniel Callahan, "Creating a Community," in *The Postconciliar Parish*, ed. James O'Gara (New York: P.J. Kenedy, 1967), p. 111.

However this critique, while having some merit, seems to go too far in stressing the human dimension of parish community to the detriment of recognizing the necessary role which the divine activity of the Spirit plays in helping to actualize the ecclesial Body of Christ in the eucharist. Most liturgists today would argue that the human and divine aspects inherent in what it means to celebrate eucharist complement one another, thus avoiding a false dichotomy. Cf. Eugene A. Walsh, "The Church Makes the Eucharist; The Eucharist Makes the Church," *Church* 2/3 (1986), pp. 24-30.

local church but the universal Church. A local community ought not merely to promote the care of the faithful within itself, but should be imbued with the missionary spirit and smooth the path to Christ for all.

What is interesting to note about this passage is the recognition that pastoral care in the local community is not just a matter of ministering to individuals, but of helping to build a genuine community.[75] Presumably, the presence of such community will also contribute to the pastoral care and support that parishioners can receive from their priests and from one another. Furthermore, this community-building activity is not just inwardly focused, but also outwardly oriented in its missionary thrust.

PO 8 recognizes that not all priests are engaged in parochial ministry. Some are engaged in "supra-parochial" ministries or in other apostolates which help in the mission of the church. An appeal is made for greater cooperation among all priests and religious on the local level. For, "they all contribute to the same purpose, namely the building up of the body of Christ, and this, especially in our times, demands many kinds of duties and fresh adaptations." What this passage reveals is that, as important as the parish is to the local church, it is not the only means for the organization of the apostolate. Furthermore, because of the "times" we live in, "fresh adaptations" are needed to carry out ministry and promote Christian community.[76]

In the Decree on the Apostolate of Lay People (*Apostolicam Actuositatem*) attention is given to the vital role of the laity in the vocation of the church. Chapter three of this decree deals with the variety of "fields" wherein the apostolate can be found and exercised. One of these fields is the parish. In AA 10 it is stated that, "the parish offers an outstanding example of community apostolate, for it gathers into a unity all the human diversities that are found there and inserts them into the universality of the Church." The parish is further described in this section as being an "ecclesial family."

---

[75] Stressing the need for the parish to be a place of genuine community, John Paul II has said that "the parish is not principally a structure, a territory, a building. The parish is first of all a community of the faithful....That is the task of the Parish today: to be a community, to rediscover itself as community." Address to Parish Focolarini, March 3, 1986. Cited in the *East Asian Pastoral Review* 3 (1988), p. 254.

[76] A call for parish adaptation was also made at the 1987 Synod of Bishops. "The Synod Fathers for their part have given much attention to the present state of many parishes and have called for a greater effort in their renewal. . . . So that all parishes of this kind may be truly communities of Christians, local ecclesial authorities ought to foster the following: a) adaptation of parish structures. . . [and] b) small, basic or so-called 'living' communities." Cf. John Paul II, *Christifideles Laici* 26.

It is also spoken of as being a "kind of cell" of the diocese.[77]

The image of family underlines the social nature of parish community. The comparison to being a cell of the diocese highlights how the parish shares in the ecclesiality of the local church. But most noteworthy of all is the recognition that lay people have a role to play in the apostolate of the parish itself. Activities geared towards the building up of the parish community are not to be carried out only by priests and religious. This is also corroborated by AA 26, where it is recommended that parish councils be set up, indicating the extent of the co-responsibility the laity are to have in the parish. Thus, the laity have an essential role to play both in the world and church at large, as well as in the specific context of the parish.[78]

The final text to be examined deals with the promotion of the liturgical life of the diocese and the parish. In SC 42 it is stated that due to pastoral necessity, the bishop should establish parishes and other groupings wherever needed so that, "they may represent the visible Church constituted throughout the world." This idea of the parish rendering visible the church was also mentioned in LG 28. But of further significance is the recognition that pastoral need plays a role in the raison d'etre of the parish community. As we have seen Congar point out, the parish originated as a "pastoral convenience."[79] But this fact does not lessen its importance nor its fundamental ecclesiality. If anything, it draws attention to the fact that the fulfilling of pastoral needs is a constitutive component *of* the ecclesiality of the parish (this has implications too for the question of the ecclesiality of SCCs).[80]

In attempting to provide a synthesis of what these indications of the parish in the Council documents represent theologically, Albert Houssiau is led to identify two major characteristics.[81] Firstly, the parish is simultaneously a visible and localized ecclesial reality, as well as a spiritual or mystical manifestation of the Body of Christ. This includes recognition of the eucharistic nature of the parish community. Secondly, the ecclesiality of the parish derives from and is dependent upon its participation in the local church. The ecclesial nature and role of the parish vis-à-vis the local

---

[77] During his 1987 pastoral visit to the United States John Paul II gave an address in San Antonio, Texas wherein this idea of the parish being an ecclesial family was reiterated. Cf. John Paul II, "The Parish: Family of Families," *Origins* 17/17 (1987), pp. 288-290.

[78] "In the present circumstances the lay faithful have the ability to do very much and, therefore, ought to do very much towards the growth of an authentic ecclesial communion in their parishes." John Paul II, *Christifideles Laici* 27.

[79] See chapter one, part III, section B § 1.

[80] The question of how SCCs can be understood to share in the ecclesiality of the parish/local church will be examined later in chapter seven, parts I and II.

[81] Cf. Houssiau, "L'approche théologique de la paroisse," p. 319.

church is analogous to the ecclesial nature and role of the local church vis-à-vis the universal church.[82]

Furthermore, because the parish as an institution or instrument of the local church does not belong historically to the *ius divinum,* but was a social construct developed to meet the pastoral needs of the people, there is nothing sacrosanct about its structure (as opposed to its nature and function). This means that the actual organizational structure of the parish is free to continue developing and adapting itself to meet these pastoral exigencies. Sabbas Kilian expresses this point very well:

> The concrete form and the precise details of the human structure [of the parish] can never be defined once and for all . . . As individual and social life evolves with the changing cultural background and rapid technological achievements, it is not only possible but also necessary that the precise structural form of the relationship of the human and the divine be questioned, reexamined, and reformulated . . . [Thus] whenever we deal with the Church and its human structure, this unique problem weighs heavily in our theological formulations.[83]

The need for adaptation is already attested to in the variety of other non-parochial apostolates and communities that operate with the blessing of the bishop in the local church. This might explain why the actual word "parish" is used so sparingly in the conciliar documents which refer to the various groupings of the faithful in the local church. The Council did not want to give the impression that parishes exhaust the compositional reality of the local church.[84] This is why a variety of other more inclusive terms are used when referring to these groups as a whole in the diocese.

---

[82] In a similar vein Gianfranco Ghirlanda concludes that the conciliar documents vis à vis the parish indicate that we can "say that in a particular way, the notion of local church can be applied to the parish, although not exclusively so, since it can also be attributed to other local communities." But the significance of the parish's ecclesiality "is why the local community can be referred to as the Church of God." Ghirlanda, "Universal Church, Particular Church, and Local church at the Second Vatican Council and in the New Code of Canon Law," p. 244.

[83] Kilian, *Theological Models for the Parish*, pp. 17-18.

[84] Grillmeier says that "the diocese, and indeed the whole Church, is reflected more clearly in the parish than in any other 'local gatherings of the faithful' of a less organic type, because the parish embodies most fully the authority of the bishop. But this characteristic of being 'an embodiment of the whole Church' is also shared by other communities dedicated to the service of God, especially (religious) communities approved by the Church." Cf. *Commentary on the Documents of Vatican II*, Vol. I, p. 224.

Our review of the conciliar theology of the parish reveals that it reflects many of the theological insights which were first articulated by various theologians in the preconciliar period. From the point of view of new theological insights, the Council did not break any new ground in its reflections concerning the parish. What is new of course is the way in which the Council can be said to have officially adopted and ratified many of these preconciliar theological insights. This fact, when seen in the broader context of the other developments in ecclesiology, theology of the laity, and liturgy at Vatican II, helps explain the considerable impact conciliar thought had, and is still having, on the parish.

However, to say, then, that there are elements of a theology of parish to be found in the documents of Vatican II, is not to say that the council articulated these elements in any kind of comprehensive or systematic manner. And it is not to imply that the Council's depiction of the vocation and mission of the parish has not met any critique. One of the more radical critiques is to be found in some theologians who object to the current diocesan parish system itself. For instance, Orthodox theologian John Zizioulas sees the historical emergence of the parish system in the early medieval period as being something which has fundamentally destroyed the ability of the local church to be truly an episcopal community.[85]

This was due to the fact that no longer did priests live in a college with the bishop. The stationing of priests in parishes led to an effective erosion of an episcopal sense of local church. Parishes became self-sufficient entities which were *presbytero-centered*, rather than *presbyterium-centered*. This development he feels has effectively made the bishop redundant in the parish. According to Zizioulas, the parish in no way qualifies theologically to be considered a truly ecclesial reality. Not even the celebration of the eucharist in the parish can be seen as "making" it church, because its fundamental nature as an episcopal community has been so undermined. "It is for these reasons that we should regard the proper ecclesiological status of the parish as one of the most fundamental problems in ecclesiology—both in the West and in the East."[86]

Although Zizioulas' critique has some merit, he seems to pay insufficient attention to the pastoral exigencies that led to the creation of the parish system in the first place. These exigencies are still with us today. Furthermore, the episcopal nature of the local church is now a prominent feature of both Orthodox and Catholic ecclesiology. While there still remains work to be done inculcating this renewed sense of the episcopal

---

[85] John Zizioulas, *Being as Communion: Studies in Personhood and the Church*, p. 250.
[86] *Ibid.*, p. 251.

nature of the local church in the consciousness of Catholics, this is pastoral problem, not a theological one.

While not taking anything away from the profound changes that Vatican II wrought in the life and theology of the church, it can be said that the Council did not really envision any radical changes to the basic parish structure itself, or to the parish system of the diocese.[87] What was revolutionized was the manner of lay and clerical participation in the life, liturgy, and mission of the parish. What was not foreseen was the way in which these latter, more fundamental changes, coupled with the effects of rapid socio-cultural changes, would lead in a very short time to new experiments in structuring parish life, epitomized in the small Christian community phenomenon.

What made the recognition of the fundamental ecclesiality of the parish possible in Vatican II was of course the recovery of an authentic understanding of local church. If the local church was a neglected feature of official preconciliar ecclesiology, this was even more so the case with the parish. As we have seen, the parish was previously treated more as an aspect of canon law than it was of theology. The new conciliar understanding helped restore the primacy of parish being a people, rather than a place.

Paradoxically, all the attention which local church has received from theologians in the postconciliar period has led to a certain diminishment in attention being paid to the theology of parish.[88] This is not to imply that there has been a complete absence of reflection in this area.[89] But most of what has been going on has been done more in a sociological or liturgical vein. One topic which has received much attention both sociologically and theologically has been the small Christian community phenomenon. This development seems to hold the most promise not only pastorally for the parish, but also for expanding theological reflection on its vocation and mission. However, before turning to this topic, a brief look at how the theology of parish is expressed in the new Code of Canon Law is needed in order to round out our understanding of the church's perception of the parish institution.

---

[87] In terms of internal organization, the call for parish councils (AA 26) is arguably the most "structural" new development Vatican II mandated for the parish.

[88] This according to Franco Brambilla, "La parrochia nella Chiesa: Riflessione fondamentale," *Teologia* 13/1 (1988), p. 29.

[89] A notable contribution is Sabbas Kilian's *Theological Models of the Parish*. Kilian applies an Avery Dulles-inspired "models of the church" analysis to the parish setting. His insights help synthesize conciliar thinking vis à vis the parish.

II THE PARISH IN THE NEW CODE OF CANON LAW[90]

In an allocution on the 9th of December 1983, Pope John Paul II said that "the Code of Canon Law, which is the last Conciliar document, will also be the first to integrate the whole of the Council into the whole of life," since "in a certain sense this new Code could be understood as a great effort to translate this same conciliar ecclesiology into canonical language."[91] We will be looking in this section at how this effort at translating the council's ecclesiology into canonical terms has affected the parish. This is not meant to be a juridical analysis of all the canons that pertain to parish life. It is simply intended to highlight some of the more significant aspects of the current legislation.

It is helpful to begin with a brief review of how the parish was treated in the old 1917 Code. This Code (in canon 216) offered no definition of parish per se, rather it set out a description of its juridical features. Thus, a parish was understood to be: (1) a territorial section of a diocese; (2) with a portion of the Catholic population assigned to it; and (3) having a proper pastor who looked after the care of souls.[92] Furthermore, the parish was considered to be a benefice to provide for the livelihood of the pastor. Summing up the basic thrust of the 1917 Code vis-à-vis the parish, John Huels states: "the emphasis of the former law was on the rights and duties of the pastor; the parishioners were referred to only indirectly and seen as the passive subjects of the care of souls with no recognition by the law of their having any active role in the functioning of the parish."[93]

The new 1983 Code takes an entirely different approach. The pertinent sections dealing with the parish, pastors, and parochial vicars (canons 515-552) are found in Book II of the Code, which is entitled *The People of God* (in accord with the second chapter of *Lumen Gentium* on which it depends).[94] It begins in Canon 515 with a definition of the parish:

---

[90]Principle sources for this section are: Victor Balke, "The Parish Pastoral Council," *Origins* 16/47 (1987), pp. 821-825; Robert Carlson, "The Parish According to the Revised Law," *Studia Canonica* 19 (1985), pp. 5-16; Eugenio Corecco, "Ecclesiological Bases of the Code," *Concilium* 185 (1986), pp. 3-13; John Huels, "Parish Life and The New Code," *Concilium* 185 (1986), pp. 64-72; Joseph A. Janicki, "Commentary on Canons 515-572," in James A. Coriden et al., eds. *The Code of Canon Law: A Text and Commentary* (New York/Mahwah: Paulist Press, 1985), Book II, pp. 414-449 and John Lynch, "The Parochial Ministry in the New Code of Canon Law." *The Jurist* XLII (1982), 383-421.

[91] Cited by Gianfranco Ghirlanda, "Universal Church, Particular Church, and Local Church at the Second Vatican Council and in the New Code of Canon Law," p. 233.

[92] Cf. Janicki, "Commentary on Canons 515-572," p. 415.

[93] Huels, "Parish Life and The New Code," pp. 64-65.

[94] Cf. John Alesandro, "General Introduction—The Code and Ecclesiology," in *The Code of Canon Law: a Text and Commentary*, p. 8.

"A parish is a definite community of the Christian faithful established on a stable basis within a particular church; the pastoral care of the parish is entrusted to a pastor as its own shepherd under the authority of the diocesan bishop."[95] The emphasis here is on the parish being a community within the local church. This receives mention ahead of any reference to the pastor and his role. Furthermore, the understanding is that the people *form* a parish community, not that they simply *belong* to it by dint of territory.[96]

This is not to imply that territoriality is no longer juridically important. Canon 518 states that "as a general rule a parish is to be territorial, that is it embraces all the Christian faithful within a certain territory." However territoriality is not the only basis on which a parish can be established. This same canon also stipulates that, "whenever it is judged useful, however, personal parishes are to be established based upon rite, language, the nationality of the Christian faithful within some territory or even upon some other determining factor."

As we have noted earlier, the existence of so-called "personal" parishes was ratified as far back as the Council of Trent, and was also a feature of the old Code. The significance of allowing other kinds of parishes is that it frees the bishop to respond creatively to the pastoral needs of diverse groups within the diocese.[97] As important as territory is as an organizing principle for the establishment of parishes, it is not the only means for effectively responding to people's pastoral needs for Christian community. Pastoral need is sometimes best served by forming parishes along other lines as well.

This principle is also attested to in Canon 516, which deals with what are known as *quasi-parishes* or *missions*. These are communities which are not full parishes because they somehow lack all the necessary resources or qualifications.[98] They tend to be smaller in size and exist some distance from a full-fledged parish center. They are usually linked to a nearby parish and served by the pastor from there and/or by an "administrator" of some kind. But other than lacking a resident pastor, they often display most of the features of a full parish community, including having their own pastoral councils, sacramental preparation programs,

---

[95] The translation of the Code used throughout this survey is from *The Code of Canon Law: A Text and Commentary.*

[96] Cf. Janicki, "Commentary on Canons 515-552," p. 416.

[97] *Ibid.,* p. 419.

[98] "Ordinarily, a quasi-parish is equivalent in law to a parish unless the law provides otherwise. A quasi-parish is one which has not been established as a parish because it lacks one or more qualifications, e.g., resident pastor; necessary financial resources; territorial boundaries or a natural grouping by way of rite, nationality, or language. Presumably, quasi-parishes could eventually become parishes in their own right." *Ibid.,* p. 417.

liturgical celebrations and so on.[99] What is significant about quasi-parishes is that they are a duly constituted ecclesial community of the parish/local church and have a corresponding juridical identity.[100]

The same thing cannot be said at this point in time about formal juridic identity and small Christian communities. This statement needs qualification. As we shall see many SCCs in Latin America, Africa, and Asia really function as quasi-parishes or missions, and are recognized and treated as such by the local bishops. SCCs in North America, because of the different pastoral and social context, are generally not seen in this light. At the time of the drafting of the new Code, SCCs had already become a sufficiently noteworthy phenomenon for some people to suggest that they be granted some kind of official canonical recognition.[101]

But it was eventually decided that it would be more prudent not to explicitly refer to them in the Code. This was not an attempt to snub their growing importance, but was a recognition that SCCs were (and still remain) a very diverse and evolving phenomenon. Premature juridic expression might result in putting SCCs into a pastoral straightjacket. John Huels comments:

> As a general rule it is preferable for the universal law to say too little rather than too much on any matter, especially regarding something new. . . . The best code for a universal Church is one which establishes general principles and essential norms while allowing the particular churches to specify the details. The Code is apparently following this principle in regard to . . . new developments in parish life, such as the division of parishes in some areas of the world into "base communities."[102]

---

[99] It is interesting to note that having a special church building has never been a requirement of being a mission or even a parish for that matter. Sometimes assemblies are held in school gymnasiums, inside people's homes, or even in settings that are outdoors. Buildings are important for facilitating liturgy and so on, but are not of the essence for what it means to be church.

[100] Recognition of the ecclesiality of quasi-parishes will be a factor in our later analysis of the ecclesiality claimed by North American SCCs. Cf. Chapter seven, part I, section A.

[101] "Some have faulted the new Code of Canon law for not covering BECs. The omission may prove providential, since it may be much too early to codify BECs in legislation." Azevedo, *Basic Ecclesial Communities in Brazil*, p. 105, note #22.

[102] Huels, "Parish Life and The New Code," p. 69.

The final point worth highlighting in regard to the new Code and the parish is the way lay people are portrayed as playing an active and collegial role in various aspects of its administration and the fostering of pastoral activity.[103] This is reflected in many canons dealing with such matters as participation in parish pastoral councils, finance councils, and other parochial ministries and activities. The ideal that is presented is one of mutual cooperation between pastors and lay people in the work of building up the parish community.[104]

But as we know, since the closing of Vatican II in 1965 and the promulgation of the Code in 1983, much had transpired in the area of clergy-laity relations in the parish. These relations have not been always idyllic. For instance Bishop Victor Balke of the diocese of Crookston, Minnesota, laments the abuse of the principle of lay co-responsibility in the parish, especially in the first decade or so of the postconciliar period. In an article about parish pastoral councils, he notes the extremes to which some councils went to in effectively undermining and usurping the pastor's proper role in the parish. He mentions this, he says, not to assign blame but to point out the difficulties the church has faced in the postconciliar period working out the practical consequences of Vatican II's ecclesiological principles.[105]

However, other commentators see these difficulties as being one of the reasons why the Code seems to downplay certain features of the Council's ecclesiology, especially in this area of lay co-responsibility for the welfare of the parish.[106] For instance, Joseph Janicki laments the fact that the new Code did not see fit to universally legislate the necessity of establishing parish councils, being content with allowing their establishment if the local bishop judges it "opportune" (Canon 536). It is further stressed in this canon that the parish council exercises only a "consultative" role in connection with the pastor. Regarding the pastor, Janicki sees generally too much mention made of and stress given to his leadership role in the canons

---

[103] The pastor's role, by virtue of his ordination, is still seen as being necessarily distinct from that of the laity. "The parallel between the office of bishop and that of the pastor of a parish can be seen particularly in their ministerial duties. Because he participates in the ministry of the bishop, the pastor's primary role is to teach, sanctify, and govern, a threefold function (*munus*) rooted basically in holy orders and determined by canonical mission." Thus, "the parish priest is the spiritual head of the parish and truly represents the invisible Lord, and it is his duty to unite the faithful in a community founded in and for Christ." Janicki, "Commentary on Canons 515-572," p. 420.

[104] Pertaining to this ideal are the fundamental values which Huels thinks are inherent in the Code's treatment of the parish: (1) fidelity to Vatican II ecclesiology; (2) subsidiarity; (3) pastoral flexibility; and (4) collegiality in the broader participation by non-priests in parish leadership. Cf. Huels, "Parish Life and the New Code," p. 67.

[105] Victor Balke, "The Parish Pastoral Council," p. 823.

[106] Cf. Janicki, "Commentary on Canons 515-572," p. 420.

on the parish. "By contrast, little attention is given to other members of the parish in the law."[107]

The Code then is not without its critics. But on balance, many canonists judge it to have given faithful juridic expression to the ecclesiology of Vatican II.[108] This canonical expression is important in that Catholic ecclesiology understands communion to have a juridic dimension. As the *Preliminary Explanatory Note* (PEN) affixed to the end of *Lumen Gentium* describes it, "communion . . . is not to be understood as some vague sort of goodwill, but as something organic which calls for a juridical structure as well as being enkindled by charity" (PEN 2). Thus, the law on the parish, while being of secondary importance theologically, is also a part of the nature of the church. It is not intended to stifle further developments in areas of church practice, but rather to act more as a safeguard against potential abuses.

---

[107] *Ibid.*

[108] John Huels for one makes this assertion, and provides a good summation of how the parish is treated in the new Code:

> In general, the innovations in the law on parishes in the revised Code indicate that its drafters were successful, both theoretically and in practice, in implementing the principles that guided the reform of the Code as a whole. The canons on parishes reflect a number of important ecclesiological principles emphasised at Vatican II, including subsidiarity, collegiality, the importance of the diocesan bishop and the local church community, and the active role of the layperson in church life. The section on parishes in the revised Code is also quite acceptable from a practical perspective. It makes provision for the church of the future that will have fewer priests to staff parishes. It shows great flexibility in permitting local adaptations and specific determinations of the various parish structures, and in some cases making them optional. Such provisions . . . suggest a sensitivity in this section of the Code to postconciliar developments and the needs and objectives of contemporary parish life.

Huels, "Parish Life and the New Code," pp. 68-69.

CHAPTER THREE

The Parish in North America

I. PARISH LIFE IN NORTH AMERICA[1]

A. Historical Significance

There are available a number of excellent histories of the Catholic church in general, and the parish in particular, in its North American setting.[2] But outlining in historical fashion the rise and development of parish life in North America is beyond the scope of our present study. What will be attempted instead is an explanation of some of the general features of this history, so as to gain an appreciation of the role the parish has played in the life of Catholics in this region of the world.

For the sake of expediency most of the references in this chapter will be to the American experience. This is not meant to slight the Canadian experience. But the reasons for this are twofold. Firstly, the church in the U.S. is much larger than in Canada and has better documented studies of the historical and cultural setting of the parish. Secondly, in general terms, the experience of the church in so-called *English* Canada parallels that of the U.S. The situation in *French* Canada (particularly Quebec) is a different

---

[1] Principal sources for this section are: Jim Castelli and Joseph Gremillion, *The Emerging Parish: The Notre Dame Study of Catholic Life Since Vatican II* (San Francisco: Harper and Row, 1987); Commission d'étude sur les laïcs l'Église, *Histoire de l'Église catholique au Québec (1608-1970)* (Montreal: Fides, 1971); Jay P. Dolan and Jeffrey Burns, "The Parish in the American Past," *Parish Ministry* 3/5 (1982), pp. 1-4; Jay P. Dolan, *The American Catholic Experience: A History from Colonial Times to the Present* (Garden City, N.Y.: Doubleday, 1985), Jay P. Dolan, "The American Catholic Parish: A Historical Perspective 1820-1980," in *The Parish in Transition: Proceedings of a Conference on the American Catholic Parish,* ed. David Byers (NCCB: Washington, D.C.: 1985), pp. 34-46, *The American Catholic Parish: A History from 1850 to the Present, 2 Vols.,* ed. Jay P. Dolan (New York/ Mahwah: Paulist Press, 1987); NCCB Parish Project, *The Parish: A People, A Mission, A Structure* (NCCB, Washington, D.C.: 1980); NCCB Parish Project, *Parish Life in the United States* (Washington, D.C.: NCCB, 1983); and Ulysse E. Paré, "The Church in Canada," *The Canadian Catholic Review* 4/7 (1986), pp. 247-253.

[2] For historical studies of the church in the United States and in Canada see some of the sources listed in note #1 above.

story. In many ways its history and culture more closely resembles that of a Catholic country or region in Western Europe.[3]

Yet Quebec is also a part of North America, and so shares in many aspects of the *North American* lifestyle as well. This diversity of experience within the church of Canada is also a fact of life in the U.S. church. Neither country as a whole has an homogenous ethnic Catholic population, and neither country has a general population wherein Catholics are in the majority. Due to these and other similarities it is possible and legitimate to speak in general terms of a *North American* experience of church in this region of the world.

The first thing worth noting about the history of the church in North America is that it is a relatively recent phenomenon. Compared with Catholic regions of Europe, the church in North America is still in its infancy. For this reason, according to Jay Dolan, "the weight of the past is quite light; it does not leave the imprint on contemporary Catholic culture in the same manner than an ancient Catholic tradition does in a country like Ireland."[4] Nevertheless, the past, however brief it has been when measured in terms of historical time, has shaped the present.

A key to understanding the history of North American Catholicism is the parish. In the nineteenth century the parish was the central gathering place for the people. It was a neighborhood institution wherein Catholics, many of whom were recent immigrants, practised their faith and also socialized. In the course of the nineteenth century many other Catholic institutions such as hospitals, orphanages, schools and colleges were developed. Nonetheless, the parish remained the most important institution in the Catholic community. Dolan goes so far as to claim that, "it is no exaggeration to say that in the nineteenth century the parish was the foundation of American Catholicism. Without it everything else would have collapsed."[5]

In other countries where religion and culture were closely interwoven, the parish was not perhaps as central in the sustenance of Catholicism. In a country such as Ireland, Catholicism had been the religion of the majority for over a thousand years, and had thoroughly penetrated its cultural bedrock. In such a setting, the parish was only one of many cultural and religious institutions that nourished the faith of the people. In North

---

[3] For a good discussion of Québécois church and culture see: Raymond Lemieux, "Le catholicisme québécois: une question de culture," *Sociologie et sociétés* 22/2 (1990), pp. 145-164.

[4] Dolan, *The American Catholic Parish*, Vol I, p. 2.

[5] *Ibid.*, p. 3.

America, except for Quebec, Protestantism was the cultural bedrock and the separation of church and state was the norm.[6]

Thus, Catholics were in the minority, and often suffered various kinds of persecution.[7] The parish became a haven from prejudice, a kind of sanctuary out of which a wide range of other social and welfare services were provided to the Catholic community. It thus functioned, in the words of Philip Murnion, as a "comprehensive community," and fostered a high degree of solidarity among its parishioners.[8] This is why the parish in its North American setting acquired such a significant role in Catholic life.

In reviewing this history, Dolan and his colleague Jeffrey Burns see four major stages or trends in the development of parish life in America.[9] They refer to these stages as: (1) The Home Parish; (2) The Congregational (Mission) Parish; (3) The Devotional (Organizational) Parish; and (4) The Voluntary Parish. These four stages are worth taking a brief look at.

The *Home Parish* was a prominent feature of Catholic life in the early Colonial period. The first "parishes" operated out of the homes of wealthier Catholics, in much the same manner as the early Christian house churches. There were generally few Catholics in the colonies at this time. From the late 18th century to the mid-19th century there developed more established congregations or missions, but actual parish buildings were still a rarity.

During this period active lay leadership was still a significant feature of these congregations due to the general shortage of clergy. What clergy there were often had to "ride the circuit" to visit various mission outposts as often as they could. The laity had to bear most of the responsibility themselves for keeping alive the faith and organizing other aspects of the community's life. This was part and parcel of what came to be known as the lay *trustee system*. Despite the inevitable tension that sometimes arose because of "irascible" trustees and "authoritarian" priests, this system worked remarkably well.[10] This system gradually disappeared

---

[6] "The dominant fact in the life of the American parish is the fact that, in the United States, Catholicism began as an immigrant religion in a nation with an overwhelmingly Protestant culture." Castelli and Gremillion, *The Emerging Parish*, p. 10.

[7] "The influx of Catholic immigrants triggered a negative reaction among many white Anglo-Saxon Protestants, who felt threatened by change and greeted newcomers with bigotry and occasional violence." *Ibid.*, p. 13.

[8] Philip J. Murnion, "The Parish as Source of Community and Identity," in *The Parish in Community and Ministry*, ed. Evelyn Whitehead (New York: Paulist Press, 1978), pp. 104-105.

[9] Cf. Dolan and Burns, "The Parish in the American Past," pp. 1-4.

[10] Cf. Dolan, "The American Catholic Parish: A Historical Perspective 1820-1980," p. 35. Commenting on this development Dolan notes: "History has not been kind to this tradition in American Catholicism and has wrongly depicted the trustee system and lay trustees as

through the course of the 19th century as church life became more formally organized and institutionalized around the bishops and priests.

With massive increases in Catholic immigrants in the 19th century, especially in urban areas, there dawned the age of the *Organizational Parish*. The parish became the base for a multitude of religious and social services for these newer immigrant communities. A significant feature of parish life at the time was the spread of various kinds of devotional and benevolent societies. These included: The Holy Name Society; The Altar Society; The Knights of Columbus; The St. Vincent de Paul Society; and so on. These various societies remained a prominent feature of parish life up until Vatican II. Although the more devotional-type societies have waned considerably since then, the other major benevolent ones are still quite active today.[11]

After the Second World War there began a massive exodus of Catholics from their largely ethnic city parishes into new suburban ones. This demographical shift also corresponded with Catholics becoming more of an integral part of "mainstream" America. They became better educated, moved up into professional jobs, and earned more income than had their forbears. This contributed to increased social mobility, and it helped usher in the era of the *Voluntary Parish*.

It became voluntary in the sense that people felt freer to choose the parish they wanted to affiliate with, and to determine the extent of their participation in it. The parish no longer needed to provide all manner of social or welfare services. The newer suburban parishes were less ethically homogeneous than their city counterparts. For a variety of reasons, the parish lost its role as being a *comprehensive* community. Coupled with the other massive cultural changes which were going on in the 1960s, and in the aftermath of Vatican II, parish participation declined dramatically.[12] Someone who has written extensively about the impact which many of these various social changes have had on American Catholic life is Andrew Greeley.[13]

---

detrimental to Catholic life. Though the system had some problems . . . it worked remarkably well in numerous parish communities."

[11] Cf. NCCB Parish Project, *Parish Life in the United States*, p. 3.

[12] *Ibid.*, p. 9. "In the 1960s and early '70s, therefore, there were many forces affecting church life as part of a broader social phenomenon that loosened the bonds of common belief, values, relationships and practices. Church attendance began to decline for the first time in our history until finally in the late '70s a third smaller percentage of Catholics were to be found at Mass on Sunday than had been present in 1967."

[13] Cf. Greeley, *The American Catholic: A Social Portrait* (New York: Basic Books, 1977); and a work he co-authored entitled *Parish, Priest and People* (Chicago: Thomas More Press, 1981).

Because this recounting of some of the important features of parish life in American history has brought us up to date, we turn now and look more closely at the contemporary situation of the parish. There are two studies in particular which are worth utilizing in this regard. The first involves the work of the *Parish Project* which was commissioned by the NCCB and begun in 1978. The second, which was inspired by the first, is the *Notre Dame Study of Catholic Parish Life*, begun in 1982. Because it is more recent in origin and more comprehensive in nature, more attention will be paid to examining the findings of this latter study.

B. The Contemporary Situation

1. The NCCB's "Parish Project"

In November of 1975 the bishops of the United States convened in Washington for their annual meeting. At that meeting, Bishop Albert Ottenweller, then Auxiliary Bishop of Toledo, Ohio, made a noteworthy appeal to his brother bishops concerning the need to renew parish life in a more fundamental way. He said that although there had been in the years after the Council an expansion of all manner of programs seeking to renew the parish, the general situation had continued to deteriorate. "My contention is that one reason the parish is so weak for our times is that one point is longer than the other—that institution is very strong but community is very weak."[14]

Ottenweller cited the book by Stephen Clark, *Building Christian Communities*, as an example of the direction needed for today.[15] Clark's major thesis is that Christian life in today's increasingly secularized world can only be sustained by creating a more comprehensive community *environment* which can truly foster and sustain personal and ecclesial renewal. Many parishes are offering many *services* to their people, but they are failing in this more fundamental need.

Bishop Ottenweller's statements had quite an impact at the time because they seemed to express and crystallize the experiences and feelings of a good many bishops in attendance.[16] The NCCB soon afterwards decided to form an *ad hoc* committee to study the matter which eventually became known as the *Parish Project*.[17] They were given a wide-ranging

---

[14] This quote is from an address he gave to the Parish Project that reflects his 1975 speech to the NCCB. See "Parish Renewal: A Process, not a Program," *Origins* 8/42 (1979), p. 674.

[15] Cf. Stephen Clark, *Building Christian Communities* (Notre Dame, Indiana: Ave Maria Press, 1972).

[16] Cf. NCCB Parish Project, *Parish Life in the United States*, p. 10.

[17] The director of the Parish Project was Philip J. Murnion.

mandate which included: identifying the critical issues in parish life; assembling and disseminating resources for parish development; undertaking studies of the parish; and so forth. It formally began its work in 1978 and completed its activities in 1982. In the course of its work it published a national directory of parish development programs and resources, a *Vision Statement* for the parish, and a *Final Report* which it submitted to the bishops in November of 1982.[18]

The *Vision Statement* is interesting to note because it attempted to enunciate a coherent and succinct description of the raison d'être of the Catholic parish. This was something its authors felt was lacking in Vatican II's documents which touched on parish life.[19] This vision statement was approved for publication by the NCCB in 1980, and was officially entitled: *The Parish: A People, A Mission, A Structure.* It calls attention to the fact that the parish is for most Catholics "the single most important part of the church."[20] Yet it also recognizes that for all its importance, it defies easy description. "So many hues would be needed to paint an accurate picture of the parish, so many shapes and dimensions to sculpt it. . . . Not only is the parish, therefore, a mystery of faith, but, even at the level of human understanding, any parish eludes neat explanation."[21]

The *Vision Statement* goes on to recognize that people respond to God's call with varying degrees and styles of commitment. This contributes to the natural diversity of parish life and to a diversity of needs within the community. But the parish is not merely a collection of individuals or families, it has a corporate nature as well. Thus, "a parish seeks to become ever more fully a people of God, sharing the mission of Christ, and developing the structure necessary for supporting its community life and carrying out its mission."[22] Rather than attempt to furnish a definition of parish, this statement goes on to elaborate a *vision* or *ideal* of how a parish

---

[18] These were published respectively under the following titles: NCCB Parish Project, *Parish Development: Programs and Organizations* (Washington, D.C.: NCCB, 1980); NCCB Parish Project, *The Parish: A People, A Mission, A Structure* (Washington, D.C.: NCCB, 1980), and NCCB Parish Project, *Parish Life in the United States: Final Report to the Bishops of the United States by the Parish Project* (Washington, D.C.: NCCB, 1983).

[19] "From the beginning it became clear that there was lacking a clear statement of ideals for parish life. Vatican II's many documents obviously had implications for parish life and the reforms of the liturgy that followed directly changed much of parish life. But the parish as such received negligible attention in the Council. [Therefore] the Committee set about a task that proved to be a centerpiece of all its work. This was to articulate a 'Vision Statement' for parishes, a description of the kind of parish life toward which renewal efforts might be directed." Cf. NCCB Parish Project, *Parish Life in the United States*, p. 12.

[20] NCCB Parish Project, *The Parish: A People, A Mission, A Structure*, p. 3.

[21] *Ibid.*

[22] *Ibid.*, p. 5.

community should understand its nature and role. Among the ideas it endorses is the formation of small groups.[23]

The 1982 *Final Report* was as equally wide-ranging as the Parish Project's activities had been. It described the nature of the cultural challenge facing parishes today, examined the variety of current approaches to parish life that are in evidence, noted the impact of many new movements and associations (mentioning in this regard the growing proliferation of small groups), identified the areas of greatest need, and made recommendations pertaining to parish life and structure.[24]

By way of conclusion, the significance of the *Parish Project*'s activities lies not only in the fact of their publication, but also in the indication it gives of the seriousness with which this topic of the parish was (and is) treated by the bishops. Its importance is really self evident, for as Archbishop Daniel Pilarczck of Cincinnati has recently opined, "either the church flourishes in its parishes or it does not flourish at all."[25]

2. The Notre Dame Study of Parish Life

The *Notre Dame Study* of Catholic parish life was a multidisciplinary research endeavour unprecedented in its scope.[26] It was undertaken by a group of scholars at the University of Notre Dame, with the help of funding from the Lilly Endowment. It resulted in a comprehensive, social-scientific survey of parishioners' beliefs, practices, and communal faith experiences, as well as chronicling other structural aspects of parish life. This *Study* provides the best data available on the current state of parishes in the United States.[27] Although it was not intended to be a theological reflection on the parish, it does offer a solid point of departure

---

[23] *Ibid.,* p. 17. "The mission of the parish is often significantly enriched when it provides the people an opportunity to meet in smaller groups in which they can speak and better understand the meaning of their faith and, by doing so, strengthen their commitment and celebrate their unity in Christ."

[24] Because the cultural challenges facing the parish and the impact of lay movements and associations will be addressed in a more thematic manner later in this chapter, no mention is being made of them at this time. Also, due to the fact that the more thoroughly researched and more recent *Notre Dame Study of Parish Life* covers much of the same ground as does this *Final Report,* we will leave this discussion for the next section which follows immediately.

[25] Daniel Pilarczck, "Does the Church Flourish in Its Parishes?" *Origins* 16/39 (1987), p. 682.

[26] Cf. Castelli and Gremillion, *The Emerging Parish: The Notre Dame Study of Catholic Life Since Vatican II,* p. 3.

[27] Dr. David Leege headed the team which compiled most of the reports which form the basis of the *Notre Dame Study.* Castelli and Gremillion's book, *The Emerging Parish,* is a summary presentation of the *Notre Dame Study's* results.

for later theological reflection. This is why some of its findings will be presented and commented upon in summary fashion.[28]

The first phase of the project began in 1981 with a general survey of 1,850 parishes, which represented about 10% of the nation's total number of parishes at the time. The second phase began in 1982 and concluded in 1985. This second part of the *Study* involved an examination of the results of the general survey by sociologists, historians, and theologians. The final phase of the project represented an effort by scholars and church leaders to interpret the significance of the findings.[29] One of the most significant conclusions was the recognition that the postconciliar parish was still very much of an "emerging" reality, even twenty-five years after Vatican II.[30]

An important feature of the *Notre Dame Study* was the way it concentrated on getting the opinions of *Core Catholics*, meaning those who participated in parish life on a regular basis. This did not mean it was trying to neglect those Catholics who were not practising or who may have been alienated from the church. But these non-practising Catholics were not its central concern. It wanted to know essentially what committed Catholics thought about parish life. Thus, the *Study* attempted to "feel the pulse" of the contemporary American parish and to view it through the eyes of ordinary parishioners.

---

[28] "Most theologians today would accept the thesis that there is an ongoing dialectical relationship between theology and the lived experience of the community. Without a certain amount of experience theological reflection is not possible, or at least not grounded in reality; without ongoing theological reflection the life of the community lacks focus and direction." T. Howland Sanks, "Forms of Ecclesiality: The Analogical Church," *Theological Studies* 49 (1988), p. 695.

In a similar vein, and apropos to our study of small Christian communities and the parish, the NCCB Parish Project said that "the continual development of parishes as significant communities of faith and conscience will call for constant development in theology and action in parishes. Continual theological study and reflection . . . will be a critical resource for ensuring depth and pertinence in all the ministries of parishes . . . [because] pastoral conflicts often arise when the proposed practice moves beyond the accepted theology." NCCB Parish Project, *Parish Life in the United States*, p. 64.

[29] The 10 official reports published by the *Notre Dame Study* team which formed the basis of Castelli and Gremillion's summary, *The Emerging Parish*, are listed on pages 212-213 of their book. They are available by writing to Notre Dame University. In addition to these reports, the other principal published product of the *Study* was *The American Catholic Parish: A History from 1850 to the Present*, ed. Jay P. Dolan.

[30] Cf. Castelli and Gremillion, *The Emerging Parish*, p. 2.

Before considering some of the attitudes of *Core Catholics*, it is worth noting some general statistics first.[31] These are presented here in point form:

- There are 19,313 parishes in the U.S.

- The average parish has 2,300 parishioners, of whom about 1,300 attend Mass in a given week.

- One parish in five has a mission attached to it.

- 11% are *national* parishes (the rest are basically territorial).

- The average parish is served by 1.7 full-time priests, .8 part-time priests, .3 permanent deacons, and .6 nuns. It also employs 1.3 laypersons for pastoral ministry. Only 3% of U.S. parishes have no full-time priest.

- 67% of Core Catholics are women.

- Average age of Core Catholics is 49.3 years (for all Catholics it is 42.6 years).

- 9% of Core Catholics attend a parish (not a *national* one) from outside its territorial boundaries.

The above statistics are helpful, but they do not really do justice to the variety of parish life in the U.S. Parishes come in all shapes and sizes. There is no such thing as a typical parish. Generally speaking, Catholic parishes tend to be much larger on average than their Protestant counterparts. But at least U.S. Catholic parishes still have a relatively high ratio of priests to people (although the average age of priests is high). Lack of priests, coupled with even larger average parish populations, is a real problem in other regions of the world.[32]

In a detailed analysis of how organizationally *simple* or *complex* a parish is, based on the number and variety of services and programs offered, it was found that most fall into one of four basic categories:

Type 1 -The Simple Parish = 18% (provides little more than Mass and some religious education for the young).

---

[31] These statistics have been gleaned from a number of different sections within the *Notre Dame Study*. There were selected because they highlight the compositional features of the parish.

[32] This will be confirmed in our next chapter. It is being pointed out because it is one of the reasons why SCC development has occurred in a different manner in North America when compared to what has happened elsewhere, particularly Latin America and Africa.

Type 2 -The Moderately Complex Parish = 28% (in addition
to the above, has youth ministry, ministry to the sick,
liturgical planning, adult education, ministry to the elderly,
and some social services to the needy).

Type 3—The Complex Parish = 19% (in addition to the above,
has prayer groups, evangelization, catechumenate, and
ministry to the separated and divorced).

Type 4 -The Very Complex Parish = 18% (similar to Type 3,
but more likely to have a parish school and more social
action programs).[33]

What this analysis indicates for Castelli and Gremillion is that a
majority of parishes have attempted to internalize the vision of Vatican II
in terms of making the parish a more participatory place. Another sign of
commitment to this ideal is the growing emphasis on parish renewal. Some
29% of parishes had made use of some form of parish renewal program.[34]

Regarding the expectations *Core Catholics* have of their parish, it
is interesting to note their responses to the question of what a parish is
suppose entail for believers. They gave their own answers to this question,
which were then grouped according to general theme. The respondents
could give as many answers as they wished. The results are as follows (% =
respondents mentioning this theme:

1) Reference to parish as People of God, Body of Christ, family,
community, fellowship of believers = 42%

2) Emphasis on charitable works, help for the poor and for those in need
= 33%

3) General reference to parish as a place for religious activity; spiritual
enrichment = 32%

4) Reference to parish as a place offering worship and sacraments; liturgies
= 28%

5) Emphasis on personal religious growth, faith, holiness, closeness to
God, getting to heaven = 26%

6) Emphasis on religious formation, socializing children, evangelizing
adults = 25%

---

[33] Castelli and Gremillion, *The Emerging Parish*, pp. 63-64.
[34] *Ibid.*, p. 76.

7) Emphasis on preservation and propagation of the Roman Catholic faith = 6%[35]

    In commenting on the significance of these particular findings, Castelli and Gremillion conclude: "these findings clearly show that American Catholics are at home with thinking about the parish as the People of God and see the purpose of the parish as communitarian in nature."[36]

    In general, *Core Catholics* are attached to and pleased with their parishes. However if most *Core Catholics* are comfortable with the vision of community and People of God, and seem to indicate that the parish is indeed just such a reality for them, for a number of others it is not. In response to the question: "How much of a feeling of community is there in your parish?" 57% said a "strong" feeling; 40% said "some" feeling; and 4% said there is "no" feeling of community.[37]

    For most parishioners, the parish is not a major social center in their lives. The best attended social activity in the parish is Bingo.[38] This is not to imply that social activity is the most important indicator of community. But it does show the extent to which the parish's role as a galvanizing social force has diminished for Catholics in the local neighborhood. *Core Catholics* say they seldom if ever talk to other parish members other than close friends. Castelli and Gremillion comment: "these findings indicate a major gap in the rhetoric and reality of community for American Catholics. Taken together, they suggest that for about half of the Core Catholic sample, the parish provide a real sense of community. But for a large minority—possibly 40%—that community does not exist."[39]

    The *Notre Dame Study* involves far more than just these few indications which have been presented here. But its basic conclusion remains the same. Despite some problem areas the post-Vatican II Catholic parish in the United States is said to be basically healthy.[40] It plays an important role in the lives of its parishioners and it displays a willingness to

---

[35] *Ibid.*, p. 57.

[36] *Ibid.*

[37] *Ibid.*, p. 58.

[38] *Ibid.*, p. 69.

[39] *Ibid.*, p. 60. Castelli and Gremillion are not contradicting the finding that some 97% of *Core Catholics* reported that there was a *strong* or at least *some* feeling of community in their parishes (see note #37). What they find odd is that many *Core Catholics* could make this claim and yet not know all that many (if any) parishioners on any kind of personal or social basis. This raises an interesting question as to what are our expectations of parish community? We will look at this issue briefly later on in this chapter (part II, section B).

[40] *Ibid.*, p. 200.

continue to adapt its structures so as to accommodate their pastoral needs. Overall then, the *Study* does present an informative picture of the current state of affairs in U.S. parish life.

But the *Study* has not been without its critics. Howland Sanks criticizes its lack of attention to the situation of alienated Catholics, and to the situation of many Hispanic Catholics who are often not formally registered members of parishes (and who are thus statistically under-represented in the study).[41] Furthermore, he fears that:

> The relative satisfaction in the U.S. with the changes in the parish since Vatican II pointed out by the Notre Dame study may stifle our imaginations and lull us into a sense of complacency about the present status of the parochial form of church. The study surveys how the parish as it now stands is functioning, but it does not consider what an ideal form of church for our time and place might be. There is no utopian ideal against which to measure the parish theologically. Participant satisfaction is not a theological criterion.[42]

In some ways the NCCB Parish Project's *Vision Statement* had attempted to enunciate just such a theological ideal for parish life. This was not to be the purpose of the *Notre Dame Study*. But Sanks' criticism still has some merit. A major concern among many observers of the parish scene in America is that, despite implementing Vatican II's vision of the church on the local level, the parish's basic structural paradigm has remained the same. The question has been asked as to whether it is really adequate to meet the needs for being a Christian community in today's social climate. For instance, Patrick J. Brennan remarks:

> Though Vatican II vocabulary resounds through our parishes, and though many parishes have experienced an explosion of lay ministries, often the paradigm for parish remains basically the same as it was for our grandparents. . . . This model or paradigm, institutionalized almost a century ago, simply is not as effective as it once was, amid the significant social changes our age has witnessed.[43]

---

[41] Sanks, "Forms of Ecclesiality: The Analogical Church," pp. 705-706.

[42] *Ibid.*

[43] Patrick J. Brennan, *Re-imagining the Parish* (New York:Crossroad, 1990), p. ix.

The significance of these social changes was not ignored by the framers of the *Notre Dame Study*. In the words of Castelli and Gremillion, it is recognized that the parish indeed embodies and profiles "the dramatic dilemma of a rock-founded church moving amidst the fast-flowing currents of American culture and society."[44] Reference was made to the cultural order and its effect on parish life. Thus, to gain a better understanding of what some of these aspects of American culture and society are that are impacting on parish life, we turn now to our next section for a more in-depth treatment of this topic.

II. CULTURAL CHALLENGES TO BEING PARISH IN NORTH AMERICA[45]

A. Modernity and Secularization: Some Preliminary Remarks

At the 1985 Synod, the bishops recognized that the "signs of the times" had changed since Vatican II had spoken about them.[46] In particular, the world had gone through, and is still in the midst of, a time of staggering social change and cultural transition. Paul VI, in a memorable phrase, had called the growing split between the Gospel and culture as being "without a doubt the drama of our time."[47] This split has had a dramatic impact on many aspects of church life and practice. *Gaudium et Spes* had indeed recognized the cultural challenges to the faith which modernity represented, and wanted the church to play more of an active role in evangelizing culture.[48]

Without getting into a lengthy excursus on the nature of this altered cultural climate a few remarks about some of its general features are called for in order to understand more adequately the challenges it poses to

---

[44] Castelli and Gremillion, *The Emerging Parish*, p. 8.

[45] Principal sources for this section are: Robert Bellah et al., *Habits of the Heart: Individualism and Commitment in American Life* (Berkeley: University of California Press, 1985); Avery Dulles, "Catholicism and American Culture: The Uneasy Dialogue," *America* 162/3 (Jan. 27, 1990), pp. 54-59; Fernand Dumont, "Crise d'une Église, crise d'une société," in *Situation et avenir du catholicisme québécois, vol II: entre temple et l'exil*, eds. Fernand Dumont et al. (Ottawa: Leméac, 1982), pp. 11-48; Stanley Hauerwas and William Willimon, *Resident Aliens: Life in the Christian Colony* (Nashville: Abington Press, 1989); Robert McElroy, *John Courtney Murray and the Secular Crisis: Foundations for an American Catholic Public Theology* (Rome: Gregorian University Doctoral Dissertation, 1990); Philip Murnion, "The Community Called Parish," *Church* 1/4 (1985), pp. 8-14; Cassian Yuhaus, ed., *The Catholic Church and American Culture* (New York/Mahwah: Paulist Press, 1990); Vatican Secretariat for Promoting Christian Unity, *Sects or New Religious Movements* (Washington, D.C.: NCCB, 1986); and Evelyn Eaton Whitehead, ed., *The Parish in Community and Ministry* (New York: Paulist Press, 1978).

[46] Cf. 1985 Synod, *Final Report*, Part II, section A § 1.

[47] Cf. *Evangelii Nuntiandi* 20.

[48] Cf. *Gaudium et Spes* 4.

Christian faith development and to the formation of effective parish communities today. This will done with particular attention being paid to the nature of the North American cultural landscape. This analysis will also help later on in understanding how small Christian communities are particularly adapted from a social point of view to help meet this "cultural challenge."

One of the most consistent and compelling themes in the writings of John Courtney Murray was his conviction that the modern world was facing a moral and social crisis of immense proportions. He termed it the "secularist crisis."[49] This crisis he saw as threatening to undermine the spiritual roots of Western culture. Murray noted that the American brand of secularism was less ideological than its European counterpart, but its practical effect was just the same. It was leading to the systematic de-Christianization of American society, and replacing it with a purely secular type of humanism as the dominant cultural ideal. This form of secular humanism Murray saw as having many diverse roots (i.e. in Enlightenment philosophy, French Revolutionary politics, Industrialization), and he noted that it had been growing for some time. But it was now in full bloom. Murray wanted to help stem the tide of this "secularist drift" in society and attempt to have Christians reclaim the cultural order once again.[50]

A defining feature of secularization then is the decline of God's place (and hence of the church) in public consciousness. The process of secularization does not specifically mean the loss of faith, but the isolation of faith and religion from the rest of life.[51] Religion becomes marginalized and explicit religious norms are no longer seen as governing everyday activities. In the 1960s and 1970s there arose two different theological approaches to the question of what to do about secularization. One school of thought welcomed it. They saw it as helping to purify and liberate the church from a host of social obligations and entanglements so as to be in a better position to be the church. The other school of thought criticized this positive assessment of secularization for being too naive and unrealistic about its far reaching consequences (Avery Dulles called it "practically suicidal" and "theologically false"[52] They stressed the fact that social embodiments of religion helped support people in their faith.

---

[49] Cf. "A Spiritual Crisis in the Temporal Realm," an Address to the Scheil School, March, 1945 (The John Courtney Murray Papers, Archives of Georgetown University). Cited in Robert McElroy, *John Courtney Murray and the Secular Crisis: Foundations for an American Catholic Public Theology*, p. 2.

[50] *Ibid.* 41.

[51] Cf. Murnion, "The Community Called Parish, " p. 8.

[52] Avery Dulles, *The Resilient Church: The Necessity and Limits of Adaptation* (Garden City, N.Y.: Doubleday, 1977), p. 18.

In terms of the impact of secularization, a region which was particularly hard hit in North America was Québécois society. There was during the years of the 1960s a massive cultural transformation that became dubbed the *Quiet Revolution.* The church in Quebec was initially happy to give control of many schools, hospitals, and other social institutions back to the government. But these actions in no way helped to prevent a massive haemorrhaging of religious practice among Quebec Catholics. Today it is estimated that less than 10% of Quebec Catholics go to church on a regular basis.[53]

The situation was slightly different in the rest of North America. There had always been more of a separation of church and state, and less homogeneity among the Catholic population. But the impact was also felt. It is estimated that at least one third of Catholics stopped going to church on a regular basis.[54] Many of these Catholics have not necessarily given up their faith. What they have given up on is the church. All of these changes have made religious practice more of a voluntary effort than at any time in North American history. It has also lessened the traditional teaching authority of the church. Many Catholics, imbued with the individualist ethos of North American culture, have opted for a "pick and choose" attitude towards church teaching and faith practice.[55]

Thus, modernity and the secular culture it helped spawn, have had a decisive hand in conditioning personal and social consciousness. This in turn has affected individual and communal faith practice on the part of Christians. Whereas faith was once supported by the cultural milieu, this is no longer the case any more.[56] Religion is continually embracing a smaller part of the cultural expression of social life. As a result, as Karl Rahner expressed it, *neo-paganism* is on the rise.[57] Clearly, the faith of past generations can be attributed to more than merely social influences and cultural factors. But culture was and is an important influence all the same.

---

[53] For an in-depth analysis of the contemporary situation of the church in Quebec, see: Fernand Dumont, "Crise d'une Église, crise d'une société," pp. 11-48.

[54] Cf. Note #12 above.

[55] Cf. Castelli and Gremillion, *The Emerging Parish*, p. 4.

[56] Karl Rahner, in describing what he calls the religio-sociological situation of Christianity in the recent past, says that traditionally it possessed a certain official status in society and was support to faith development. But today the situation is much different. "Our present situation is one of transition from a Church sustained by a homogeneously Christian society and almost identical with it . . . to a Church made up of those who have struggled against their environment in order to reach a personally clearly and explicitly responsible decision of faith. This will be the Church of the future or there will be no Church at all." Rahner, *The Shape of the Church to Come,* p. 24.

[57] *Ibid.,* p. 32.

Rahner thus saw the modern age as marking the return of the "church of the little flock."[58] The church finds itself once again in a diaspora situation, like that of the early Christians. In this minority situation, if the church is to survive and thrive, it will have to become more self-consciously a living faith community. It cannot depend on culture to pass on Christian values and beliefs any more. The church, and especially the parish, cannot be satisfied with catering only to the private needs of individuals. It will have to function as a comprehensive counter-cultural community.[59]

It is not only Catholics who feel this way about the state of things. Rahner's thoughts are echoed more recently by Stanley Hauerwas, an American Protestant moral theologian. His recent book, *Resident Aliens: Life in the Christian Colony*, is subtitled: *A Provocative Christian Assessment of Culture and Ministry for Those who Know Something is Wrong*.[60] Despite its somewhat alarmist title, it is a very sober account of the issue of faith and culture. Hauweras sees as being especially debilitating the impact modern culture is having on the church's role as a formator of Christian virtue and moral character. He attributes this to the demise of what he refers to as the *Constantinian* status quo regarding the unity of faith and culture in Western civilization.[61] He also laments the inadequacy of much of today's theology to effectively deal with the fundamental question of *how* to be church in this radically changed cultural milieu.

Hauerwas sees the church on the local level as needing to become "a community of character."[62] He thinks that genuine Christian moral and spiritual formation cannot occur outside of a truly communal context. This entails a recovery of the notion of *discipleship*.[63] This will entail a need for Christians to become more involved with their church communities, not less. Hauerwas states: "As Christians we believe we not only need a community, but a community of a particular kind to live well morally. We need a people who are capable of being faithful to a way of life, even when that way of life may be in conflict with what passes as 'morality' in the larger society."[64]

---

[58] *Ibid.*, p. 29.

[59] Cf. Rahner's remarks about these matters in "Structural Change in the Church of the Future," *Theological Investigations*, Vol. XX (London: Darton, Longman and Todd, 1981), pp. 115-132.

[60] Co-authored with William Willimon.

[61] *Ibid.*, p. 18.

[62] Cf. Hauerwas, *A Community of Character* (Notre Dame: University of Notre Dame Press, 1981).

[63] *Ibid.*, p. 49.

[64] Stanley Hauerwas, "On Keeping Theological Ethics Theological," in *Revisions: Changing Perspectives in Moral Theology*, eds. Stanley Hauerwas and Alisdair MacIntyre (University of Notre Dame Press, 1983), p.35.

The reflections of Murray, Rahner, and Hauerwas provide just three examples of how the problem of modernity and secularization is seen as negatively affecting the church. There are of course many others Christian writers who could be cited in this regard, as well as a multitude of statements by the magisterium on this topic.[65] However, it would be a mistake to conclude from these observations that modernity is somehow intrinsically evil. In many instances it has helped spur developments which have been very beneficial to social progress and harmony.[66] It would be wrong to cast *modernity* and *secularization* in the role of scapegoat for all the problems in the world today. However, this point being recognized, it is justifiable to see in the *secular mindset* and *lifestyle* which modernity has helped engender, definite challenges for the church in its promotion of a gospel lifestyle for believers.[67] To see this in more concrete terms we now turn to an analysis of some specific traits of North American culture.

B. North American Culture and the Church

North American *culture* is not an easy concept to define. If culture can be broadly construed as involving a set of assumptions embodied in a way of life, then American culture is not a unitary phenomenon.[68] It is more accurate to speak of a *mosaic* of American cultures and life styles. Even when one attempts to generalize about American culture, one is struck not only by its diversity, but also by its ambiguity. As one author has stated in trying to paint a portrait of contemporary cultural attitudes, "Americans seem at one and the same time individualistic and conformist, tolerant and intolerant, materialistic and idealistic, the most religious and the most secular of peoples."[69] So there is always a need to proceed carefully and in a balanced manner when addressing this matter.

---

[65] As an indication of the seriousness with which this subject is taken by the church, Pope John Paul II decided in 1982 to create a new Pontifical Council for Culture, as a means of addressing in an ongoing manner the issues involved in this cultural challenge.

[66] Speaking of the benefits of modern scientific and technical progress, as well as some of the problems this progress has created, *Gaudium et Spes* says that "these drawbacks are not necessarily due to modern culture and they should not tempt us to overlook its positive values" (GS 57).

[67] It is within the context of these challenges that John Paul II has frequently called for a "re-evangelization" of people and culture. Cf. *Redemptoris Missio* 32.

[68] Cf. David J. O'Brien, "The Church and American Culture During Our Nation's Lifetime, 1787-1987," in *The Catholic Church and American Culture*, ed. Cassian Yuhaus (New York/Mahwah: Paulist Press, 1990), pp. 2-3.

[69] *Ibid.*, p. 3.

Another danger that sometimes exists in talking about culture (especially from a religious perspective) is the tendency to dwell on its negative qualities and to moralize about them. However, as we have previously stated, not everything about modernity and contemporary culture is necessarily bad or morally flawed.[70] Modernity has brought about many lasting benefits and there are many positive values to be found in secular culture. But granted this fact, it is true nevertheless that there are many ways in which modernity and contemporary culture have proven to be problematic for both individuals and society. This in turn has also affected the church, particularly in the areas of faith development and community formation.

Most often these problematic aspects are the result, not of a particular trait of modernity or culture in and of itself, but of a distorted emphasis placed on it.[71] In the following list an attempt has been made to express in summary fashion some prominent features of North American life and culture (this list is by no means exhaustive). Beside each point, in brackets, is a brief mention of how this particular feature can have problematic repercussions. Some of these prominent features are:

1) Stress on Individualism and Personal Freedom (which can breed privatism and lead to alienation and social fragmentation)

2) Capitalistic Economic Orientation (which can promote narcissistic consumerism)

3) Philosophical and Moral Pluralism (which can promote moral relativism and *anomie*)

4) Technological Affluence (leading to greater mobility and self-sufficiency, contributing to an erosion of natural community)

5) Media Saturation (i.e. "T.V. culture"—leading to the media taking over as the dominant purveyor of cultural values and ideals)

6) Liberal Democratic Political System (involving the separation of church and state, which makes it difficult to publicly refer to the religious dimension of policy issues)

---

[70] In characterizing the effects of modernity and secularization, one author has stated: "These are sometimes good, sometimes evil, and often ambiguous. Modernity can lead to human community and comfort or to pollution and poverty for millions; it can facilitate or disrupt human values; it can enrich a poor country or steal its unrenewable sources of energy; it can help in the diffusion of truth or of lies through the media, and it can pass on productive information or child pornography." Desmond O'Donnell, "An Introduction to Modernity," in *Trends in Mission*, eds. W. Jenkinson and H. O'Sullivan (Maryknol, N.Y.: Orbis, 1991), p. 118.

[71] For a more in-depth discussion of this point see: John Coleman, "Values and Virtues in Advanced Modern Societies," *Concilium* 191 (1987), pp. 3-13.

7) Compartmentalization of Work and Social Life (can promote a self-centered and often frenetic lifestyle)

These features of modern North American life and culture have been chronicled in numerous studies.[72] Perhaps the best known recent work in this field was written up in the book *Habits of the Heart*.[73] What Robert Bellah and his fellow sociologists from the University of California found in their research into this area was that the sometimes exaggerated stress placed on individualism in American culture was a leading factor contributing to social fragmentation. This fact, when coupled with other features of modern life such as increased mobility, the growth of suburbs, the rationalization of the workplace, and so on, was contributing to a significant loss of natural community and overall social coherence. This fragmentation is manifested in higher levels of family breakdown and divorce, drug and alcohol addiction, urban violence and decay, and so forth.

In many ways the Hippie movement and corresponding *Commune* phenomenon of the 1960s was a quest to recover a more basic sense of community and simpler lifestyle, in order to counter these dominant cultural values and social paradigms. But these often romantic attempts at engendering a more personal and spontaneous sense of community failed for the most part to live up to expectations. They invariably fell apart after experiencing much internal conflict and disappointment. Avery Dulles thinks that part of the reason for their failure was due to a lack of appreciation for some needed degree of traditional structure and discipline.[74]

Another postconciliar sign of the times in this regard is the explosive growth in cults, sects, and new religious movements. This is a global phenomenon, but it is also very characteristic of the North American situation. In the 1986 Vatican document *Sects or New Religious Movements*, particular note was taken of the reasons for this growth and the pastoral challenge it poses to the church. It notes that many Catholics are being drawn into these various groups. In attempting to understand the reasons why people are attracted to them, the following points are outlined: (1) The quest for belonging; (2) The search for answers; (3) The search for wholeness; (4) The search for cultural identity; (5) The need to be recognized, to be special; (6) The search for transcendence; (7) The need for

---

[72] The traits listed above have been extracted from a number of articles in Cassian Yuhaus, ed., *The Catholic Church and American Culture*.

[73] Cf. Robert Bellah et al. *Habits of the Heart: Individualism and Commitment in American Life*.

[74] Avery Dulles, *The Resilient Church*, pp. 15-16.

spiritual guidance; (8) The need for vision; and (9) The need for participation and involvement.

In reference to the first point listed above, the document states that "the fabric of many communities has been destroyed; traditional life styles have been disrupted; homes are broken up; people feel uprooted and lonely. Thus, the need to belong."[75] It is also observed that a major factor contributing to the growth of these sects and new religious movements has been the failure of mainline churches to adequately respond to the legitimate spiritual needs of many people, and to provide them with a meaningful experience of Christian community. In describing the suggestions and responses the Secretariat for Promoting Christian Unity received to a questionnaire it had sent to church leaders around the world, the document states that "almost all the responses appeal for a rethinking (at least in many local situations) of the traditional parish community system; a search for community patterns that are more fraternal, more to the measure of man, more adapted to people's life situation."[76]

This sentiment was also reaffirmed in Cardinal Arinze's address to the 1991 Consistory of Cardinals. He dealt with this same topic of new religious movements. Comparing the approach taken by many of these new movements to that of many Catholic parishes, he states:

> Where parishes are too large and impersonal, they install small communities in which the individual feels known, appreciated, loved and given a meaningful role. Where lay men and women feel marginalized, they assign leadership roles to them. Where the sacred liturgy is celebrated in a cold and routine manner, they celebrate religious services marked by crowd participation. . . . Not all such methods deserve to be frowned upon.[77]

Thus, the effects of secularization and social fragmentation have heavily impacted on the parish's ability to function as a meaningful faith community. Communal support is a vital means for sustaining the faith of individuals. In fact, personal spirituality depends to a large degree on community. Communal support is all the more critical in the current situation wherein the church finds itself having diminished influence in

---

[75] Vatican Secretariat for Promoting Christian Unity, *Sects or New Religious Movements*, p. 7.

[76] *Ibid.*, p. 13.

[77] Francis Arinze, "The Challenge of New Religious Movements," *Origins* 20/46 (1991), p. 750.

shaping or affecting the secular culture at large. Sociologist Peter Berger has described the functioning of community in terms of being the establishment of a "plausibility structure." This is a way of thinking and acting, shared among a group of people, that enables them to maintain a minority position with confidence in the face of contrary cultural pressures.[78]

The traditional conception of the parish was that it was a family-based community. But with the family facing increasing pressure by destabilizing socio-cultural influences, a healthy family life is becoming more difficult to sustain. Many Catholics still look to the parish for support in family life. Yet, the same social forces that are undermining the family are also present in the parish, making the engendering of authentic Christian more problematic. In commenting on this state of affairs Evelyn Whitehead observes:

> Recent efforts to move parishes toward more communal forms of interaction have neither been easy nor very successful. Many reasons are offered to explain this difficulty—numbers, apathy, distance, time, inertia. The explanation perhaps runs deeper. Perceptive critics of American life have underscored a contemporary ambivalence regarding community. An expressed desire to live in trust and fraternal cooperation stands alongside an enduring cultural commitment to individualism and the autonomous pursuit of one's own destiny. American Catholics have not been spared the experience of these cultural contradictions.[79]

Whitehead goes on to raise the question of what *parish community* is suppose to mean. Does it mean primarily that more emotional intimacy is required? French theologian Christian Duquoc is one person who is wary of a tendency on the part of some people to exalt, in an exclusive fashion, the idea that personal and direct relationships are the dominant values needed in Christian community.[80] Another critic of this tendency is American

---

[78] For more insight into the sociological imperatives inherent in being a functional Christian community see: Peter Berger, *The Sacred Canopy* (Garden City, N.Y.: Doubleday, 1967); and Peter Berger and Richard Neuhaus, *To Empower People* (Washington, D.C.: The Enterprise Institute, 1977).

[79] Evelyn Eaton Whitehead, "The Structure of Community: Toward Forming the Parish As a Community of Faith," in *The Parish in Community and Ministry*, p. 36.

[80] "A number of sociologists have drawn the attention of theologians to the problems of an indiscriminate use of this term [community]. In fact the study of community movements in Europe shows that this is to exalt a single form of belonging to the church, one in which

Quaker Parker Palmer. He sees it as being a form of idolatry to exalt a purely familial and intimate understanding of what community entails. The Christian community must always make room for the "stranger." It can never close in on itself to the exclusion of others. Thus, he thinks it would be a mistake to make church community into some kind of escape from an increasingly depersonalized society.[81]

In chronicling the responses of Catholics to the question of how to engender a greater degree of community in the parish, Philip Murnion notes five basic positions or approaches which are most often advocated.[82] The first is what he terms the *traditionalist* response. This response advocates a return to the structures and practices of the past as being the best means for reviving Catholic identity and parish community. A second response is what he labels the *sectarian* strategy. This strategy advocates seeing the church as invariably comprising only a relatively small band of the elect. It sees it as being futile to think of community as being something that the masses can meaningfully participate in. Because of this fact, the best place to realize authentic Christian community is *outside* the parish, in the context of a movement that is better able to inculcate a deeper commitment in this regard.

The third response involves stressing the *emotional intimacy* dimension to community that we have already noted above. Murnion sees this as epitomized in the community of the encounter weekend or retreat. The fourth approach is to actually give up on the idea of creating a more personal and fraternal sense of parish community altogether, and to settle instead for the idea of parish being akin to a religious *association*. An association, according to Murnion's characterization, helps its members individually to participate in its various activities, without demanding much in the way of inter-relating or community building.

The fifth and final approach Murnion terms *community as solidarity*. This is the approach favoured by Murnion. Community is seen here as being best realized when all the various sub-groupings of the parish act in solidarity with one another and with the tradition of the church. Murnion is a little vague however in detailing how this solidarity is to be achieved in practice. But despite this shortcoming, his overall account does help to bring into sharper focus the polarization of attitudes toward community that are prevalent in many parishes today. It is recognized in most of these approaches that *more* or *better* community is needed if people

personal and direct relationships are dominant." Christian Duquoc, *Provisional Churches* (London: SCM Press, 1986), p. 37.

[81] Parker Palmer, *The Company of Strangers* (New York: Crossroad, 1986), pp. 119-130.

[82] Cf. Murnion, "The Community Called Parish," pp. 8-14.

are to be supported in their faith, given the current socio-cultural environment. The question of *how* this is to be achieved is the real debate. Murnion expresses the nature of this challenge in the following terms: "Thus, church efforts to address precisely our challenge of faith must be directed not so much at shoring up doctrine and orthodoxy, however important these may be, but at reestablishing the link between faith and life."[83]

Murnion's characterization of approaches to parish community parallels that of Avery Dulles' recent characterization of American Catholic strategies that deal with the problem of church and culture in general.[84] Dulles notes four basic responses: traditionalism, neo-conservatism, liberalism, and radicalism. An elaboration of these positions is not required here. But what is interesting to note is Dulles' conviction that none of these four strategies is outrightly wrong. All have laudable features that incorporate important insights into the nature of the church-world relationship. But each also has certain limitations and drawbacks.[85]

Dulles sees the most fundamental question raised by this analysis as being how the church can be in their best senses both *counter-cultural* and *accomodationist* in its relation to contemporary culture and society. By way of conclusion he states:

> Pope John Paul II, like Paul VI before him, has repeatedly called upon Catholics everywhere to evangelize their cultures. He recognizes that faith cannot survive without cultural embodiment, and that faith can have no home in a culture untouched by the Gospel. . . . They must, through their parishes, their families, prayer groups or basic ecclesial communities, find an environment in which they can interiorize their religious heritage. In this way they can prepare themselves to become agents in the evangelization of the secular culture. Such cultural evangelization, in turn, may help to establish an atmosphere in which Catholic Christianity can be lived out more faithfully by greater numbers.[86]

---

[83] *Ibid.*, p. 9.

[84] Cf. Dulles, "Catholicism and American Culture: The Uneasy Dialogue," pp. 54-59.

[85] "None of the four strategies, I submit, is simply wrong. The realities of American Catholicism and of American culture are complex and many-faceted. American life has aspects we can praise with the neo-conservatives and the liberals, and other aspects we must deplore with the traditionalists and the radicals." *Ibid.*, p. 57.

[86] *Ibid.*, p. 59.

In the following section, a closer look is taken at the role played by various recent lay movements, associations, and parish renewal programs in this process of helping to engender Christian community and evangelization. This survey will provide the final insights needed in order to furnish a general context wherein the subsequent treatment of small Christian communities can be better situated and understood.

III. RESPONSES TO THE CHALLENGE[87]

A. Lay Movements and Associations in the Church Today and Their Impact on Parish Life

In the latter part of the nineteenth century their arose in many lay people a new consciousness of the need to play more of an active role in the Christian renewal of society.[88] In the face of increasing secularization, many outstanding individual efforts were made to spread and defend the faith, to promote Catholic social action, and to try and reanimate society with Christian values. This activity was recognized and encouraged by the Holy See. Pius X spoke of this "Catholic action" as being an important means of helping "to restore all things in Christ."[89] But it was Pius XI (1922-39) who gave this activity the official name of *Catholic Action* and launched it as a mandated activity in the church. He spoke of Catholic Action as being an expression of "the lay apostolate." He even sought to give it further theological legitimation by defining it as "the participation of the laity in the hierarchical apostolate."[90]

Beyond this generic definition, Pius XI left the specific nature of Catholic Action flexible. Because of this fact, there arose many different lay

---

[87] Principal sources for this section are: Debra Campbell, "The Heyday of Catholic Action and the Lay Apostolate, 1929-1959," in *Transforming Parish Ministry,* eds. Jay Dolan et al. (New York: Crossroad, 1990), pp. 222-251; Yves Congar, *Lay People in the Church* (London: Geoffrey Chapman, 1985 Revised Edition); Gianfranco Ghirlanda, "Movements within the Ecclesial Communion and Their Rightful Autonomy," *The Laity Today: Bulletin of the Pontifical Council for the Laity* 32/33 (1989-90), pp. 46-68; John Jacoby, "A Parish Renewal Program: *Christ Renews His Parish,*" in *Evangelization Portrait of the Month* (Washington, D.C.: Paulist Catholic Evangelization Center, n.d.), pp. 11-15; Philip Murnion, "Parish Renewal: State(ments) of the Question," *America* 146 (1982), pp. 8-14; Angelo Scola, "Associations and Movements in the Communion and Mission of the Church Today," *The Laity Today: Bulletin of the Pontifical Council for the Laity* 32/33 (1989-90), pp. 37-45; and Leo Ward, *Catholic life, U.S.A.: Contemporary: Lay Movements* (St. Louis: Herder, 1959).

[88] Cf. Congar, *Lay People in the Church,* pp. 359-362.

[89] Cf. Pius X, *E Supremi* (1905), in *The Papal Encyclicals,* Vol. III (1903-1939), ed. Claudia Carlen (Raleigh: The Pieran Press, 1990), pp. 7-10.

[90] Cited by Yves Congar, *Lay People in the Church,* p. 362. In pages 362-399 Congar gives an excellent account of the emergence and nature of Catholic Action, including discussion of this famous, though somewhat problematic, definition given by Pius XI.

initiatives, in many different fields, which came to be seen as expressions of the lay apostolate and of Catholic Action. From the 1930s to the 1950s, the terms *Catholic Action* and *lay apostolate* were used extensively by bishops, priests and lay people to refer in a general way to the laity's responsibility to engage in apostolic activities on behalf of the church. This activity contributed greatly to a renewal in the theology of the laity that was to be embraced in a decisive way by Vatican II.

Historian Debra Campbell describes the years 1929-1959 as being the heyday of Catholic Action and the lay apostolate in the United States.[91] There arose many new organizations which were directly inspired by the Catholic Action mandate. These included: the Young Christian Workers (or *Jocist*) movement; the Christian Family Movement (CFM); the Catholic Worker movement; Madonna House; the Grail; the Cana movement; and a host of smaller or more regional initiatives. Even existing lay organizations and parish programs were influenced by Catholic Action and were given a new focus or received a new impetus during this era. These included: the Knights of Columbus; the St. Vincent de Paul Society; the Holy Name Society; the Legion of Mary; the Catholic Evidence Guild; the National Conference of Catholic Charities (NCCC); the Confraternity of Christian Doctrine (CCD); the Catholic Youth Organization (CYO); as well as other sodalities, auxiliaries, associations, leagues, and fraternities of various kinds.

Some of these new movements were imported from Europe, while others were indigenous. For instance, the *Jocist* movement was founded in Belgium by Canon Cardijn in 1912.[92] The term *Jocist* was an abbreviated form of *Jeunesse Ouvrière Chrétien*, otherwise known as the Young Christian Workers. It never became much of a force in the American lay apostolate, but its basic format and method were to become very influential. Jocist groups were called cells. They were composed of small groups of parishioners who met regularly to discuss how the gospel might be applied to the particular problems they faced at work. A central feature of their discussions was the application of the *inquiry method* of *See, Judge, Act.*[93]

It was out of a Jocist cell that the Christian Family Movement (CFM) was founded in Chicago in 1943.[94] CFM became a movement of Catholic couples who focused on ways to strengthen family life. They

---

[91] Cf. Campbell, "The Heyday of Catholic Action and the Lay Apostolate, 1929-1959," p. 222.

[92] *Ibid.,* p. 233.

[93] This inquiry method was to become very influential in the development of Latin American BECs. Cf. Chapter four, part II, section A § 2.

[94] Cf. Campbell, "The Heyday of Catholic Action and the Lay Apostolate," p. 248.

maintained the essential Jocist format and method in their meetings. CFM groups were usually composed of six-eight couples and a chaplain, who would meet every second week in each others' homes. Their meetings began with a brief time of gospel reflection followed by a discussion period. The chaplain would usually lead the gospel reflection, and the couples would lead the discussion. The discussion revolved around topics of Christian family life, as well as other matters of broader social concern. Various projects and activities were initiated to help respond in a concrete fashion to these family needs, and to address other social concerns on both local and national levels.

Both CFM, and the similar Cana movement, represented a new phenomenon in that they were small group lay apostolates based in the homes of lay people.[95] This did not mean they were not tied into the local parish. Each group had a chaplain who was usually the pastor or assistant pastor of the parish. But the fact of meeting in homes anticipates more recent developments with SCCs and other parish renewal programs that got under way in the postconciliar era. Also of lasting significance has been the influence of the Jocist *inquiry method*. This method was to become a prominent feature of Latin American base community meetings. For these reasons, some commentators on the lay apostolate speak of the Jocist movement, and the other groups it inspired, as being forerunners of small Christian communities.[96]

CFM reached its peak in 1959 when some 40,000 couples were involved. It still operates today, but with a greatly reduced profile. The real successor to CFM in the postconciliar era is Marriage Encounter, which itself began as a CFM initiative.[97]

Despite the importance of Catholic Action and the various forms of preconciliar lay movements and apostolates, some people think they were hampered in their activity by an inadequate theology of the laity.[98] Debra

---

[95] *Ibid.*, p. 250.

[96] Bob and Irene Tomonto, "Basic Christian Communities: The Christian Family Movement Model," in *Basic Christian Communities:The United States Experience* (Chicago: National Federation of Priests' Councils, 1983), p. 42. Gottfried Deelen also describes these lay movements as having had a role in laying the groundwork for the emergence of base communities, especially in their contribution to the general spiritual-formation of the people. See: "The Church on its Way to the People: Basic Christian Communities in Brazil," *Pro Vita Mundi Bulletin* 81 (1980), p. 4.

[97] Cf. Tomonto, "Basic Christian Communities: The Christian Family Movement Model," p. 42.

[98] Giuseppe Alberigo sees the phenomenon of Catholic Action as having been a surrogate for what was really needed in the church, namely a more comprehensive theology of the laity. This partially explains the reason why Catholic Action, as such, faded after Vatican II. Cf. Alberigo, "The Christian Situation After Vatican II," in *The Reception of Vatican II*, eds

Campbell notes that because lay leadership was not yet fully appreciated in the parish itself during this era, some of these movements grew up or operated on the "fringes" of the parish system.[99] She thinks this development contributed to a degree of impatience and frustration which some lay people felt towards the so-called *institutional* church.

Regardless of what one thinks about Catholic Action and preconciliar lay movements and associations, there is little doubting the fact that they made a significant contribution to the life of the church at the time. This contribution is still being felt today. This is because since Vatican II the church has witnessed as even greater proliferation of lay movements and associations.[100] If many of the older, more traditional movements and associations experienced an identity crisis and decline, many newer ones soon took their place. In North America, movements such as Marriage Encounter, Cursillo, the Charismatic Renewal, and many others, attracted participants in large numbers and on a scale not seen in preconciliar times. In Europe, movements and associations such as Communion and Liberation, Focolare, the Neo-Catechumenal Way, and many others rose to new prominence. Many of these groups had already begun to emerge before the Council began, but they grew exponentially afterwards.[101]

The overall impact of these newer movements and associations on the postconciliar church has been essentially positive. They have helped amplify in Catholics a new community consciousness and have promoted Christian spirituality and social outreach. Although many of these newer movements and associations are not parish-based to the same degree as their predecessors were, they nevertheless, in the findings of the *Notre Dame Study*, "energize their members for more active parish life."[102] This is why the work of the movements has been credited with helping to promote and realize the renewal of the church envisioned by Vatican II. There are even those who are comparing their impact to that of the Dominican and Franciscan revivals of the thirteenth century.[103]

Giuseppe Alberigo et al. (Washington, D.C.: Catholic University, 1987), p. 17, note # 55.

[99] Cf. Campbell, "The Heyday of Catholic Action and the Lay Apostolate," p. 228.

[100] "In recent days the phenomenon of lay people associating among themselves has taken on a character of particular variety and vitality. . . . In modern times such lay groups have received a special stimulus . . . we can speak of a new era of group endeavors of the lay faithful." John Paul II, *Christifideles Laici* 29.

[101] For more information about European lay movements see: F. Blachnicki et al. *I movimenti nella chiesa* (Milano: Jaca, 1981).

[102] Castelli and Gremillion, *The Emerging Parish*, p. 26.

[103] Author Unknown, "The Challenge of the Movements," *The Tablet* (March 19, 1988), p. 323.

But there have also been problems. In the words of the *Parish Project*, they sometimes have had the effect of turning people *on* to the movement, but *off* of the parish.[104] However, as the *Parish Project* itself recognizes, this is not directly the fault of these movements. In some cases the parish was not meeting the needs for community and spiritual formation which people were experiencing. These movements were providing the kind of holistic environment for evangelization, community, ministry, and faith development, which was often still missing in many parish settings despite the renewal of Vatican II. For many participants, the parish remained the place for Sunday worship, but their primary Christian "community" became identified with their movement or association group.

At the Synod on the Laity in 1987, this topic of lay movements and associations in the church occasioned much stirring debate by the bishops.[105] The bishops applauded the work these movements have accomplished, and wanted them to continue to grow and flourish, but to do so in closer union with the local church. They observed that despite good intentions, some lay movements and associations had become a source of tension. The bishops recognized that the new Code of Canon Law grants lay movements and associations a certain rightful autonomy.[106] But they requested better guidelines from Rome pertaining to how new groups could go about attaining proper ecclesiastical recognition, and maintaining a more direct link with the local bishop. In the apostolic exhortation which followed the Synod, *Christifideles Laici*, John Paul II attempted to address some of these concerns, and outlined what are referred to as the "criteria for ecclesiality of lay groups."[107]

Despite these efforts to clarify the situation, there remains much work to be done in this area. For instance, Pope John Paul II made this a topic of his 1992 Ad Limina address to the bishops of southern France. He applauded the progress that is being made to foster dialogue with these lay associations and told the bishops that "it is part of your pastoral task to welcome the initiatives and promote the complementarity of the movements of different inspiration. You must watch over the leadership of these groups,

---

[104] Parish Project, *Parish Life in the United States: Final Report* (Washington, D.C.: NCCB, 1983), p. 60.

[105] Cf. 1987 Synod, "The Synod Propositions," *Origins* 17/29 (1987), pp. 499-509.

[106] Cf. Gianfranco Ghirlanda, "Movements within the Ecclesial Communion and Their Rightful Autonomy," pp. 46-68.

[107] Cf. *Christifideles Laici* 30. Because these criteria also pertain to an evaluation of the ecclesiality of SCCs, we will review them at a later stage in this thesis (see chapter seven, part II, section A).

the theological and spiritual formation of their leaders, and their proper insertion into the diocesan community."[108]

In general, these problems with lay movements and associations are really a postconciliar phenomenon. One observer of this development credits this to the fact that the parish is no longer the setting for many of these movements, and the parish priest no longer the person exercising as much direct pastoral control or leadership.[109] This was how the church in the past was better able to ensure the proper supervision and accountability of various groups. The parish priest usually had more theological education and a better ecclesiological awareness of the significance of the diocesan church. Structurally speaking, he had more of a direct link to the bishop, and lines of communication were clearly established.

With the advent and growth of lay leadership and non parish-based lay groupings, the parish and the parish priest have declined somewhat in overall significance in the local church. They are still vitally important of course, but nevertheless the diocese has become less exclusively a parish-based reality. Thus, new diocesan structures and lines of communication need to be established to ensure the overall unity and catholicity of the diocesan church. This is a welcome development, but it will still take more time and effort before it becomes fully rooted and operational.[110]

B. Some Recent Approaches to Parish Renewal

Another major development in the postconciliar North American church has been the proliferation in the number and variety of renewal programs aimed specifically at the parish.[111] In many respects these parish programs have aims which are similar to those of the lay movements and associations, namely: to stimulate further personal conversion and growth in faith, to help engender a deeper awareness of Christian community, and to help promote lay ministry and social outreach. But rather than take people outside of the parish context in order to achieve these goals, these programs seek to work within an existing parish community. They are not intended or

---

[108] Pope John Paul II, "Ad Limina Address to the Bishops of Frances' Midi Region," *L'Osservatore Romano* (English edition—April 15, 1992), p. 3.

[109] Cf. Johannes Farnleitner, "Developments in the Lay Apostolate During the Last 20 Years and Challenges for the Laity," *The Laity Today* 32/33 (1989-90), p. 10.

[110] In a similar vein vis à vis parishes and SCCs there is a need to clarify the pastor's role and supervisory responsibility. We will see later how various types of North American SCCs approach this issue (chapter five).

[111] The *Notre Dame Survey* indicated that 29% of U.S. parishes had made use of one or more renewal-type programs. Cf. Note #34 above.

designed to be diocesan or intra-parochial in nature, as are many movements and associations.

This is not to imply that lay movements and associations do not have a specific concern for parish life. Many of them are explicitly committed to helping renew the parish. But although their concern may be the same, their strategy and focus is different. This may be illustrated by comparing for example the Cursillo movement with the parish renewal program *Christ Renews His Parish*, begun in the diocese of Cleveland in 1969.[112] The *Christ Renews His Parish* program is similar in nature to that employed by the Cursillo movement.[113] Both begin with a retreat experience for their participants which is structured around talks and small group sharing. Both encourage follow-up after the retreat by forming small groups that meet on a regular basis to continue the process of faith sharing and community support. Both encourage their participants to act as team members for an upcoming retreat experience wherein the process is begun again for a new group of people.

The only real difference is that *Christ Renews His Parish* is geared towards, and restricted to, members of a particular parish, whereas Cursillo operates on more of a diocesan level, drawing participants from many different parishes simultaneously. Both have a concern then for individual and ecclesial renewal. But the *Christ Renews His Parish* program is designed to lead in more of a direct and immediate manner to *parish* renewal and the fostering of *parish* community, than is Cursillo, which lends itself more readily to *individual* renewal and the fostering of a *Cursillo* community. This is not intended to be a criticism of Cursillo, merely an observation of the community dynamic that is at work within it and many other lay movements.[114]

Another parish renewal program which operates in a similar vein is called the *Parish Renewal Experience*. It is modelled after Marriage Encounter and employs many of the same features noted above for *Christ Renews His Parish*.[115] Fr. Charles Gallagher, its founder, estimates that since its inception in 1978, some 5,000 priests have gone through the training to host the *Parish Renewal Experience* in their own parishes. He

---

[112] Cf. John Jacoby, "A Parish Renewal Program: *Christ Renews His Parish*," pp. 11-15.

[113] For information about Cursillo see: Marcene Marcoux, *Cursillo: Anatomy of a Movement* (New York: Lambeth Press, 1982).

[114] The *Parish Project* had criticized lay movements for sometimes having the effect of turning people *on* to the movement, but *off* of the parish. Cf. Note #104 above.

[115] Cf. *Parish Project*, "Worldwide Marriage Encounter: *Parish Renewal Experience*," in *Parish Development: Programs and Organizations* (Washington, D.C.: NCCB, 1980), pp. 213-216.

estimates that between 1000-1500 U.S. parishes have operated with the program, directly involving over 500,000 parishioners.[116] The purpose of the program is described as follows:

> To create unity and a sense of belonging among the parishioners through a process of prayer, immersion in scripture, and personal sharing with one another which is learned on the weekend and then practised on a continuing basis in the normal parish life. It is not intended to be a separate organization in and of itself, but merely a means that can be utilized within the parish to create an atmosphere of listening, of growth and of closeness.[117]

The parish renewal program which has had the most impact to date, and which has involved the most participants, is called *RENEW*.[118] It too is very similar in nature to *Christ Renews His Parish* and the *Parish Renewal Experience*. However, since *RENEW* is treated in an upcoming chapter dealing with small Christian communities, there will be no further discussion of it at this time.

What is significant about these kinds of parish renewal programs (i.e. *Christ Renews His Parish, Parish Renewal Experience, RENEW*) is their all-inclusive nature. They are not simply intended to renew or support one particular segment of the parish population, as do many other kinds of worthwhile parish programs or groups.[119] This is not to imply that those groups which support only one particular segment of the parish population are somehow deficient. It is simply to indicate that there is a difference in scope. This is being pointed out here because, as we shall see, most North American SCC programs also view themselves as being a parish renewal process which is all-inclusive in nature.[120]

---

[116] Statistics cited in a letter from Charles Gallagher to the author (dated Feb. 14, 1992).

[117] *Parish Project*, "Worldwide Marriage Encounter: *Parish Renewal Experience*," p. 214.

[118] Cf. Chapter five, part II, section A.

[119] For example, parish groups created for the renewal and support of: Separated and Divorced Catholics; Widowers; Parents; Seniors; Single Adults, Homemakers; and so forth.

[120] The benefit of having an approach to parish renewal which is more all-inclusive in scope is illustrated in an observation made by Earnest Larsen: " One major problem in parish renewal is that we lack a center or focal point of what we are trying to accomplish. A parish is such a diverse, complex, random kind of thing that most of us don't know where to focus. We do not have a base broad enough to encompass all the parts. Therefore, what we wind up doing is trying to 'renew a part,' and somehow sooner or later it seems to fall apart under its own weight." Larsen, *Spiritual Growth: Key to Parish Renewal* (Ligouri, Missouri: Ligouri

What really sets SCC programs/organizations apart from the parish renewal programs we have mentioned above is the stress SCCs place on being a permanent fixture of the parish scene. Although *Christ Renews His Parish* and the *Parish Renewal Experience* encourage their small groups to continue meeting after the initial weekend retreat, there is very little in the way of on-going pastoral support for them. Furthermore, they are not seen as restructuring the parish or as redefining what it means for parishioners to participate in the parish community in quite the same manner as do most SCCs. They are seen more in terms of being a catalyst to community development, rather than as an integral and on-going feature of what being a parish community structurally entails.[121]

Having noted some of the ways and means in which the quest for parish renewal has been pursued in its North American context, and having drawn attention to the fact that SCCs are in one sense a part of this movement for parish renewal, let us now finally turn our attention directly to the BEC/SCC phenomenon. In our subsequent analysis of BECs/SCCs, further distinctions will be made so as to properly identify both their ecclesiality and their ecclesiological significance.

Publications, 1978), p. 9.

[121] For example Arthur Baranowski, author of one of the SCC programs we will examine later in chapter five, states that SCCs are different from other kinds of parish renewal programs in that SCCs are a process which aims to permanently restructure the way parishioners experience and participate in the parish community. Cf. Baranowski, *Creating Small Faith Communities* (Cincinnati: St. Anthony Messenger Press, 1988), p. 1.

Part Two:
Small Christian
Communities

CHAPTER FOUR

The Emergence
of Small Christian Communities

I. THE MANY FACES AND NAMES OF SMALL
CHRISTIAN COMMUNITIES

At the 1968 Conference of Latin American bishops (CELAM) held in Medellin, Colombia, Brazilian Archbishop Ivo Lorscheiter described the existence of Basic Christian Communities as being, for both church and society, "the most important event of our epoch."[1] Regardless of whether or not the Archbishop was historically justified in making such a claim, such was the impact that he, and many others, felt that BCCs were having in Brazil. This statement is all the more remarkable when you consider that BCCs had only just recently appeared on the scene there. Within a short time they had multiplied and spread all over Latin America, and were being imitated in other areas of the world. This rapid cross-cultural spread, coupled with indigenous developments of a similar nature in other regions, has led some commentators to conclude that it must be a movement inspired by the Holy Spirit.[2] Others have described it in terms of having touched a deep nerve in the corporate psyche of believers.[3] In any event, it is not an exaggeration to say that this movement has become a very significant ecclesial phenomenon.

At the 1991 Notre Dame University International Consultation on the topic of small Christian communities, it was recognized that this was a

---

[1] Cited in the Medellin document on "Joint Pastoral Planning," in Vol. II of *The Church in the Present-Day Transformation of Latin America in the Light of the Council* (Washington, D.C.: NCCB, 1970), pp. 10-11.

[2] "Many pastors and teachers in the church judge the small Christian community movement to be a visible expression of the work of the Spirit within the church at the present time." Raymond Collins, "Small Groups: An Experience of Church," *Louvain Studies* 13 (1988), p. 130.

[3] Cf. Bernard Lee and Michael Cowan, *Dangerous Memories: House Churches and Our American Story* (Kansas City: Sheed and Ward, 1986), p. 3.

world-wide phenomenon "which goes by many names and has many faces."[4] This diversity is one of the striking features of the small Christian community movement as a whole. It is thus helpful to begin an examination into this topic by briefly noting the various "names" by which this phenomenon is known. An awareness of the variety in the nomenclature, and the fact that terms are sometimes used interchangeably, will prevent possible terminological confusion arising in our subsequent deliberations on this subject.

In Latin America they were first called *Communidades de Base* or *Basic Communities*. In order to distinguish them from non-religious groups the adjective *Christian* was sometimes added to make the term *Basic Christian Communities* (BCCs). Later, another designation developed in order to heighten the ecclesial nature of these groups, thus came the term *Communidades Eclesailes de Base* (CEBs) or *Basic Ecclesial Communities* (BECs).[5] In Africa they are generally known as *Small Christian Communities* (SCCs) in english-speaking regions, and as *Communautés Ecclesiales Vivantes* (CEVs) or *Living Ecclesial Communities* in french-speaking areas. Influenced by Latin American nomenclature, the term *Basic Christian Communities* (BCCs) became an early (and still quite common) appellation for this phenomenon in Europe, North America, and Asia. The terms BECs and SCCs are also in use in these other regions.

In addition to these major designations there are a host of other minor ones that can be found in the literature. Most of these are variations on the terms listed above. One finds references to these groups as being *Small Basic Christian Communities, Small Church Communities, Small Faith Communities, Christian Faith Communities, Church Cell Communities*, and so forth.[6] Another category of terms are to be found in attempts to characterize their general function or significance from a sociological perspective. These include such designations as *Intentional Communities, Critical Communities*, and *Grassroots Communities*.[7]

For the purposes of consistency and clarity, the term *small Christian communities* (SCCs) has been used throughout this study as the common way of referring to this phenomenon. This is not an arbitrary

---

[4] 1991 International Consultation on Basic Christian Communities (University of Notre Dame), *Final Statement*, p. 1.

[5] *Eclesiales* is used in spanish-speaking regions of Latin America, while *Eclesiais*, which is portuguese, is used in Brazil.

[6] Joseph Healey has compiled an extensive list of these general designations. See the paper he presented to the 1991 Notre Dame University International BCC Consultation entitled, "Evolving a World Church From the Bottom Up," pp. 1-30.

[7] "Intentional Christian Communities" (ICCs) is a term frequently used by Bernard Lee and Michael Cowan in their book: *Dangerous Memories: House Churches and Our American Story*.

choice, but reflects the fact that this is the designation most widely in use in North America.[8] However, it is by no means the only term in use. Generally speaking therefore, when referring specifically to either another region of the world which uses a different term, or to North American groups which designate themselves in a different way, the alternate usage of choice will be followed in the interests of accuracy.

This plethora of terms used by advocates and practitioners of small Christian community is not just a matter of rhetorical whimsy, but is sometimes indicative of different theological and ecclesiological emphases. Thus, in the literature on SCCs one finds that "sometimes the emphasis is upon *being church* and sometimes upon the *new ways* of doing it."[9] Additional differences are to be found in the variety of roles SCCs play in different social and cultural settings. For instance, some observers claim that the Latin American model of basic communities is not readily transferable to North America because of the great differences in their respective social and ecclesial settings.[10] Another explanation sees the difference in terminology as being a deliberate choice, "in order to avoid the false impression that the Latin American model of Basic Christian Communities is *the* paradigm of small Christian communities."[11]

Because SCC development has proceeded in different ways in different places, it is beneficial to begin this analysis with a brief review of how it has emerged, and what some of its major ecclesiological characteristics are, in various regions of the world. This will provide a context for understanding the nature of the influences on North American efforts in this field. It will also furnish us with a means for understanding what some of the special traits of North American SCCs are, and how they in turn are impacting on efforts that are currently underway world-wide to assess their ecclesiological role and status within the parish and the local church.

---

[8] "In the literature of North America *Small Christian Communities* seems the preferred terminology at the present time." Raymond Collins, "Small Groups: An Experience of Church," p. 120, note #44.

[9] 1991 International Consultation on Basic Christian Communities (Notre Dame University), *Final Statement*, p. 3.

[10] Cf. Raymond Collins, "Small Groups: An Experience of Church," p. 120, note # 44.

[11] *Ibid.*

II. A SURVEY OF THE SCC PHENOMENON IN OTHER REGIONS OF THE WORLD

A. Latin America[12]

1. Emergence

Basic Christian Communities first came to prominence in Brazil, and from there quickly spread to other regions of Latin America.[13] However, since Brazil still has the largest concentration of BECs in Latin America, this country provides a good focus for studying their general features in this region of the world.[14] Historical studies of the emergence of these Brazilian BCCs point to "three convergent forces" or stimuli which spurred their initial development in the 1950s.[15] The first stimulus was that of lay catechists being used in Rio de Janeiro State to teach people about the faith and assemble them for liturgical services when a priest was not available for Sunday Eucharist. The second stimulus was the effort of the Basic Education Movement and the Natal Movement, which helped to educate, evangelize and address social concerns, especially by means of radio broadcasts. The third stimulus came from the impact of various lay movements and lay apostolates in their efforts to bring about personal and ecclesial renewal.

---

[12] Principal sources for this section are: Marcello de Carvalho Azevedo, *Basic Ecclesial Communities in Brazil: The Challenge of a New Way of Being Church* (Washington, D.C.: Georgetown University Press, 1987); Alvaro Barreiro, *Basic Ecclesial Communities: The Evangelization of the Poor* (Maryknoll, N.Y.: Orbis Books, 1982); Leonardo Boff, *Ecclesiogenesis: The Base Communities Reinvent the Church* (Maryknoll, N.Y.: Orbis Books, 1986); CELAM, *1968 Medellin Conference Final Document* (Washington, D.C.: NCCB, 1970); CELAM, *1979 Puebla Conference Final Document* (Washington, D.C.: NCCB, 1980); CELAM, *1992 Santo Domingo Conference Final Document* (Bologna: Edizioni Dehoniane, 1992); W.E. Hewitt, "Christian Base Communities (CEBs): Structure, Orientation, and Sociopolitical Thrust," *Thought* 63/249 (1988), pp. 162-175; and Sergio Torres and John Eagleson (eds.), *The Challenge of Basic Christian Communities* (Maryknoll, N.Y.: Orbis Books, 1981).

[13] Besides efforts in Brazil, the most notable other early development in this area was that of the "San Miguelito Experiment" in Panama. It represented the efforts of some American missionary priests to organize smaller communities for the purposes of scripture reflection and faith sharing in a Panama City parish in 1963. It gained a lot of media attention and helped popularize the concept in North America and further abroad. Cf. Sabbas Kilian, *Theological Models for the Parish*, pp. 62-66.

[14] Azevedo points out that Latin America is a diversified region, ecclesially, geographically, culturally, socially, and politically. It is therefore "risky" to generalize about the situation of BECs in Latin America (the same holds true for Brazil itself). But it is true nevertheless that Brazilian BECs share many of the same traits as those of their neighbors in this region. Cf. Azevedo, *Basic Ecclesial Communities in Brazil*, p. 7.

[15] Cf. Azevedo, *Basic Ecclesial Communities in Brazil*, pp. 23-28.

This activation of the laity, together with the pastoral emphasis on integral evangelization, were the two central features of these stimuli.[16] They led to a new awareness in many lay people of their role in the life and mission of the church. This new awareness received a strong boost from Vatican II. Together these influences, coupled with the fact of rapid secularization of Brazilian society which was occurring at the time, prompted the Brazilian bishops to advocate the formation of *basic communities* as part of their first joint pastoral plan issued in 1965. In this plan it is stated that:

> There is an urgent need to decentralize the parish, not necessarily in the sense of creating new juridical parishes, but in the sense of awakening and activating basic communities (such as the existing rural chapels) within the parish territory. In them Christians would not be anonymous persons seeking merely the performance of a service or the fulfilment of an obligation. They would be faithful members feeling accepted and responsible as an integral component, living in communion with Christ and all their brothers and sisters.[17]

Within twenty years of the launching of this pastoral plan, which many see as having been the official birth of the BEC phenomenon, estimates placed the numbers of BECs in Brazil at between 50,000—80,000 (involving 1—1.5 million people).[18] As impressive as these numbers are, they do not mean that BECs suddenly burst onto the scene there. They had a slow gestation and a gradual emergence. It is difficult in fact to pinpoint historically the first actual BEC. It was more the case of a continuum in the development of efforts to re-establish rural chapels, the work of small neighborhood groups to raise people's consciousness about social problems, and other efforts which utilized the small group dynamic. These developments gradually coalesced into the prototype of the base community of today. Azevedo finds it striking that in much of the early literature on

---

[16] *Ibid.,* p. 27.

[17] Cited by Azevedo, *Basic Ecclesial Communities in Brazil,* p. 28.

[18] *Ibid.,* p. 11. These statistics are based on 1984 estimates. Some current estimates place the number of BECs over the 100,000 mark. The situation is complicated by the fact that BECs range in size from groups as small as five people, to those numbering up to fifty or more (the average size is reported to be in the 20-50 person range). Thus Azevedo cautions: "the more I have studied BECs, the more convinced I have become that it is too difficult to make a reliable survey that would yield indisputable statistics." As we shall see, a similar problem exists in getting accurate statistics on the numbers of North American SCCs.

BCCs, while mention is made of their "novelty," no claims or hints are made as to their possible future prominence.[19]

In much of Brazil, BECs have tended to flourish mainly in rural areas and on the peripheries of big cities. They have not been as prevalent in metropolitan urban centers or in more affluent surrounding neighborhoods. BECs have been thus welcomed to a great extent by the poor and needy. But it would be incorrect to say, as is sometimes claimed, that BCCs somehow "spontaneously" arose from this poorer *base* of Brazilian society. As one commentator has said, "CEBs are not examples of ecclesial spontaneous combustion: they do not grow where no one sows."[20] Much of this pastoral effort came from priests and other religious, working in conjunction with their bishops.

Another myth which needs dispelling is that BECs were somehow the direct product of Latin American *Liberation theology*. BECs were not really the product of any particular theology, but were the fruit of pastoral experimentation.[21] Both BECs and Liberation theology arose separately. But they soon began to mutually influence and nourish one another. Liberation theology helped many BECs reflect in a beneficial way on the theological, ecclesiological, and social implications of their existence. But it also radicalized some BECs, leading to tensions with the hierarchy. These tensions were most in evidence in Nicaragua in the 1970s and 1980s, when the bishops there accused BECs of undermining their pastoral authority and trying to establish a "parallel church."[22]

But at the time of the Medellin meeting of CELAM in 1968, no such misgivings were in evidence. BCCs were enthusiastically hailed as a revolutionary new means of furthering evangelization. At the 1974 Synod on Evangelization in Rome, the Latin American experiment with BCCs received more international attention and acclaim.[23] We shall leave until chapter six a detailed examination of the mention made of BECs in the apostolic exhortation *Evangelii Nuntiandi* which Pope Paul VI wrote following this Synod. We shall also return momentarily to the ecclesiological implications for BECs found in the Medellin document, as well as to those found in the documents of the following CELAM meetings held in Puebla, Mexico in 1979, and Santo Domingo, Dominican Republic

---

[19] *Ibid.*, p. 36.

[20] David Regan, *Church for Liberation: A Pastoral Portrait of the Church in Brazil* (Dublin: Dominican Publications, 1987), p. 47.

[21] Azevedo, *Basic Ecclesial Communities in Brazil*, p. 177.

[22] Cf. Jeanne Gallo, *Basic Ecclesial Communities: A New Form of Christian Organizational Response to the World Today* (Boston University: Doctoral Dissertation, 1989), p. 440.

[23] Cf. Paul VI, *Evangelii Nuntiandi* #58.

in 1992. What is needed first is a brief explanation of some of the major characteristics of BECs in their Latin American setting.

2. Characteristics

Many explanations of BECs begin with an elaboration of the terms *basic*, *ecclesial*, and *community*, so as to provide a generic portrait of their characteristic features. *Basic* is said to mean several things. It refers to the idea that BECs are: (1) a basic cell of the church; (2) go back to the basics of Christianity; (3) belong to the base of society—the poor; and (4) belong to the base of the church—the laity.[24] BECs are *ecclesial* in that they are both an integral *part* of the church, and represent "a new way of being the church."[25] Finally, they are a *community* in that they are composed of people who personally know and support one another.[26]

It is difficult for many North Americans to appreciate the extent of the grinding poverty, oppression, and deprivation faced by many of the poor in Latin America. In years past, politically and socially, they had no voice, no power, and little hope for improvement. Ecclesiastically, they had little active role or responsibility in the church. But through the efforts of BECs, many poor have discovered once again their God-given human dignity and their rightful role in church and society. This new awareness has energized them for social, ecclesial and political action that would have been unthinkable in the past. This is why Gustavo Gutiérrez describes BECs as representing an "irruption of the poor" into the mainstream of church and society; the "absent ones" are making their presence felt.[27] This new awareness of the poor, and the important role they play, was expressed at Puebla in terms of the church needing to have a "preferential option for the poor."[28]

---

[24] Cf. Margaret Hebblethwaite, "Christian Cells," *The Tablet* (April 30, 1988), p. 498.

[25] The phrase "a new way of being church" has become a popular means of characterizing the BEC phenomenon. It appears semi-officially for the first time in a text emanating from the Seventh Ordinary Meeting of the Permanent Council of the National Conference of Brazilian Bishops, *As Comunidades Eclesiais de Base na Igreja do Brazil* (San Paolo: Ed. Paulinas, 1982), Doc. #25, p. 5.

[26] In a 1974 report, the Brazilian Bishop's Conference stated that *community* is not the primary goal of BECs. Rather, it should be seen as a natural consequence of Christian interaction in the areas of faith support and social outreach. Cited by Gottfried Deelen, "The Church on its Way to the People: Basic Christian Communities in Brazil," *Pro Vita Mundi Bulletin* 81 (1980), p. 3.

[27] Cf. Gustavo Gutiérrez, "The Irruption of the Poor in Latin America and the Christian Communities of the Common People," in Torres and Eagleson (eds.), *The Challenge of Basic Christian Communities*, pp. 107-123.

[28] Cf. CELAM's Puebla *Final Document*, part four, chapter one.

As central as the poor are to the Latin American experience of BECs, it would be a mistake to assume that only poor people qualify as members. Azevedo criticizes what he sees in some Latin American theologians as being "a tacit assumption that dire poverty is a precondition for BECs."[29] There is a tendency to glorify the poor, and to claim that only a church from "the base" can be the true church. This approach seems to programmatically exclude from the church people from other social classes, and even the hierarchy. This in effect is a kind of reverse discrimination. It also ignores the fact that most BECs were established with the help of clergy, religious, and laity from the middle-class.

The two major features of a typical BEC meeting are the Scripture reading/reflection time and the discussion period which follows. According to Carlos Mesters, the simple act of having Latin American Catholics actually read and reflect together on the biblical Word of God, has had enormous consequences.[30] It has opened up for them new horizons in understanding how God acts and how Christians should respond. It has led to the inculcating of a biblical spirituality which is less individualistic and more communitarian in nature. It has also helped to purify popular religiosity of superstitious and other syncretistic elements. Furthermore, BECs provide a Catholic alternative to the growing popularity of sects and Protestant Evangelical churches in Latin America.[31]

The discussion period is usually focused on issues of faith and social concern. It involves making a concrete link between the Word of God and the present situation of the people. It further involves a determination of what *praxis* the group should undertake to make improvements in the local community. This discussion involves the application of the classic "see, judge, act" methodology.[32] Sometimes discussion outlines are provided to BECs from the diocese to help in the Scripture reflection and discussion period. The result of this discussion and corresponding action is said to lead to a dynamic of "consciousness raising" and "empowerment" taking place in the lives of the people.[33]

---

[29] Azevedo, *Basic Ecclesial Communities in Brazil*, p. 89.

[30] Cf. Carlos Mesters, "The Use of the Bible in Christian Communities of the Common People," in Torres and Eagleson (eds.) *The Challenge of Basic Christian Communities*, pp. 197-210.

[31] This "Protestant explosion," especially in Evangelical and Pentecostal churches, has seen the number of Protestants in Latin America increase from 4 million in 1967 to 30 million in 1985. Fully 10% of Latin Americans are now Protestant. According to some estimates only 15% of Latin Americans are active Catholics. Statistics cited by Ralph Martin, "Sects Education," *New Covenant* (Oct. 1991), p. 26.

[32] This method originated with the Catholic Action *Jocist* movement. Cf. Chapter three, part III, section A.

[33] Cf. Paulo Freire, *Pedagogy of the Oppressed*, (New York: Seabury Press, 1970).

The social action which is undertaken may include such things as organizing literacy classes and neighborhood crime watches, building and maintaining community centers, aiding those most in need of economic assistance, petitioning the local government for better municipal services, helping the formation of labor unions and food cooperatives, and so forth. It must be remembered that in many of the poorer areas of Latin America, there is very little in the way of government assistance or basic municipal services. If the people do not organize and mobilize themselves for these tasks, they will not be realized in the local community.

This fact underlines one of the major differences between Latin American and North American SCCs. Because of the relative affluence and political stability of North America, SCCs do not have the same social or political function as do their Latin American counterparts. This is not to say that North American SCCs do not or need not reach out to assist the local community. We will see later how they approach this dimension of community action. For now we simply make this observation by way of highlighting the role played by the social and cultural milieu in the functioning of SCCs.

Besides social action, there is also much liturgical activity and sacramental preparation undertaken by the groups. Most BECs function as quasi-parishes, gathering for Sunday Liturgy of the Word services when then there is no priest present to celebrate Eucharist. They help in the sacramental preparation of children and in marriage preparation. They also help organize community social events such as festivals and celebrations which coincide with Holy Days and other liturgical feasts. This activity is a practical necessity in many areas given the chronic shortage of clergy in Latin America, and the large size of many parishes.[34] As we shall see, due to different circumstances in this regard, North American SCCs generally do not have this same liturgical function as do many of their Latin American counterparts.

There is in fact quite a variety in size, function, and socio-political orientation in Latin American BECs. There is a tendency in the literature to talk about Latin American BECs as if they were all of one basic type, or else to idealize a particular type. But as one studies Latin American BECs it soon becomes apparent that there is no single paradigm out of which they all operate. Instead, there is a remarkable diversity in evidence. For instance, in a socio-scientific random sampling of the 800 BECs operating in the Archdiocese of São Paolo, Brazil, W.E. Hewitt identified six different *types*

---

[34] Cf. Azevedo, "Basic Ecclesial Communities: A Meeting Point of Ecclesiologies," *Theological Studies* 46 (1985), p. 603.

of BECs.[35] These types can be described from a sociological point of view as follows:

Type 1—*Simple Devotional Groups* (23%). This is the organizationally simplest type of BEC. Groups belonging to this category meet weekly, usually in the home of a fellow member. Their meetings consist primarily of prayer, Bible reading and reflection. Outside the meeting they will engage in some form of charitable work in the local community. There is no engagement in political activities or highly organized community social action projects.

Type 2—*Devotional Miniparishes* (4%).[36] Aside from the small group meeting, these BECs host weekly Sunday liturgies for the area residents at a nearby chapel or community center when a priest is not available for Mass. They also engage in sacramental preparation and some other basic forms of social outreach. They are more organizationally complex than Type 1 groups, being usually directed by a steering committee (*conselho*).

Type 3—*Elementary Devotional/Political Groups* (18%). Similar to Type 1 groups in nature and scope. The major difference being their involvement in certain activities of a limited political character. There is a more explicit attempt made to facilitate consciousness-raising and to discuss social and political problems.

Type 4—*Politically Oriented Miniparishes* (23%). Represent a combination of Type 2 and Type 3 BECs. They function as mini-parishes, but with a more pronounced involvement in political and social action. They have a more organized internal structure. In addition to the steering committee or *conselho*, they will have various sub-committees or tasking groups to oversee particular initiatives.

Type 5—*Politically Oriented Missionary Groups* (4%). What characterize these BECs is their almost total emphasis on political causes and social action. Bible reading/reflection and other religious services and practices are held only infrequently. They undertake community action projects in less affluent neighborhoods, located at some distance from the group itself (thus the so-called "missionary" dimension to their sociopolitical action).

---

[35] Cf. W.E. Hewitt, "Christian Base Communities (CEBs): Structure, Orientation, and Sociopolitical Thrust," pp. 162-175.

[36] Hewitt's use of the expression "mini-parish" is equivalent to the canonical term "quasi-parish" we have used earlier in this thesis.

Type 6—*Classic or Ideal-Type BEC* (28%). These groups come closest to the description of BECs which are frequently portrayed in the general literature. They are essentially the same as the Type 4 miniparishes, but have an even higher degree of involvement in community action projects and political causes. There is a higher degree of organizational complexity as well.

Not only is the above mentioned *classic* or *ideal* type the kind which is most frequently portrayed in the general literature, it is often presented as being the "highest" expression of what constitutes a BEC. The other simpler forms, which lack an explicit socio-political commitment, are either dismissed as being mere "prayer groups," or else described as being lower down the ladder of evolutionary development.[37] Leaving aside the question of bias, what this raises is the fundamental issue of BEC identity. This is a problem that exists in classifying SCCs in North America as well. Is it the fact that small parish groups reflect on Scripture and carry out some manner of charitable work that characterizes them as SCCs, or is it also necessary to have an official mandate and/or some accompanying self-awareness of having an abiding ecclesial role?

Regarding the socio-political activity of BECs, Hewitt notes that the Brazilian bishops have been lately trying to de-emphasize the more explicitly political nature of some of these undertakings. For these activities, they are encouraging BEC members as individuals to join existing trade unions and political parties in order to promote social change through political channels.[38] They fear BECs becoming manipulated by political groups.[39] They want BECs to focus on their inherently religious purpose, and to keep their social action in proper balance. As Cardinal Arns, Archbishop of Saõ Paulo has observed, BECs are primarily a faith reality. If they only engage in social action, however laudable, they soon exhaust themselves and die out.[40]

Although Hewitt's analysis is based on only one diocese, it appears to be indicative of the general state of affairs existing elsewhere in Brazil

---

[37] Cf. Gottfried Deelen, "The Church on its Way to the People: BCCs in Brazil," *Pro Vita Mundi Bulletin* 81 (1980), p. 5.

[38] Hewitt, "Christian Base Communities (CEBs)," p. 174.

[39] This same fear was voiced by Pope John Paul II in a message that was delivered to BECs during a visit to Brazil. Cf. "Message for Basic Christian Communities," *Origins* 10/9 (1980), p. 140.

[40] Cited by Richard Schaull in *Heralds of a New Reformation* (Maryknoll, N.Y.: Orbis Books, 1984), p. 122.

and in Latin America.[41] The same can be said for Hewitt's conclusion that most São Paulo BECs saw themselves as being "firmly rooted" within the institutional structure of the church.[42] Most of them operated as miniparishes of one kind or another, being approved sub-divisions of a particular parish, and were in regular contact with the priests and other pastoral agents from the parish church. Only a relatively few BECs operated on the "periphery" of the parish system, distancing themselves from official contact with any outside form of pastoral supervision.[43]

This decision to minimize contact with legitimate pastoral authority, and to claim a certain degree of autonomy within the local church, goes to the heart of the ecclesiological debate pertaining to the conception of the leadership role of laity in BECs, and to the question of BECs' ecclesiality in the church in Latin America. For a brief look at this debate, as well as other ecclesiological reflection in this area, we turn now to the following section.

3. Ecclesiological Reflection

One of the documents from CELAM's 1968 Medellin meeting states that BECs are "the first and fundamental ecclesiastical nucleus," and represent "the initial cell of the ecclesiastical structures."[44] This terminology was invoked because BECs were seen at the time as being primarily sub-divisions of the parish.[45] This explains the reason why the bishops felt no qualms in describing the ecclesiality of BECs in such strong terms. They were seen as being different in nature from other lay movements and associations in that they were an integral part of the overall diocesan parish system, and were the ultimate responsibility of the local parish priest.

---

[41] For confirmation of this state of affairs Hewitt cites the similar findings of John Welsh, "Comunidades Eclesiais de Base: A New Way to be Church," *America* (Feb. 8, 1986), pp. 85-88, and Thomas C. Bruneau, "Basic Christian Communities in Latin America," in *Churches and Politics in Latin America*, ed. Daniel Levine (Beverly Hills: Sage, 1980), pp. 225-237. Cf. Hewitt, "Christian Base Communities (CEBs)," p. 165.

[42] *Ibid.,* p. 167.

[43] Many commentators have pointed to the fact that BECs are changing the role of parish priests in the church today. But there is controversy over what this new role entails. For instance, as advocates of a reduced role, José Marins et al. state that: "given our recent experience of a very clerical, pyramidal church in Latin America, it is imperative that the priest today knows how and when to intervene and not to interfere in the growth of the community. He must be sensitive to a process that is emerging and to allow a seed just sown to grow. His role is one of helping the communities to form and not being the central authority deciding what the community does." Marins et al., "The Church in Latin America: Basic Ecclesial Communities" in *Trends in Mission*, eds. W. Jenkinson and H. O'Sullivan (Maryknoll, N.Y.: Orbis, 1991), p. 69.

[44] CELAM, "Joint Pastoral Planning" (a Medellin document), section #15.

[45] Cf. Azevedo, *Basic Ecclesial Communities in Brazil*, p. 16.

But in the intervening years between Medellin and the next CELAM meeting in Puebla in 1979, many developments occurred both pastorally and theologically, which resulted in a different set of challenges being posed to the question of the ecclesiality of BECs. They were still very much endorsed by the bishops at Puebla. They were referred to as being "an important ecclesial event" and "the hope of the church" (the latter being a quote taken from *Evangelii Nuntiandi #58*).[46] But unlike Medellin, there is also a strong cautionary note sounded. The document, after expounding on the valuable role played by BECs, warns that: "not enough attention has been paid to the training of leaders. . . . Perhaps that is why not a few members of certain communities, and even entire communities, have been drawn to purely lay institutions or have been turned into ideological radicals, and are now in the process of losing any authentic feel for the Church."[47]

In an attempt to express what an authentic expression of being a BEC entails, the following description is given:

> As a community, the CEB brings together families, adults and young people, in an intimate interpersonal relationship grounded in faith. As an ecclesial reality, it is a community of faith, hope, and charity. It celebrates the Word of God and takes it nourishment from the Eucharist, the culmination of all the sacraments. It fleshes out the Word of God in life through solidarity and commitment to the new commandment of the Lord; and through the service of approved coordinators, it makes present and operative the mission of the Church and its visible communion with the legitimate pastors.[48]

The Puebla document goes on to refer to the role of the parish vis-à-vis BECs. The parish is seen as having "an integral ecclesial function" within the local church. This function of ecclesial integration is described thus:

> It is a center of coordination and guidance for communities, groups, and movements. In it the horizons of communion and participation are opened up even more. The celebration of the Eucharist and the other sacraments

---

[46] CELAM, Puebla *Final Document*, section #629.

[47] *Ibid.,* section #630.

[48] *Ibid.,* section #641.

makes the global reality of the Church present in a clearer way. Its tie with the diocesan community is ensured by its union with the bishop, who entrusts his representative (usually the parish priest) with the pastoral care of the community. For the Christian the parish becomes the place of encounter and fraternal sharing of persons and goods; it overcomes the limitations inherent in small communities.[49]

This stress on BECs being an integral part of the local church, subject to its bishop, and finding its usual home in the context of the parish system, was made to counter the claims which some Liberation theologians had voiced as to the relative independence or autonomy of BECs. Between the time of Medellin and Puebla there had in fact arisen in Latin America two competing ecclesiologies of BECs. From the point of view of some Liberation theologians, BECs were not just "obedient agents" of the hierarchy in carrying out an evangelization dictated "from the top," but represented a "reversal" of the hierarchical concept of church altogether.[50]

One of the best known proponents of this line of thinking is Leonardo Boff. In his book *Ecclesiogenesis*, he describes BECs as "reinventing" the church from the "grassroots."[51] He thinks BECs should be seen as replacing the parish, not as restructuring it.[52] This is because the parish, as traditionally found in Latin America, is too large and institutional an entity. Only small groups can keep alive the communitarian nature of the church. But this task will be facilitated only if the groups keep small and refuse to allow themselves to become "bureaucratized" and "institutionalized." Thus, a certain independence from ecclesial structures and clerical interference is necessary for their well-being, and for the welfare of the wider church.

Boff is not trying to argue that institutional features such as the hierarchy have no role to play in the life of the church. But he wants to claim that the generative priority for being church belongs to the grassroots. This is because he sees "charism" as being the real organizing principle of what

---

[49] *Ibid.*, section #644.

[50] This is Rosemary Radford Ruether's characterization of the position held by many Liberation theologians. Cf. Ruether, "Basic Communities: Renewal at the Roots," *Christianity and Crisis* 41/14 (1981), p. 236.

[51] Leonardo Boff, *Ecclesiogenesis*, p. 23.

[52] *Ibid.*, pp. 6-9. Boff actually says that BECs should "not" replace the parish. But what he means by this is that traditional parishes "cannot" emulate the personal communitarian nature of BECs, no matter how hard they try. They are simply too big from a sociological point of view. In this sense the parish should not be "replaced" by one big BEC, but should be done away with entirely.

it means to be church.[53] BECs are effective because lay people are free to use their personal charisms, and share in a democratic, participatory way in the leadership and life of the community. Thus, Boff describes the ecclesiology of BECs as being "grounded in the categories of People of God, *koinonia* (communion), prophecy, and *diakonia* (service)."[54]

A fundamental question Boff asks is to what degree lay-led BECs can claim to be "fully church," and not be seen simply in terms of possessing certain "ecclesial elements."[55] He acknowledges that historically, the parish has been seen as the basic cell of the diocese, the smallest of the ecclesiastical structures that qualifies theologically for being considered "church" (the family as a "domestic church" is really another matter).[56] But with the advent of BECs, this line of thinking should be expanded to confer a similar ecclesial status on these smaller groups. Why? Because they are said to participate in the universality and catholicity of the church in the same way as parishes.

Boff bases his opinion on a number of different sources. First, he claims that Paul in his epistles refers to the ecclesiality of house-churches, which were run by "ordinary" Christians. Second, he cites Vatican II's conception of the local (particular) church and the fact that *Lumen Gentium* spoke of the church being present "in all legitimate local congregations" (LG 26). And finally, he quotes what Medellin had to say about the ecclesiality of BECs. He concludes: "Taking these reflections as consistent and conclusive, we may say that the basic church communities, in all theological rigor, are true, universal church, concretized on this small-group level. [Because therein] . . . lives the totality of the life of the church, as expressed in service, celebration, and evangelization."[57]

A full critique of Boff's analysis is not really needed. Suffice it to say that he has been highly selective in his use of the theological "sources" he bases his argument on (as this study shows in its earlier treatment of these same sources).[58] Azevedo states that Boff's ecclesiology is simply not

---

[53] Boff explains this idea more thoroughly in his book *Church: Charism and Power* (New York: Crossroad, 1985).

[54] *Ibid.,* p. 9.

[55] Boff, *Ecclesiogenesis*, p. 11.

[56] An explanation of the ecclesiological meaning of the term "domestic church," as it is sometimes applied to the family, will be featured in chapter seven, part III, section C § 1.

[57] *Ibid.,* p. 20.

[58] Our earlier overview of the Pauline house churches shows that Boff's depiction of their leadership and ecclesiality is deficient (cf. chapter one, part I, section C). So too is his interpretation of *Lumen Gentium* 26 (cf. chapter two, part I, section B § 1). Furthermore, he cites Medellin out of context (the bishops had described BECs as being an "ecclesiastical nucleus" because they viewed them as being essentially sub-structures of the parish community—cf. note

Catholic. He says Boff "won't make a contribution by denying meaningfulness or apostolic continuity to the hierarchy, or by claiming to originate the church power of governing and pastoring solely on their own; the mere existence of a community of faith does not suffice for that."[59] Azevedo recognizes that BECs represent a new means for going about the task of being church, but this fact does not change the church's fundamental ontological or theological identity. Azevedo would prefer to express the significance of the BEC phenomenon thus: "without ceasing to be what it intrinsically is, then, the Church is moving toward a new concrete and historical way of being church."[60]

This attempt to define BECs as churches in their own right has been condemned by the bishops, and even by some other Liberation theologians. For instance, Enrique Dussel characterizes such an attempt as being a form of "ecclesial narcissism."[61] The promotion of the term "basic *ecclesial* communities" (BECs) by the hierarchy, rather than simply "basic Christian communities" (BCCs), was made to emphasize the ecclesial link BECs have to the wider church, not to indicate their independent ecclesial identity.

This point was recently reiterated at CELAM's 1992 Santo Domingo conference. BECs are described as being "living cells of the parish," whose animators "must be in communion with their parish and their bishop."[62] If sincere communion is not maintained, then such BECs "cease to be ecclesial," becoming the victims instead of ideological or political manipulation.[63] Thus, CELAM continues to promote the development of BECs, but under the condition that they remain in solidarity with, and integrated into, the parish, diocese, and universal church.[64]

Azevedo reports that most Brazilian BECs strive to be "ecclesial" in the fullest sense of the word, and are happy to be an integral part of the diocesan structure.[65] There is not as much anti-institutional or anti-clerical sentiment in evidence among BECs as is sometimes claimed.[66] BECs are not seen as destroying or replacing the parish, but as being a fundamentally new way of revitalizing it. They are not a transitory phenomenon, but represent

---

#45 above).

[59] Azevedo, *Basic Ecclesial Communities in Brazil*, p. 206.

[60] *Ibid.,* p. 195.

[61] Cited in Azevedo, *Basic Ecclesial Communities in Brazil*, p. 106, note #28.

[62] CELAM, Santo Domingo *Final Statement*, #61.

[63] *Ibid.,* #62.

[64] *Ibid.,* #63.

[65] Cf. Azevedo, *Basic Ecclesial Communities in Brazil*, p. 66.

[66] For corroboration of this point see Gary MacEoin and Nivita Riley, *Puebla: A Church Being Born* (New York: Paulist Press, 1980), pp. 17-18.

the emergence of a new structure which is part of the on-going evolution of the parish in history. But BECs have not simply impacted upon parish organization. They have had the effect of leaven in the dough, renewing not just a part of the church, but helping in the transformation of the whole organism. They do indeed seem to represent "a new way of *living* as Church, of *being* Church and *acting* as Church in Brazil."[67] They have had this impact on the church in Brazil because they have been legitimated on three fronts: theologically, juridically, and sociologically.[68] But Azevedo thinks it would be a mistake to become too enthusiastic about BECs if the result is a downgrading of other forms of pastoral activity.[69] BECS are not the only locus of community and evangelization in the church today.

Azevedo laments the fact that the growing polarization and radicalization of theology in Latin America is preventing genuine dialogue from taking place between opposing camps. Such dialogue would hold much promise for the opening up of new avenues for much needed ecclesiological reflection and synthesis. This is why he characterizes the BEC phenomenon as representing "a meeting point of ecclesiologies."[70] But instead of dialogue, one finds mainly "sterile polemics." Media sensationalism has also taken its toll. What in actual fact is a theological debate among a small minority of theologians, becomes amplified in the press. The result is increasing confusion and perplexity among the common people.[71]

It has been worthwhile recounting the major features of Boff's ecclesiological assessment of BECs, because this line of thinking has influenced a certain strand of North American reflection in this area, as we shall see. It also serves to bring into sharper focus the nature of the current ecclesiological debate pertaining to BECs, and the quest for new categories by which to express their ecclesial significance. In a sense, every new phenomenon creates its own language and establishes new categories for its self-expression. The same thing can be seen as happening today with BECs. Despite the inadequacy of Boff's analysis and his fundamental conclusions, it is hard to argue with his recognition of this essential dynamic:

> The basic communities are generating a new ecclesiology, formulating new concepts in theology. This is still just beginning, still in process. It is not an accomplished

---

[67] Azevedo, *Basic Ecclesial Communities in Brazil*, p. 5.

[68] *Ibid.*, p. 41.

[69] *Ibid.*, p. 80.

[70] Cf. Azevedo, "Basic Ecclesial Communities: A Meeting Point of Ecclesiologies," pp. 601-620.

[71] Cf. Azevedo, *Basic Ecclesial Communities in Brazil*, pp. 108-109, note #40.

reality. Pastors and theologians, take warning! Respect this new way that is appearing on the horizon. Do not seek to box this phenomenon within theological-pastoral categories distilled from other contexts and other ecclesial experiences. . . . We must . . . stay open. Otherwise we may smother the Spirit.[72]

B. Africa[73]

1. Emergence

As was the case with Latin America, it is not possible to present an overview of SCC development for all of Africa. The continent is a vast one, comprising many different countries with a wide array of different cultural, linguistic, and religious affiliations. Generally speaking, sub-Sahara Africa is where the majority of Christians make their home. Within this domain, in addition to many local indigenous languages, there are two main linguistic regions. These are English-speaking East and South Africa and French-speaking West and Central Africa.

Of these two main linguistic regions, SCCs have achieved special prominence in the so-called AMECEA countries of East Africa.[74] Developments of a similar nature had also gotten underway in other regions around the same time. But because the bishops of the AMECEA countries have been in the forefront of SCC development in Africa, this region provides a good focal point for our analysis of the "African" situation regarding their historical emergence and chief characteristics. So only brief mention will be made of developments in other areas. This is because, as was the case before with the situation of Brazilian BECs vis-à-vis the rest of Latin America, there is enough similarity in the situation of SCCs in this region of Africa to warrant generalizations based on the AMECEA experience.

The pastoral challenges posed to being an effective parish community in Africa are similar in many ways to what we have noted about the church in Latin America. A major shortcoming is the large territorial

---

[72] Boff, *Ecclesiogenesis*, p. 2.

[73] Principal sources for this section are: Patrick Kalilombe, *From Outstations to Small Christian Communities* (Eldoret, Kenya: Gaba Publications, Spearhead #82-83, 1984); Eugène Lapointe, *Une expérience pastorale en Afrique Australe* (Paris: Editions L'Harmattan, 1985); Silverio Twinomugisha, *Ecclesiological Meaning of Small Christian Communities in Uganda Today* (Rome: Urbaniana University Doctoral Dissertation, 1991); Bernard Ugeux, *Les petites communautés chrétiennes, une alternative aux paroisses? L'expérience du Zaire* (Paris: Cerf, 1988); and various articles in the *African Ecclesial Review* (AFER) and *Pro Vita Mundi Bulletin*.

[74] The Association of Member Episcopal Conferences of Eastern Africa (AMECEA) comprises 82 dioceses from the countries of Kenya, Uganda, Tanzania, Zambia, and Malawi.

size of many parishes (especially in rural areas). This is a consequence of too few clergy to pastor them. To cope with this situation, the early missionaries set up *Outstations* or *Mass Centres* in many rural parishes. These outstations, usually located in outlying villages, functioned as chapels or missions of the mother parish. A priest from the parish church would come around on a regular basis (usually monthly) to provide for Eucharist and other sacramental celebrations.[75]

But it became apparent that this system was inadequate to meet all the pastoral needs of the people. Competition from smaller-based Protestant churches was also being felt. In the 1920s and 1930s, with the impetus provided by Catholic Action, many lay catechists and other church elders from the outstations were trained to teach in outstation schools, prepare catechumens for baptism, and to assist in other apostolic activities such as conducting Sunday prayer services. Vatican II was to provide a major stimulus to further developments in this area of lay pastoral ministry and leadership.[76]

Despite the improvement to parish life represented by the development of outstations and trained lay leaders to help in the pastoral ministry, these groupings were still too large in many instances to facilitate effective Christian formation and to promote further lay participation in the life of the local church. This was made evident by the continuing loss of Catholics to other smaller sects and Protestant churches that was occurring even after the Council. In order to address this problem, Marie-France Perrin Jassy, a cultural anthropologist, was requested by the Maryknoll Fathers to investigate this situation in the North Mara region of Tanzania. Her conclusions, published in 1973, became an influential factor in the AMECEA bishops' decision to advocate the formation of SCCs in their dioceses.[77]

Perrin Jassy's investigation highlighted many significant points that helped explain why the Luo in North Mara were leaving the Catholic church and joining independent African churches. Among her findings, it was stated

---

[75] For insight into what this situation concretely entails, Mbarara diocese in Uganda serves as a good example. It covers an area of 10,980 sq. klms. It has a Catholic population of 400,000, out of a general population of about one million. There are 20 parishes and quasi-parishes, encompassing 155 outstations, and served by 27 priests and 120 lay catechists. The average parish has a Catholic population ranging between 15,000—40,000, which includes the population of the outstations (which range in size from 500—3,000). Statistics cited by Bishop John Baptist Kakubi, "Christian Communities in Mbarara Diocese," *AFER* 21/5 (1979), p. 299.

[76] Bishop Patrick Kalilombe of Lilongwe, Malawi provides an excellent historical account of these developments in his book: *From Outstations to Small Christian Communities*, pp. 25-43.

[77] Cf. Marie-France Perrin Jassy, *Basic Community in the African Churches* (Maryknoll, N.Y.: Orbis Books, 1973).

that for people to feel they *belong* to a group, they need to take an active role in that group. Experience shows that people can become more *involved* in a group, and become more easily *recognized* if the group is of a smaller nature. She found that the Catholic church had played an important role in the life of the Luo, but she noted that nevertheless: "It is separated from the Luo by a gap which the years have not closed . . . In most cases the faithful play an essentially passive role. . . . The faithful, for different reasons, have never had to take a hand in the fortunes of their Church and assume their responsibilities."[78] In contrast, the independent African churches were usually small, neighborhood-based groups that engendered a stronger sense of community and wherein leadership and ministry was shared by many, not just a few.

Although the idea of organizing the parish apostolate around even smaller units than those of the outstations had been in practice in many regions of Africa since the early 1960s, it had not yet matured.[79] In hindsight, what was still missing was a more complete reception of Vatican II's vision of the church and recognition of the role of the laity. This was happening in some areas more quickly than in others. Eventually, through a convergence of factors that coalesced in the 1970s (including the influence of the 1974 Synod on Evangelization in Rome—at which the Latin American experience with BECs received much publicity), the African model of "small Christian communities" became a reality.[80]

It was during the 1976 plenary meeting of the AMECEA bishops that SCCs were launched as an official pastoral policy. A major recommendation of that meeting was "that the systematic formation of Small Christian Communities should be the key pastoral priority in the years to come within Eastern Africa."[81] Three years later, the subject of SCCs was again the major topic of reflection at the AMECEA plenary meeting. It was found that in the intervening years the implementation of the 1976 pastoral plan was proceeding unevenly. Some bishops and their priests had not really grasped how the concept of SCCs differed from the older strategy of outstations. Thus, the 1979 meeting helped in the dissemination of more information about SCCs, and set up more realistic guidelines for their

---

[78] *Ibid.,* p. 247.

[79] The bishops of the former Belgian Congo (now Zaire) had called for the establishing of cell-like sub-structures known as *communautés chrétiennes vivantes* (CCVs) in parishes there as early as 1961 (they were later renamed *communautés ecclésiales vivantes* or CEVs). Cf. Ugeux, *Les petites communautés chrétiennes, une alternative aux paroisses?,* p. 9.

[80] Cf. Twinomugisha, *Ecclesiological Meaning of Small Christian Communities in Uganda Today,* p. 30.

[81] Cited by Joseph Kelly, "The Evolution of Small Christian Communities," *AFER* 33/3 (1991), p. 115.

establishment. Particularly helpful in this regard was the detailed and practical information about SCCs that had come out of the Lumko Institute in South Africa under the guidance of Fr. (now bishop) Fritz Lobinger.[82]

2. Characteristics

In a recent article Joseph Healey, a Maryknoll priest based in Tanzania, lists ten major characteristics of a typical SCC in East Africa.[83] Before listing these features, Healey begins by stating what SCCs are not. They are not "prayer groups." As important as prayer is to an SCC, they are said to be much more all-encompassing and integrated into the total life of church than is a simple prayer group. They are not "apostolic groups" or other traditional forms of parish organizations (i.e. Legion of Mary, St. Vincent de Paul, The Altar Society, etc.). Finally, they are not traditional outstations. Outstations usually involve a larger grouping of local Catholics and are the setting for Sunday Liturgies and other forms of Sacramental preparation and celebration. SCCs on the other hand are smaller, and supplement outstation liturgical activity.

The major characteristics of an SCC according to Healey are listed here as follows:

(1) An SCC is small, usually no more than 15-20 adults (with varying numbers of children).

(2) The SCC is usually a neighborhood group. The rural model is a communion of extended families in the same neighborhood. The urban model usually groups people who live in an apartment or row of houses or housing project.

(3) The SCC usually meets in the home of one of its members.

(4) The SCC meeting is held in addition to, and outside the context of, Sunday Eucharist/Liturgy of the Word Services.

(5) The leadership of the SCC comes from within its own ranks.

(6) The SCC meeting has some kind of Bible Sharing/ Reflection on a regular basis.

---

[82] The Lumko Institute published a variety of easy-to-read tracts and pamphlets about SCCs for laity and pastoral workers alike. Also important in the dissemination of information was AMECEA's own documentation service and the numerous articles on SCCs that began appearing in African journals such as *AFER*. For insight into the Lumko approach to SCCs see Fritz Lobinger, *Building Small Christian Communities* (South Africa: Lumko Missiological Institute, 1981).

[83] Cf. Joseph Healey, "The Option for Small Christian Communities," *Pro Vita Mundi Bulletin* 12 (1989 90), pp 11-12.

(7) The SCC emphasises personal relationships and solidarity (sharing together, working together, celebrating together) within the context of African values and customs.

(8) The SCC has some kind of planned practical action, mutual aid and social outreach.

(9) The SCC participates in the parish structures, for example, each SCC (or group of SCCs) has a representative on the outstation or parish council. There is also some kind of coordination and networking among SCCs of a given parish.

(10) There are regular meetings and training sessions for SCC leaders.

Healey remarks at the end of this list that not all of these ten characteristics are present in every single SCC, but that most SCCs either already have them, or are in the process of incorporating them.[84]

In comparisons which are made between African SCCs and Latin American BECs, it is often noted that African SCCs lack the same kind of political dimension and commitment to social change which mark many of their Latin American counterparts. There is very little in the way of consciousness raising, the struggle for liberation, or in-depth social analysis evident in an SCC meeting. The Bible reading/reflection component is similar. But the missionary activity of SCCs is usually of a basic charitable or evangelistic nature, such as visiting the sick, meeting with a lapsed Catholic, helping out someone in financial need, etc. There is also little anti-clerical or anti-institutional sentiment evident in African SCCs, and little clamouring for a more autonomous status within the parish or local church.[85]

African SCCs then are of a predominately "pastoral" nature. They are seen primarily as a means of helping to strengthen the overall experience of Christian community and mission in the parish\outstation. In the words of Bishop Kalilombe, SCCs are a way of helping to make the church more "self-ministering, self-propagating, and self-supporting."[86] They are also part of the larger effort that is underway in the African church to help inculturate the faith.

---

[84] *Ibid.*, p. 12.

[85] Cf. John Guiney, "Comparing BCCs in S. America and Africa," *AFER* 30 (1988), pp. 167-180.

[86] Patrick Kalilombe, "Building Christian Communities," *Lumen Vitae* 32/2 (1977), p. 177.

3. Ecclesiological Reflection

In the published conclusions of the 1979 AMECEA plenary meeting, many aspects which touch on the nature of SCC ecclesiality are outlined.[87] The bishops begin by affirming a statement they made about SCCs at their previous meeting in 1976. "The Christian communities we are trying to build are simply the most local incarnations of the one, holy, Catholic and apostolic Church."[88] SCCs are to be seen then as attempts to *incarnate* and *localize* the church. "Small Christian Communities are means by which the Church is brought down to the daily life and concerns of people to where they actually live. In them, the Church takes on flesh and blood in the life situation of the people . . . In them, they can truly experience the Church as a new way of being together."[89]

The size of an SCC is variable, but it should be neither too large, resulting in people not being able to effectively know one another, nor too small, resulting in a lack of needed charisms for its proper functioning. "It is the experience of sharing the love of Christ together in a familiar circle that is the defining element of a small Christian community, compared with the larger ecclesial groupings of outstation, parish, and diocese."[90] The bishops further explain that a more intimate experience of Christian community is needed for the effective catechesis and spiritual support of its members. SCCs do not replace the parish or outstation, but renew and complement them in the task of being the church.

Structurally, the SCC is described as being "the most local unit of the church."[91] This is not to take anything away from the role of the family in the church. Family life is still of the utmost importance. SCCs are viewed in fact as being essentially groupings of families, and as being an effective means of supporting family life. But the family, as *domestic church*, has a different role to play than does the SCC. The SCC has more of an explicit ecclesial function, integrating families more effectively into the parish, and providing a means for greater lay participation in the life of the church. Thus, SCCs are seen as occupying a new niche in the parish system. This conception is brought out in the following statement:

> Since "the ideal way of renewing the parish is to make it
> a community of communities" (Synod 1977, Proposition

---

[87] Cf. AMECEA Bishops, "Conclusions of the Study Conference of the AMECEA Plenary 1979," *AFER* 21/5 (1979), pp. 265-272.

[88] *Ibid.,* pp. 265-266.

[89] *Ibid.,* p. 266.

[90] *Ibid.,* p. 267.

[91] *Ibid.,* p. 268

on the Parish), small Christian communities together make
up the parish; united with the local pastor, they form part
of the parish, of the diocese, of the universal Church. It is
the ordained ministry (of Bishops and priests) which is the
link among the communities in time and space, and
between them and the universal Church. This role is
essential in preserving the ecclesial bond among the
communities.[92]

The SCC is seen as changing the role of both priests and the laity.
The priest still exercises an overall leadership role in the parish community,
but increasingly his task is to enable the laity to exercise their charisms in
a mutually supporting manner. The SCC helps in the basic Christian
formation of the laity. Reflection on the Word of God is a vital part of this
formation. But this stress on the Word of God, "must not be allowed to
diminish the centrality of the Eucharist in the worship of the community."[93]

Patrick Kalilombe states that the AMECEA bishops' commitment
to SCC development represents a decisive landmark in East African pastoral
policy:

It is deliberately intended to modify deeply our pastoral
system, policy, and practice. Until now the avowed
common system was to base the life of the Church on the
parish level, rather than on the sub-parish level. The
parish was taken for granted as the basic or nuclear
expression of the local church. Any sub-parish division
was not really considered as an adequate realisation of the
Church, capable of being the centre or basis of a full
ecclesial existence. It could only be an administrative
component of the parish, with no real life of its own, that
looked up to the parish even to enable it to live and
function in an elementary way. Concretely speaking, the
parish was the lowest division of the diocese.[94]

Kalilombe points out that a fundamental reason for this new
thinking is the recognition that the parish system as it exists in Africa, is of
a very different kind than ones existing in Europe or North America. The
large territorial size of many parishes, coupled with often times inadequate

[92] *Ibid.*

[93] *Ibid.,* p. 271.

[94] Kalilombe, "Building Christian Communities," p. 183.

means of transportation, make it difficult for many Catholics to participate in "parish" activities. Thus, "in the circumstances in East Africa, it is impossible to consider the missions or the parishes as the basic units of the local church. If we do so, the Church will be doomed to failure. We must adopt a new system in which the basic units of the Church will be these smaller communities in which the ordinary life of the people takes place."[95]

It is not just the shortage of priests which is a factor in the development of SCCs. It is more a recognition of the need for the laity to take more of an active role in the process of sustaining their faith. The bishops of Uganda recognized that as important as Eucharist and other liturgical services are to the maintenance and celebration of the faith, they are nevertheless "not enough" on their own to help people grow to Christian maturity.[96] SCCs are seen as being an ideal way of fostering such Christian maturity and expanding the sense of what it means to be church on the local level.

Eugène Lapointe, in reflecting on the ecclesiological significance of SCCs in South Africa, makes some observations which are similar to those outlined above by the AMECEA bishops. He describes three fundamental ecclesiological principles involved in SCCs.[97] The first is the principle of subsidiarity. SCCs not only decentralize the parish for the benefit of the apostolate, but they take over certain roles and activities of the parish according to their own ecclesial "competence." The second is the principle of legitimate diversity. Not all SCCs have to be carbon copies of one another. The third is the principle of co-responsibility. The laity are active collaborators with the ordained ministers in realizing the task of being the church in today's world.[98]

In reflecting on the situation of SCCs in french-speaking Africa, one bishop from Zaire sees them as embodying an approach to being church that is of a more "human size and scale."[99] They are not an alternative to the parish, but a means of restructuring and renewing it. SCCs should not be described in terms of being "miniature parishes," for this skewers their ecclesial function and role.[100] It can also inadvertently promote an

---

[95] Kalilombe quote cited by Jan Gootaers, "Laity in the Field: Polarities and Convergences," *Pro Vita Mundi Bulletin* 110/3 (1987), p. 16.

[96] Cf. Twinomugisha, *Ecclesiological Meaning of Small Christian Communities in Uganda Today*, pp. 29-30.

[97] Cf. Lapointe, *Une expérience pastorale en Afrique Australe*, pp. 228-231.

[98] Further elaboration of these principles will be undertaken in the final chapter dealing with an ecclesiological reflection of the North American experience of SCCs (cf. chapter seven, part III, section B § 2).

[99] Cf. Bishop Monsengwo Pasinya, in the Preface to Bernard Ugeux's *Les petites communautés chrétiennes, une alternative aux paroisses?*, p. 13.

independent mindset among SCCs. Generally speaking, the problem that the Latin American church has had with some SCCs clamouring for more autonomy, is not a major issue in the African church at this time. The problems or weaknesses that do exist in french-speaking African SCCs include: insufficient grasp of doctrine—resulting in a lack of a proper sense of what it means to "belong" to the church; lack of sacramental nourishment; and lack of juridical identity.[101]

Some critics of African SCCs see these problems or weaknesses as being partially the result of the hierarchy *imposing* SCCs as a pastoral strategy "from above." They should have been allowed to spontaneously arise "from below."[102] But as we have noted in regards to the Latin American emergence of BECs, most of them did not arise spontaneously from below. Generally speaking, John Guiney does not see this criticism as being much of a shortcoming. He notes that where a serious pastoral effort has been made to set up SCCs, "they have been warmly received by the people."[103]

These observations about the characteristics and ecclesiality of African SCCs serve to highlight the points of continuity and discontinuity they share with their Latin American counterparts. They should not be treated as "poor copies" of the Latin American model, but as an African response to different pastoral exigences.[104] To complete our survey of the diverse ways in which SCCs have come to function and be understood in the parish/local church, we turn now to briefly comment upon the European and Asian experience.

C. Other Regions

1. Europe

It is far more difficult to generalize about the situation of BCCs in Europe than in Latin America and Africa. Though it does seem clear that they have a much lower official profile and are a relatively minor phenomenon in the European church at this time. Those BCCs that do exist tend to be marked by a strong tinge of social protest.[105] They have grown

---

[100] Bernard Ugeux, *Ibid.,* p. 289.

[101] Cf. A. Kalonji Ntekesha, *Les communautés ecclesiales de base: Foyers d' un Christianisme Africain?* (Rome: Gregorian University Doctoral Dissertation, 1983), p. 45.

[102] Cf. Guiney, who cites a report by A. Shorter in "Comparing BCCs in S. America and Africa," p. 168.

[103] *Ibid.*

[104] This is an opinion noted by Kelly, "The Evolution of Small Christian Communities," p. 108.

[105] Cf. Gottfried Deelen, "Basic Christian Communities in Europe," *Pro Vita Mundi Bulletin* 81 (1980), p. 30.

up on the fringes of the official church and often times express vocal opposition to it. Not surprisingly, the hierarchy has not been as enthusiastic about their activities, tending to view them with a mixture of suspicion and mistrust.

Another problem is identifying what a BCC is in Europe. In Italy, for example, some commentators lump all the small groups that have been spawned by such lay movements as the Neocatechumenal Way, Focolari, and Communion and Liberation, into the general category of "BCCs."[106] But these groups, while often times operating out of a parish setting, are not really parish-based, nor do they consider themselves part of a wider "BCC" movement. They really have a different ecclesial identity and purpose. The BCCs that do go by that name in Italy have aligned themselves often times with political movements such as *Christians for Socialism*. Hence, "the leftist character of many grassroots communities—one might even say the majority—explains why the Italian communities have strong political convictions . . . and why church authorities more often than not are very chary of or opposed to them."[107]

The situation is not really that much different in France. Many of these BCCs emerged out of the 1968 student protests there. They tend to want to remain on the fringes of the official church so as to better preserve their autonomy and supposedly be more effective in their quest to transform the church.[108] While other lay groups such as Jean Vanier's *L'Arche* communities, the ecumenical *Taizé* community, and various Charismatic communities have flourished, the French BCCS have tended to remain a rather "peripheral phenomenon."[109]

Spain seems to be the country in Europe with the largest numbers of BCCs. Many of these are similar in their characteristic features to those in Latin America. The Spanish bishops have also taken more of an active role in monitoring and attempting to guide BCC activity and development. In spite of some opposition to the hierarchy, Cardinal Tarancón of Madrid indicated that these groups were a Spirit-inspired phenomenon that should be encouraged as well as subject to on-going discernment.[110]

In the Germanic and Anglo-Saxon countries of Northern Europe (and for that matter Eastern Europe too) BCCs are in even less evidence. The exception to this situation is the Netherlands. There is a small but active network of BCCs in operation in the Netherlands. They derive their

---

[106] *Ibid.*, p. 32.

[107] Jan Kerkhofs, "Basic Communities in Europe," *Pro Vita Mundi Bulletin* 62 (1976), p. 24.

[108] Cf. Deelen, "Basic Christian Communities in Europe," p. 32.

[109] Cf. Kerkhofs, "Basic Communities in Europe," p. 24.

[110] Cf. Collins, "Small Groups: An Experience of Church," p. 123.

fundamental inspiration from Latin American BCCs and from Liberation theology. Often added to this is a strong commitment to the Peace movement and to ecumenical concerns.[111]

Attempts to explain why BCCs in Europe have not experienced the same success as their Latin American and African counterparts vary. Some observers point to the different role BCCs play in the church and society in these regions of the world. Michael Winter gives three reasons for this difference. First, the shortage of clergy is not as acute yet in Europe. Second, most Catholics live within a reasonable distance form a parish church and have an easier time getting there due to better means of transportation. Third, the relative affluence of Europe has lessened the need for political action to remedy social ills due to poverty (though there are a host of other social problems in Europe that need addressing).[112]

2. Asia

Outside of the Philippines, the Catholic church is in very much of a minority situation in the rest of Asia. And except for the Philippines, the same thing applies to the situation of BCCs in this region of the world. While experiments with BCCs are reported to be underway in many Asian countries (i.e. India, Taiwan, Korea, Pakistan, Malaysia, Thailand, Indonesia, New Guinea, Laos), it is difficult to ascertain how prevalent they are in the local churches. Generally speaking though, the Asian bishops have made parish revitalization one of their top pastoral priorities, and they have expressed an openness to and support for BCC development.[113]

In the Philippines, BCC formation and development has been an important pastoral priority of the bishops there since the 1970s.[114] BCCs have achieved a level of growth and prominence not unlike some of their Latin American or African counterparts. In fact, some commentators have characterized the Filipino experience of BCCs as representing a "bridge" between the Latin American model (with its social justice emphasis) and the African model (with its pastoral focus).[115]

Because of these similarities with the Latin American and African situations vis-à-vis BECs/SCCs, it is not necessary to review the

---

[111] Cf. Healey, "Evolving a Church from the Bottom Up," p. 19.

[112] Cf. Michael Winter, *What Ever Happened to Vatican II?* (London: Sheed and Ward, 1985), p. 149.

[113] Cf. Grootaers, "Laity in the Field," p. 21.

[114] Cf. Julio X. Labayen (Bishop of Infanta, Philippines) "Basic Christian Communities," *AFER* 30 (1988), p. 142.

[115] Cf. Lee and Cowan, *Dangerous Memories*, p. 43.

characteristics of Filipino BCCs or their perceived ecclesiality.[116] By way of conclusion, a quote from Bishop Orlando Quevedo provides a good example of how BCCs are viewed in the Philippines:

> The GKK [*Filipino for SCC*] is simply the Church in miniature. It makes the Church concrete and local at the grassroots. Its impact is on the whole of life, though it is not political or ideological. It is ecclesial. The GKK is a community of faith, hope and love. In it, the people of God pray and reflect on the Word of God, as the Word bears upon their life situation. It is a community of action for the building up of a people, based on God's Word. It supports no movement except the movement towards Christ.[117]

III. AN INTRODUCTION TO NORTH AMERICAN SCCs

A. Challenges Posed to Understanding the North American Experience of SCCs

As was previously mentioned in the introduction to this thesis, there exists a general lack of awareness in the international Catholic community of the specific characteristics of the North American experience of SCCs. At the time when BCCs were first emerging in force onto the international scene in the 1970s, little was really known about developments happening in North America. For instance, the *Pro Vita Mundi Bulletin* in 1976, and again in 1980, devoted an entire issue to the topic of BCCs worldwide. Developments were reported on in Latin America, Africa, Europe, and Asia. But not in North America. The editor of the *Bulletin* acknowledged that this omission represented a "gap" in their information about BCCs.[118]

In retrospect, this omission was not a glaring one. The fact of the matter was that very few typical BCCs/SCCs were in existence in North America during the 1970s. There was also a further difficulty involved in identifying what should or should not be considered a "BCC." For example

---

[116] For information about the ecclesiology of Filipino BCCs, see: Ruben Birondo, "Basic Christian Communities: The Experience of the Philippines," *The Clergy Review* 70 (1985), pp. 249-252; Francisco Claver, " The Basic Christian Communities in the Wider Context," *East Asian Pastoral Review* 23/2 (1986), pp. 362-368; and Edmundo Valera, "Theology of Struggle: the Philippines' Ecclesial Experience," *New Theology Review* 5/2 (1992), pp. 62-83.

[117] Cited by Collins, "Small Groups: An Experience of Church," p. 125.

[118] Cf. Editor's note, "Basic Communities in the Church," *Pro Vita Mundi Bulletin* 81 (1980), p. 2.

Richard Westley, in a 1975 article in *Concilium*, attempted to explain the features of the American experience with "base communities."[119] But Westley doesn't mention any specific names in his description, except for the various lay communities of the Charismatic Renewal movement. But should these groups be considered "SCCs"? (More about this classification problem in a moment).

Even Avery Dulles, in the mention he makes of "North American BECs" his 1977 book *The Resilient Church*, does not shed much light on the situation. At the time, he too considered Charismatic communities and prayer meetings, along with Marriage Encounter groups and fellowships that have grown up around Catholic student associations, to be representative of this phenomenon.[120] Another category of groups frequently associated with BCCs at this time were various kinds of "social justice" advocacy and action groups. In a 1981 article describing the Canadian Catholic experience of small communities, which the author compares to that of Latin American BCCs, included are such entities as factory worker union groups, various cooperatives, and refugee support groups.[121] In a similar vein, an American commentator writing in 1983 considered the Catholic social justice lobby group NETWORK to be an example of a "small community," even though its members are reported to meet only eight times per year.[122]

Kate Pravera, in a 1981 article describing the U.S. experience of BCCs, noted this problem in categorizing the phenomenon in this region of the world. "At present, the phrase *basic Christian community* is rapidly being appropriated by groups with a wide range of ideological and ecclesiological assumptions, thereby creating confusion about their form and purpose."[123] Pravera described the promotion of BCCs in the U.S. as being spearheaded by two major groups: those seeking to revitalize parishes, and those involved in Hispanic ministry. Complicating the task of getting accurate information about these efforts was (and still is) the absence of any national network or organizing body. She notes that some kind of typological classification of BCCs would be helpful, but doubts it this is

---

[119] Cf. Richard Westley, "Base Communities in the United States," *Concilium* 104 (1975), pp. 35-42.

[120] Cf. Avery Dulles, *The Resilient Church* (Garden City, N.Y.: Doubleday, 1977), p. 14.

[121] Cf. Tony Clarke, "Communities for Justice," *The Ecumenist* 19/2 (1981), pp. 17-25.

[122] Cf. William Newell, "The Reflection Groups," in *Tracing the Spirit: Communities, Social Action, and Theological Reflection*, ed. James Hug (New York/Ramsey: Paulist Press, 1983), pp. 38-59.

[123] Kate Pravera, "The United States: Realities and Responses," *Christianity and Crisis* (Sept. 21, 1981), p. 251.

possible at this "embryonic stage" in their American development.[124]

In 1991, Joseph Healey presented a paper to the Notre Dame International Consultation on BCCs, in which he describes a variety of approaches to this problem of classification.[125] One approach is to base the distinction on whether its members actually live together in a residential setting, or else live apart and come together only for meetings and other activities (residential vs. non-residential type of BCC). Another approach is to base the classification on whether or not the BCC is a parish group or else exists outside of an explicit parish context (parish-based vs. non-parish-based types of BCCs). Yet another approach would be to look at the major task or avowed purpose of the group (i.e. social justice, ecumenical, prayer, pastoral/therapeutic support). Healey notes that such diversity at the basic level of classification "clearly indicates that SCCs/BCCs mean many different things to many different people."[126]

Mindful of this diversity, the problems associated with defining "small Christian community," and the variety of ways one could go about categorizing this phenomenon, one must nevertheless opt for some form of typological classification of North American SCCs in order to begin a study of this topic. The classification opted for in this study will be briefly outlined in the following section. The three major categories of SCCs are said to be: Movement-based; Private Association; and Parish-based.[127] The reasons for dividing North American SCCs along these lines will be explained next, as will the reason for making parish-based SCCs the major focus.

B. A Typological Classification of North American SCCs

1. Movement-based

The importance of lay movements in the postconciliar church has been referred to earlier.[128] There is no doubt as to their great impact and abiding value. Many such movements have sought to provide their participants with an experience of Christian community and conversion, so as to help them grow in faith awareness and service. But generally speaking, while being often times very supportive of parish life and parish involvement for their members, the locus of this community experience is

---

[124] *Ibid.*

[125] Cf. Healey, "Evolving a Church from the Bottom Up," p. 6ff.

[126] *Ibid.,* p. 4.

[127] Robert Baldwin refers in a general way to this categorization of American SCCs in his article "Think Small," *New Covenant* (Nov. 1991), p. 12.

[128] Cf. Chapter three, part III, section A.

outside of a single parish setting.

The Charismatic Renewal movement, which began in the U.S. in the late 1960s and rapidly spread worldwide, is a good example of this dynamic. There are two main ways of participating in the movement. One way is to attend a weekly prayer meeting. Another way is to take a further step and join some kind of "Covenant" community.[129] The prayer meetings, while sometimes small, can also be quite large. The setting is more often than not a church basement or parish hall. But the participants at a local prayer meeting are usually drawn from a number of nearby parishes. The prayer group is often advertised in the parish bulletin as a "parish activity," but it is usually responsible for the organization of all its own internal affairs. While some pastors take an active role in supporting the group, most do not have the time or inclination to get involved on a regular basis. Thus, the prayer group is treated from a pastoral perspective as being just one of many worthwhile activities in the parish.

The joining of a Covenant Community usually entails more of a commitment than does simply being a member of a prayer group. These communities can take many forms (i.e. small or large, residential or non-residential, Catholic or ecumenical). But they are usually even less connected to a specific parish than is a prayer meeting. While individual members remain good parishioners of a nearby parish, the focus is on their own community.[130]

The Charismatic Renewal, and the communities it inspired to form in North America, did not come about as a result of the influence of Latin American experiments with BECs. It was clearly a separate development. Nevertheless, the same concern for a more meaningful sense of Christian community is shared by both groups. This explains the reasoning behind some commentators referring to these Charismatic groups as being North American "manifestations" of the basic community phenomenon.

However, the Charismatic Renewal, and other lay movements in North America, do not see themselves in this light. They have not appropriated this terminology. They do not call their meetings or communities BECs or SCCs. Theirs is not the same kind of role within or relationship to the parish as is the case with most Latin American BECs and African SCCs. For many of these reasons, American sociologist of religion Joseph Fichter does not consider these kinds of North American lay

---

[129] For information about Charismatic prayer meetings and Covenant communities see: Kevin and Dorothy Ranaghan, eds., *As the Spirit Leads Us* (Paramus, New Jersey: Paulist Press, 1971).

[130] For a good description of one how one such Covenant community organizes itself, see the mention made of the New Jerusalem community of Cincinnati, Ohio, in Newell, "The Reflection Groups," pp. 38-40.

movement "communities" as being representative of what "basic Christian community" has come to mean and entail.[131]

Before leaving this subject of lay movements, there is one other important *type* that bears mentioning. It often gets overlooked, but there are a significant number of *Third Order* lay associations which incorporate a small community meeting format. They are called Third Orders because they are lay associations affiliated with a specific Religious Order or community in the church. Usually, what is mainly involved by a lay participant in such an association is a commitment to live out the spirituality or charism of the particular congregation. But in the case of the Jesuit-inspired *Christian Life Communities*, a commitment to meet on a regular basis with other members in a small group for continued support is also a standard feature.[132] These meetings, and the service to the church and local community that flows out of them, are remarkably similar to those of a typical BEC/SCC. But again, due to a lack of an explicit parish affiliation or grounding, they cannot be considered representative of what a typical BEC/SCC has come to mean and entail.

2. Private Association

As was noted in recounting the Brazilian experience of BEC formation, most groups were established with the help of pastoral workers and integrated into the parish\diocesan network. However, some of these groups developed or demanded more autonomy as communities, and began to maintain only a nominal link with the parish or diocese. Other groups were established with this bent from the outset. From the point of view of the Brazilian bishops, all legitimate BECs must have an identifiable pastoral link to the local church (however minimal). Those that refuse to consider this an important aspect of what being a BEC entails, are not really ecclesial entities. For all intents and purposes they are independent groupings of a sociological kind.

The same story holds true for a small segment of the North American SCC phenomenon. But to explain this properly some distinctions must first be made. There are some SCCs in existence who, through no fault of their own, have only a tenuous link to the parish or diocesan church

---

[131] Cf. Joseph Fichter, "Parochial Realities in America," in *A Sociologist Looks at Religion* (Wilmington, Del.: Michael Glazier, 1988), p. 205.

[132] Strictly speaking, the Christian Life Communities are not a "Third Order" Jesuit association. But its lay members have close ties to the Jesuits and are committed to an Ignatian spirituality. For an explanation of this relationship, as well as insight into the nature of the Christian Life Communities, see the letter of Jesuit Superior General Peter-Hans Kolvenbach printed in *Harvest* 24/2 (1991), pp. 21-22.

structure. These are groupings of lay people who self-consciously see themselves as SCCs in form and purpose, but who have been either given the proverbial "cold shoulder" by their respective parish priests. Thus, some may actively seek more integration, but for a variety of reasons they are not able to realize this in any kind of meaningful way.[133] These SCCs can be described then as operating more along the lines of private lay associations (from a canonical point of view).

There are also other lay groups calling themselves BCCs/SCCs who, like some of their Brazilian counterparts (and frequently imbued with the same kind of extreme form of Liberation ecclesiology), have self-consciously distanced themselves from any kind of pastoral link to the parish or diocesan church. For instance David Power, in an 1983 article, described these groups as having "little to do" with ecclesiastical structures. They are communities who are "disenchanted" with the established ecclesial order.[134] In a similar vein, Virginia Hoffman describes some such groups as seeing "little hope" for a meaningful renewal of parish structures, thus they "need" to grow up "outside" these structures (but not be in "opposition" to them).[135]

Some of these groups are in a sense reminiscent of the *Underground Church* phenomenon of the 1960s, wherein groups therein expressed a deep-seated *anti-institutional* sentiment, and sought to have a fully autonomous existence while somehow still considering themselves to be "in" the church.[136] It is thus often difficult to ascertain whether or not these kinds of groups should be also classified as private lay associations, or whether they have severed true communion with the church in the manner of some "independent" Latin American BECs.[137]

Complicating matters in determining what SCCs are of the private association/independent type, is the *ideology* problem which Azevedo lamented had divided theologians into opposing camps over this issue in Brazil. Some commentators may be reading more into the supposed autonomy of these groups than is really there. Another problem we have

---

[133] We will examine this type of SCC group in the next chapter when dealing with the activity of the *Buena Vista* network (cf. chapter five, part I, section F).

[134] Cf. David Power, "Households of Faith in the Coming Church," *Worship* 57 (1983), pp. 237-255.

[135] Cf. Virginia Hoffman, *Birthing a Living Church*, (New York: Crossroad, 1988).

[136] For an account of this phenomenon see Malcolm Boyd, *The Underground Church* (New York: Sheed and Ward, 1968).

[137] Even private lay associations have the duty to remain in full and sincere communion with the church. Because the issue of what this communion practically entails is an important criterion in determining the ecclesiality of SCCs, we will examine these and other papal and synodal criteria for BEC/SCC ecclesiality in greater detail later in chapter seven, part II, section A.

seen is how some commentators tend to lump all manner of social justice reflection groups, ecumenical groups, and other private lay associations under the banner of BCCs/SCCs. There are in fact many recognized forms of lay association and "community" in the church today. But the BCC/SCC phenomenon is really a very specific kind of ecclesial community (even though it has a diversity of expression).

In surveying the North American literature then, it is difficult to tell how prevalent these kinds of either private association or independent types of BCCs/SCCs are in the church today. While some authors frequently talk about how such groups are establishing informal networks across the land, they are remiss in providing much information as to their names or sizes. One thing does seem clear however, is that when compared to the efforts that are underway in regards to parish-based SCCs, these so-called private association and independent groups are in the minority today.[138]

3. Parish-based

The term *parish-based* is meant to be broad enough to include any initiative in the area of small community development which is explicitly linked to a parish setting, but which is not tied into some other form of outside lay movement or association in the church. This is not meant to include just any and all small parish groups (such as bible-studies, reflection groups, and so forth) or short-term small group renewal programs, but only those which resemble in form and function a typical SCC, and who aim for some degree of lasting stability. This usually entails some self-conscious recognition on the part of the participants that they are seeking to emulate what has come to be known as *small Christian community*. Thus, they are seeking to play an *ecclesial* role in the life of the parish (as opposed to being seen purely as a means of pastoral support).

There has been a considerable amount of activity in the promotion of parish-based SCCs in North America since the late 1970s. In addition to various kinds of individual initiatives, a host of SCC organizations have sprung up to spearhead development in this area. The major programs/organizations include: *RENEW*; Buena Vista; The National Alliance of Parishes Restructuring into Communities (NAPRC); The North American Forum for Small Christian Communities (NAFSCC); the St. Boniface Parish Cell System, Systematic Integral New Evangelization (SINE); various Hispanic ministry initiatives, and others. Because the above mentioned SCC programs/organizations represent the major activity in this area to date in North America, they have been selected for closer study in

---

[138] Cf. Baldwin, "Think Small," p. 8.

the next chapter. As was the case in our survey of Latin American and African BECs/SCCs, attention will be paid to the matter of their emergence, chief characteristics, and perceived ecclesiological significance.

By studying these parish-based manifestations of the SCC phenomenon, it is hoped that a profile of the North American experience in this area can be outlined. Of particular importance will be the ecclesiological reflection on the nature and role of SCCs which has arisen out of this experience. This reflection will be marshalled for a more comprehensive look in the final chapter at the major issues pertaining to the ecclesiality of SCCs and how to assess the ecclesiological significance of their impact on the vocation, mission, and theology of the parish church in North America.

CHAPTER FIVE

Parcel-Based SCCs in North America

I. NORTH AMERICAN SCC PROGRAMS/ORGANIZATIONS

A. Hispanic Ministry Initiatives[1]

1. Emergence

The term *Hispanic* is a very broad one. It has come to be used in the United States as an umbrella term that covers what in fact are a diversity of ethnic groups which share a Spanish-language heritage.[2] The majority of Hispanics are of Mexican, Puerto Rican, and Cuban descent, but there are others from many different regions of Central and South America as well. Some are recent arrivals, struggling to establish themselves, while others have been living in the U.S. for many generations and are fully assimilated into the social mainstream. Thus, a certain degree of caution is needed when attempting to generalize about the situation of Hispanics.

By some accounts, Hispanics are the fastest growing segment of the U.S. Catholic population.[3] Many dioceses have responded to this development by establishing offices to coordinate Hispanic ministry. In 1983, the U.S. National Conference of Catholic Bishops (NCCB) issued an important pastoral letter which addressed the issue of Hispanic ministry. It was entitled *The Hispanic Presence: Challenge and Commitment*. This

---

[1] Principal sources for this section are: Allan Figueroa Deck, *Hispanic Ministry in the United States: Pastoral-Theological Research* (Rome: Gregorian University Doctoral Dissertation, 1988); The U.S. National Conference of Catholic Bishops, "The Hispanic Presence: Challenge and Commitment," in *Pastoral Letters of the United States Catholic Bishops*, Vol. V, ed. Hugh Nolan (Washington, D.C.: NCCB, 1989); The National Conference of Catholic Bishops, *National Pastoral Plan for Hispanic Ministry* (Washington, D.C.: NCCB, 1987); and The U.S. National Conference of Catholic Bishops' Secretariat for Hispanic Affairs, *[Draft] Guidelines for Small Church-Based Communities* (Washington, D.C.: NCCB, 1991).

[2] Because of this diversity, some people have questioned the adequacy of the single word "Hispanic" to designate these groups as a whole. Nevertheless, the term has gained a certain currency in common usage, and can legitimately be used so long as this heterogeneity is not forgotten. Cf. Deck, *Hispanic Ministry in the United States*, p. 12.

[3] "Demographic projections based on birth rate and immigration indicate that by the year 2000 fifty percent of U.S. Catholics will be of Latin American origin." A quote of Enrique Dussell cited by Alfred Hennelly, "Grassroots Communities: A New Model of Church?" in *Tracing the Spirit*, ed. James Hug (New York/Ramsey: Paulist Press, 1983), p. 71.

letter, in conjunction with the deliberations of the third national *Encuentro* conference of Hispanic pastoral leaders held in 1985, led to the publication in 1987 of an official *National Pastoral Plan for Hispanic Ministry*. An integral feature of this plan was the call to promote "small ecclesial communities" within the parish framework.[4]

The NCCB Secretariat for Hispanic Affairs is currently in the process of drafting a set of concrete guidelines for dioceses to use in the promotion of BECs. In their working document, a valuable historical sketch of the emergence of Hispanic BECs in the U.S. is recounted.[5] The major influences on the development of U.S. Hispanic BECs are said to include: Vatican II; the 1968 Medellin Conference of CELAM; the first National *Encuentro* Conference on Hispanic Pastoral Ministry in 1972; Pope Paul VI's *Evangelii Nuntiandi* (1975); the second National *Encuentro* Conference in 1977; the 1979 Puebla Conference of CELAM; the NCCB's 1983 Pastoral Letter on Hispanic Ministry; the third National *Encuentro* Conference in 1985; and the NCCB's 1987 National Pastoral Plan for Hispanic Ministry.[6]

Much of the early activity with Hispanic BECs can be traced to efforts that emanated from the first and second National *Encuentro* Conferences (1972 and 1977). In March of 1974, the first *National Course on Small Church-Based Communities* took place involving 68 participants from various regions of the U.S. This course was a joint effort of the Secretariat for Hispanic Affairs with Pablo Sedillo and Edgar Beltran, and Fr. Virgilio Elizondo of the Mexican American Cultural Center (MACC) based in San Antonio, Texas. Other courses and symposia soon followed in many other areas throughout the country.

Because of the variety of efforts which were underway at this time, "there was no single model established in the development of a small church-based community."[7] Each region had (and continues to have) its own unique experience with the development of BECs. Some groups quickly flourished, while others quickly faded. Some regions attempted to coordinate BEC development, while others left things up to the individual initiatives of pastoral agents. This explains, in part, the desire of the Secretariat to draft a set of guidelines which would make more explicit what

---

[4] Cf. NCCB, *National Pastoral Plan for Hispanic Ministry*, p. 12.

[5] Cf. Secretariat for Hispanic Affairs, [1991 Draft] *Guidelines for Small Church-Based Communities*, pp. 7-18.

[6] *Ibid.*, p. 10.

[7] *Ibid.*, p. 13.

it perceives should be the "ecclesiology" and "methodology" inherent in BEC development.[8]

The Secretariat is also attempting to conduct a census of Hispanic BECs in the U.S. To date, no one really knows how prevalent a phenomenon they are. In a 1990 general survey of Hispanic ministry, many dioceses reported having at least "some" BECs in existence, but no specific numbers were cited.[9] Other sources indicate that the numbers of Hispanic BECs range from a high of 400 in the diocese of Brownsville, Texas, to only a handful in other places.[10] Based on his own research, Allan Deck concludes that "BECs are not as widespread as the enthusiasm and commentary on them would indicate."[11]

A problem in ascertaining the numbers involved lies in determining what groups qualify as quintessential Hispanic BECs. In the literature one finds that small Hispanic groups that are affiliated with Cursillo or the Charismatic Renewal are frequently designated as BECs. But as this thesis has already explained, such movement-based small groups are of a different type than the more true-to-form parish-based variety. Another complication stems from the fact that the majority of Hispanics who are currently involved in small faith-sharing groups of the parish-based type participate in one or another of the major national programs such as *RENEW* or SINE.[12] Leaving aside for later the study of these other programs, we will first examine the characteristic features of the prototypical Hispanic BEC.

2. Characteristics

According to Bernard Lee and Michael Cowan, U.S. Hispanic BECs are not identical with, but are certainly much closer to, the Latin American model and ethos than are other indigenous SCC initiatives such as *RENEW*.[13] There is a similar kind of broader social concern and role played by many U.S. Hispanic BECs. Social action projects such as COPS (Communities Organized for Public Service) have helped many predominately Hispanic parishes address social, political, and economic issues that are of immediate concern to their local neighborhoods and cities. Through their parishes, many Hispanic BECs are involved in these efforts

---

[8] *Ibid.,* p. 4.

[9] Cf. Secretariat for Hispanic Affairs, *National Survey on Hispanic Ministry* (Washington, D.C.: NCCB, 1990), p. 4.

[10] This information was obtained by the author in an August 1992 telephone conversation with a director of the MACC in San Antonio, Texas.

[11] Deck, *Hispanic Ministry in the United States,* p. 38.

[12] This observation was made by Allan Deck in a letter to the author dated Feb. 6, 1992.

[13] Cf. Lee and Cowan, *Dangerous Memories,* p. 55.

as well. There is more of a pronounced need for this kind of activity in the Hispanic community because many recently arrived Hispanic immigrants (and illegal aliens) to the U.S. tend to be relatively poor, and are hence in need of basic assistance in these areas.

Many early BECs got their start in the context of family and neighborhood groupings, not the parish per se. This was partially the result of a lack of outreach to recently arrived Hispanics in parishes where Anglos constituted the majority. The National Pastoral Plan recognized that "the great majority of our Hispanic people feel distant or marginated from the Catholic Church."[14] To respond to this situation many diocesan offices of Hispanic Ministry were established in the 1970s and 1980s to spearhead efforts in this regard. Part of their *Pastoral de Conjunto* (coordinated pastoral planning) often included an attempt to establish BECs. This explains why some Hispanic BECs arose outside of a specific parish structure. As a result, some BECs suffered an identity crisis of sorts, not really knowing how or where they fit into the local church.

This also helps to explain the reasons behind the Secretariat for Hispanic Affairs' desire to draft a set of guidelines that would elaborate on the constitutive elements of a BEC. As their draft document states, "for many years the Hispanic community in the United States has been in search of these elements."[15] In an attempt to articulate what these constitutive elements are, the following nine traits are outlined:

(1) *Small.* BECs are small so that its members are able to relate to one another on a personal level.

(2) *Communitarian.* People are in committed relationships that reflect and foster the community life of the church.

(3) *Ecclesial.* BECs are in ecclesial communion with its legitimate pastors and with rest of the church.

(4) *Prophetic.* BECs are meant to be a leaven for the promotion of the Kingdom of God in the world.

(5) *Celebrative.* BECs celebrate the faith through means of group prayer and para-liturgies.

(6) *Missionary.* BECs are a means for the evangelization of its members and for the evangelization of the world.

---

[14] NCCB, *National Pastoral Plan for Hispanic Ministry*, p. 11.

[15] Secretariat for Hispanic Affairs, [Draft] *Guidelines for Small Church-Based Communities*, p. 19.

(7) *Example and Promoter of Justice.* BECs seek to live out the church's preferential option for the poor.

(8) *Ministerial.* Members make use of their own gifts and charisms in service to one another and to the world.

(9) *Of the Grassroots.* BECs are from the grassroots and are intended to serve the grassroots church and community.[16]

Further on in this same document a brief description of what should constitute a "model agenda" for a BEC meeting is outlined.[17] The meetings should be held weekly, if possible (usually in member's homes), and begin with a period of prayer and/or scripture reflection. This can be supplemented by a time of "life-sharing." This is followed by a study and discussion time that revolves around the "See, Judge, Act" methodology characteristic of many Latin American BECs. Concrete plans are drawn up and for later action by BEC members. A review of past BEC activities should also be included so as to evaluate the effectiveness of what has been done and to guide future initiatives.

The document also addresses the manner in which BECs should be coordinated at the parish and diocesan levels. The parish is seen as offering a natural point of unity and a home for BECs. But such grassroots communities are not always as territorial as parishes. Some may involve members from several parishes. So a certain sensitivity and flexibility is needed on behalf of pastors in dealing with BECs. The parish and/or diocese should have a steering committee to coordinate BEC growth and development. But it is also important that BECs do not end up being burdened with an excess of organization.

3. Ecclesiological Reflection

Allan Deck, in reflecting on the situation of Hispanic BECs in California, noted a tendency on the part of some communities "to become parallel churches imbued with the idiosyncrasies of the leaders who initiate them."[18] However this problem does not appear to be widespread. Interestingly enough, Deck's research further reveals that these kinds of independent BECs do not seem to last very long, disintegrating usually within three to five years. According to Deck, a major factor in this disintegration is a basic lack of institutional security and continuity. This security, as well as ecclesial grounding and liturgical nourishment, is best

---

[16] *Ibid.,* pp. 19-23.

[17] *Ibid.,* pp. 36-39.

[18] Deck, *Hispanic Ministry in the United States,* p. 45.

provided by the parish. He concludes: "Efforts to establish BECs that prescind from, ignore, or oppose competent ecclesial authority at the parish level have shown to be problematic. Generally they do not survive."[19]

Part of the problem in this regard seems to stem from the early perception some BECs had of themselves as being essentially free or private associations of the faithful. They were not established, as were many of their Latin American counterparts, as quasi-parishes. They did not have the same kind of pastoral link to the parish or liturgical role within the wider parish community. Some were established through individual pastoral initiative, others from a diocesan office. Thus, an explicit link to the parish was not always made.

But the importance of the parish to the life of BECs was underlined in the NCCB's 1983 Pastoral Letter on Hispanic Ministry: "The role of the parish, in particular, is to facilitate, coordinate, and multiply the *communidades eclesiales de base* within its boundaries and territories. The parish should be a community of communities."[20] A similar stress on the role of the parish is found in the NCCB's 1987 National Pastoral Plan for Hispanic Ministry:

> The Hispanic community recognizes that the parish is, ecclesiastically and historically speaking, the basic organizational unit of the Church in the United States, and will continue to be so; at the same time it is affirmed that conversion and a sense of being Church are often lived out in smaller communities within the parish which are more personal and offer a greater sense of belonging.[21]

In their Pastoral Letter, the NCCB also quote CELAM's Medellin statement that a BEC is "the first and fundamental ecclesiastical nucleus."[22] But there is no further explanation given here, or in the National Pastoral Plan, as to what they interpret this statement to mean. Clearly, BECs are seen as being sub-units of the parish. Any ecclesial status one may want to ascribe to BECs is derived from this fundamental relationship. This is all the NCCB seems to say about this matter. But in the Secretariat's draft Guidelines for BECs, a more comprehensive explanation of their ecclesiality is offered:

---

[19] *Ibid.*, p. 47.

[20] NCCB, *The Hispanic Presence: Challenge and Commitment*, p. 60.

[21] NCCB, *National Pastoral Plan for Hispanic Ministry*, p. 11.

[22] NCCB, *The Hispanic Presence: Challenge and Commitment*, p. 42.

Theologically, the CEB is a PORTION of the Church and, at the same time, the whole Church. It is a portion because it is small; the parish is a PORTION of the diocese, which is a PORTION of the Church in a country and of the universal Church. Each of these levels of the Church is the whole Church because it contains all the elements, in smaller or greater portion, of the Church of Jesus.[23]

Unfortunately, this explanation seems similar to, and just as problematic as, Leonardo Boff's description of BECs recounted earlier in chapter four. While the intent is not to convey some form of autonomous ecclesial status or role on BECs, the ecclesiological inaccuracies inherent in such a statement could possibly lead to this kind of conclusion. At any rate, these guidelines are only in draft form, and do not as yet represent the Secretariat's official policy.

What this analysis reveals is that at the level of the NCCB, while there is acceptance and praise for Hispanic BECs, there is also a reluctance to invest them with the same kind of ecclesiological weight as do their Brazilian or AMECEA counterparts. This is understandable given that BECs do not have the same kind of liturgical role, nor as pronounced a social role, in the U.S. church. Nevertheless, the NCCB sees BECs as being an important innovation, describing them as being "a prophetic challenge for the renewal of our Church and humanization of our society."[24]

B. RENEW[25]

1. Emergence

The *RENEW* program traces its inception to 1976, when then Archbishop Peter L. Gerety of Newark, New Jersey, asked two of his diocesan priests, Thomas Kleissler and Thomas Ivory, to devise a program which would help prepare Newark parishes to establish parish councils, as had been requested by Vatican II. Kleissler and Ivory reflected on this task, and reasoned it would do little good to erect such parish council structures

---

[23] Secretariat for Hispanic Affairs, [Draft] *Guidelines for Small Church-Based Communities*, pp. 49-50.

[24] NCCB, *National Pastoral Plan for Hispanic Ministry*, p. 12.

[25] Principal sources for this section are: James R. Kelly, "Does the *RENEW* Program Renew?" *America* (March 7, 1987), pp. 197-199; Thomas A. Kleissler, Margo A. LeBert, and Mary C. McGuinness, *Small Christian Communities: A Vision of Hope* (New York/Mahwah: Paulist Press: 1991); Maurice L. Monette, *RENEW Small Group Leader's Workbook* (New York/Mahwah: Paulist Press: 1990); National Office of *RENEW*, *RENEW: An Overview* (New York/ Mahwah: Paulist Press, 1988); and The NCCB Committee on Doctrine, "The *RENEW* Process: Strengths and Areas for Improvement," *Origins* 16/30 (1987), pp. 547-549.

unless parishioners first had an adequate grasp of Vatican II's vision of the church and of the heightened role of the laity within it. Added to this was a concern for spiritual renewal, which they saw as being a necessary precondition for lasting institutional transformation. So they proceeded to invite a small group of sisters and lay people to join them in a year-long process of prayer and discussion in order to develop a suitable approach to this task at hand. Out of this process the *RENEW* program was born.[26]

It was first implemented in the archdiocese of Newark in the years 1978-1980. While *RENEW* was underway in Newark, officials from other dioceses heard about it and asked permission to use it in their own parishes. Because of the many requests, the archdiocese established a national *RENEW* office to help other dioceses implement the program. The program spread rapidly, not only in the United States, but in Canada and then further abroad as well. Since 1980, over 100 U.S. dioceses and 85 international ones have availed themselves of the *RENEW* program in one form or another. Kleissler estimates that over two million people have participated in *RENEW* small groups as a result.[27]

2. Characteristics

RENEW describes itself as a spiritual renewal "process" which is aimed at deepening personal faith and creating a new awareness of Christian community in the parish.[28] It pursues this goal through the implementation of a comprehensive 2 1/2 year program which is comprised of five "seasons." These seasons, consisting of six weeks, focus respectively on the following themes: The Lord's Call; Our Response to the Lord's Call; Empowerment by the Spirit; Discipleship; and Evangelization. These seasons are first preceded by a year of preparation and training for lay leaders in the parish, which is usually spearheaded by the local diocesan office of *RENEW*. In addition to this preparation there are no less than ten other committees that each parish is asked to establish to oversee the successful implementation of the program. The *RENEW* office provides detailed instructions on how the various components of the program are to be coordinated. This massive organizational effort has led one wit to remark that *RENEW*'s program instructions "must rival a modern general's war plans."[29]

---

[26] Cf. Kelly, "Does the *RENEW* Program Renew?", p. 198.

[27] Cf. Kleissler et al., *Small Christian Communities*, p. 2.

[28] Cf. National Office of *RENEW*, *RENEW: An Overview*, p. 1.

[29] Kelly, "Does the *RENEW* Program Renew?" p. 197.

At the heart of the *RENEW* process are the small groups of 10-12 people that are formed for the duration of the 2 1/2 year program to facilitate faith sharing and reflection. Scripture is central to this reflection process. Each group is provided with the necessary materials to guide them in this activity for each meeting, which usually takes place in the homes of the various participants. The purpose of the small group meeting is not formal Bible study, nor theological discussion, but reflection on how the participants discern God to be present and at work in their own lives. The faith sharing is suppose to be of a personal nature. But the groups are not intended to be an "encounter group or group therapy."[30]

In describing the purpose and focus of the small group sharing, the following point is stressed:

> *RENEW* does not attempt to be a systematic catechetical program. Instead, it can be called a process of spiritual formation with a sound catechetical basis. By process we mean that people are on a journey of conversion. *RENEW* does not convert people, but creates a climate where God's grace can touch people's lives.[31]

Kleissler stresses that the point of *RENEW* is conversion, not education. He found early on in the formation of the program that attempts to include small group discussion of more explicitly doctrinal material "did not work."[32] Much of *RENEW*'s basic thrust reflects this pragmatic approach.

Besides fostering the inner spiritual formation of its participants, *RENEW* has an outward directed goal of evangelization and promotion of the broader social mission of the church. The evangelization effort is directed especially at non-practising or alienated Catholics. By trying to get some of them involved in the small groups, it is hoped that they will experience a spiritual reawakening and come back to the church. In a similar vein, *RENEW* is also seen as being an effective follow-up component to the *Rite of Christian Initiation of Adults* (RCIA) in parishes.[33]

In the third season of the program, participants are introduced to the idea that action on behalf of social justice is constitutive of the gospel and is also an integral feature of evangelization. By the fifth season, they are encouraged to find concrete ways of getting involved in specific projects of one kind or another where they can but this mission into practice. Although

---

[30] Cf. Monette, *RENEW Small Group Leader's Workbook*, p. 10.

[31] National Office of *RENEW*, *RENEW: An Overview*, p. 23.

[32] Cited by Kelly, "Does the *RENEW* Program Renew?" p. 198.

[33] Cf. National Office of *RENEW*, *RENEW: An Overview*, pp. 39-52.

many social justice advocates initially felt that *RENEW* did not emphasize this component enough in its program materials, there has come to be a growing recognition of the valuable role it has played in helping to raise awareness of these issues in the minds of average parishioners and promote action in the field.[34]

The goal of *RENEW* is not just personal renewal and small group activity, but overall parish renewal as well. It seeks to achieve this by changing people's awareness of their role in the parish community, and their perception of what it means to be church. To successfully achieve this it depends heavily on the pastor's active support and involvement. "Without his personal interest and support of and enthusiasm for *RENEW*, nothing will happen in the parish."[35] The pastor's role as shepherd of the parish is strongly affirmed, while at the same time redefined. "*RENEW* sees the priest not as the manager of the parish plant but as the spiritual leader of a ministering community of disciples."[36] This is part and parcel of what *RENEW* understands Vatican II's ecclesiology to be all about:

> The crucial issue for renewal is naming our ecclesiology.
> Once we clarify our vision of church, the ministry
> question falls into place . . . .Vatican II's ecclesiology,
> which views the church as a people of God, is the
> ecclesiology which *RENEW* promotes. The people of God
> is specified as a community of disciples who hear the
> Good News, are changed by it (formed and converted),
> respond to it with specific action; celebrate the story and
> action in sacrament, life and mission. Those "disciples"
> serve in the Church and the world according to the gifts
> they have received from the Spirit.[37]

After the 2 1/2 years of *RENEW* formally ends in a parish, the question naturally arises as to what to do with the small groups? When it was originally conceived, the groups were to simply disband. In this respect, *RENEW* can be said to have initially resembled many other short-term parish renewal programs that have a definite beginning, middle, and end. But to the surprise of organizers, many *RENEW* groups wanted to continue meeting, seeing the experience as being crucial for their continued faith support. Seeing this development, *RENEW* organizers encouraged dioceses to set up

---

[34] Cf. Kelly, "Does the *RENEW* Program Renew?" p. 198.

[35] National Office of *RENEW*, *RENEW: An Overview*, p. 63.

[36] *Ibid.*

[37] *Ibid.*, p. 61.

offices for small Christian community, to help nurture post-*RENEW* groups and other similar small group entities. Out of this development was born the North American Forum for Small Christian Communities which we will take a closer look at later in this chapter.

Thus, a distinction should be made between small groups that are formed and meet for the duration of the *RENEW* program, and those that continue meeting afterwards. According to Kleissler, it is this latter category of post-*RENEW* groups that can be said to have evolved into small Christian communities.[38] Now that *RENEW* has run its course in many dioceses in North America, the pastoral focus of its organizers has shifted to the ongoing support of these SCCs and the task of making the parish a community of communities on a more permanent basis. Philip Murnion characterizes this development as representing a "second-stage" in the impact that *RENEW* is now having on the life of the U.S. church.[39]

3. Ecclesiological Reflection

RENEW seeks to be very clear about the relationship of SCCs to the parish and local church:

> Small Christian communities are part of the parish. Small community leaders are clear that as leaders they are a necessary link to the larger parish. Leaders know that these small communities exist in order to be at the service of the parish, the larger church, and the world. As leaders they are sent to serve by the parish and they serve the parish. Small community leaders are always encouraged to have respect for the teaching authority of the church and to recognize that it is through the body of the entire church that truths are revealed. To be pastoral means to have a firm commitment to the church and to look to the church for guidance.[40]

Because of this stance, and due to the fact that *RENEW* only operates in a parish context, Allan Deck notes that "the *RENEW* process defuses fears about small faith-sharing groups becoming parallel or underground churches."[41]

---

[38] Cf. Kleissler et al., *Small Christian Communities*, p. 2.

[39] Cf. Philip Murnion in the Foreword to Kleissler et al. *Small Christian Communities*, p. x.

[40] Kleissler et al., *Small Christian Communities*, p. 166.

[41] Deck, *Hispanic Ministry in the United States*, p. 47.

RENEW prides itself on having a program and an approach to the promotion of parish-based SCCs that is quite Catholic. But this fact has not spared it some criticism from the U.S. National Conference of Catholic Bishops. In 1986 the program was formally evaluated by the NCCB's Committee on Doctrine to see if it was fully pastorally and doctrinally sound.[42] It is worthwhile to review some of these findings because many of them apply as well to any number of other parish renewal programs and SCC initiatives.

The Committee's report begins by commending *RENEW* for being a significant instrument of personal and parish renewal. But it proceeds to note four major concerns. The first is a tendency to promote "a generic Christianity," with insufficient attention being paid to the specific nature of Roman Catholicism. "Basic Christian themes are presented without sufficiently relating them to their specific form as experienced in Roman Catholic tradition and practice. The literature does not identify, to the extent that we think it should, what is distinctly Catholic in our faith process."[43] Despite the fact that *RENEW* does not see itself as being an educational or catechetical program, it does provide doctrinal and formational information about many matters. So by stressing certain worthwhile elements, while not mentioning others, an indirect message is being communicated to participants regarding what is important vis-à-vis the faith.

This point is reiterated in the second concern the Committee has, namely, that there is a need for greater balance and completeness in the program. For instance, there is great stress placed on the immanence of God in people's lives, but not as much mention made of his transcendence. The same thing goes for *RENEW*'s ecclesiology. There is a laudable stress placed on the church and parish as being a community of disciples, but not as much attention paid to the church as also being "a structured, hierarchical, visible, sacramental community."[44] The same lack of balance is evident in the program's treatment of ministry. While the Committee applauds *RENEW*'s emphasis on the laity taking more responsibility for the mission of the church, there is a lack of mention made of the sacrament of orders. "Unless the necessary and unique ministerial priesthood is constantly balanced with emerging lay ministries in the church, a distorted vision about the future of ministry can develop, and a confused ecclesiology."[45]

---

[42] Cf. The NCCB Committee on Doctrine, "The *RENEW* Process: Strengths and Areas for Improvement," *Origins* 16/30 (1987), pp. 547-549.

[43] *Ibid.*, p. 548.

[44] *Ibid.*

[45] *Ibid.*

The third concern is that the cognitive dimensions of the faith need more emphasis. While the stress *RENEW* places on the affective, emotional, and personal aspects of faith are important, they need to be balanced with the intellectual dimension so as to avoid "fundamentalism and the privatization of religious truth."[46] The fourth concern is that the eucharist needs broader treatment so as to also emphasize the dimensions of worship and sacrifice, not only the aspects of friendship and community. In its suggestions to *RENEW*, the Committee recommends that the small group discussion material include more content data of a doctrinal nature so as to rectify these imbalances. "It is our conviction that any process or program of renewal and formation in the church must have a well-articulated doctrinal base which is both comprehensive and balanced."[47]

The organizers of *RENEW* took serious stock of these recommendations and rewrote much of the program material to provide a greater and more balanced doctrinal base to their program. It is not known if the changes made were sufficient enough to alleviate all the concerns of the Committee. But the fact that *RENEW* continued to be adopted by dioceses across the country points to the favorable opinion many bishops still had of it. Because the post-*RENEW* small Christian communities go on meeting indefinitely, there is actually ample opportunity to cover an almost unlimited amount of doctrinal ground in group discussions, without undermining the principle focus of faith-sharing.[48]

RENEW, in its "second-stage" emphasis, is committed to the idea that catechesis and evangelization go hand in hand. What they seek in promoting the restructuring of the parish into a community of communities is a means of making this dynamic normative to parish life. "By restructuring the parish into a community of small communities, the parish could move beyond sporadic, periodic evangelization events to becoming a consistently evangelizing parish."[49] Kleissler sees this development as being one of the best ways to implement Pope John Paul II's call for a new evangelization of all Christians. For all of these reasons and more, Kleissler believes this to be the most opportune "moment" for the church to take more of an official leadership role in the promotion of parish-based SCCs.[50]

---

[46] *Ibid.*, p. 549.

[47] *Ibid.*

[48] Cf. Kleissler et al., *Small Christian Communities*, p. 104.

[49] *Ibid.*, p. 176.

[50] *Ibid.*, p. 45.

C. National Alliance of Parishes Restructuring Into Communities (NAPRC)[51]

1. Emergence

The National Alliance of Parishes Restructuring into Communities (NAPRC) is an organization dedicated to "corporate change" in Catholic parishes. "NAPRC is about doing the parish differently, not about improving the present parish structure."[52] It seeks to promote the concept of small communities as something that is both normative and essential for parish life. But as an organization, the NAPRC is not formally tied to any particular ways or means of restructuring. It is really a network of like-minded parishes and individuals who share in and promote a common vision.

This point having been noted, it is also the case that many of the parishes who belong to the NAPRC have adopted what one could call the "Baranowski Model" of parish-based SCCs. Arthur Baranowski, who is the head of the NAPRC, is a priest of the diocese of Detroit, Michigan. He has been involved in working to establish SCCs in various parishes there since the early 1970s. In 1988 he published a book entitled *Creating Small Faith Communities*, which contained his plan or approach to restructuring parishes. This plan was the fruit of his efforts over the previous ten years to establish SCCs in St. Elizabeth Seton parish in Troy, Michigan. Baranowski is aptly described on the back cover of the book as being just an ordinary priest, working in an ordinary middle-class parish, with ordinary Catholic parishioners.[53]

Since the mid-1980s, Baranowski has been extensively involved in giving workshops to priests and parish staff personnel throughout North America and even further abroad in order to explain the concept of SCCs and parish restructuring. To date, out of some 500 parishes in the United States, Canada, and Australia that have participated in his workshops, 300 have formally adopted his approach. He has also spent some time working at the National Office of *RENEW* with Msgr. Kleissler, sharing ideas and insights into his experiences with SCCs. He is currently involved in a coalition task force, together with representatives from Buena Vista and the

---

[51] The principal source for this section is a book written by the founder of the National Alliance of Parishes Restructuring into Communities, Arthur R. Baranowski, *Creating Small Faith Communities* (Cincinnati, Ohio: St. Anthony Messenger Press, 1988).

[52] This quote is taken from an unpublished position paper that was made available to participants at the NAPRC National Colloquium held in Belleville, Illinois, Aug. 20-23, 1992.

[53] These remarks were made by James Dunning, President of the North American Forum on the Catechumenate.

National Forum for Small Christian Communities, in order to foster dialogue with the U.S. NCCB about the issue of SCCs and parish restructuring.[54]

2. Characteristics

In the Introduction to his book, Baranowski notes that since Vatican II, many parishes have tried a great number of programs to help renew the church and renew individual parishioners. Many of these programs have been very creative and worthwhile. Yet a deficiency he sees in many of these programs is that they are temporary and do not attempt to change the parish structure itself. But the parish structure itself is where he believes the "primary need" for renewal is to be found.[55]

Parishes need to restructure because they are no longer as effective as they once were in sustaining Christian community, given the radically altered cultural and social climate of today. Because of these pressures, and other factors of modern living such as increased mobility and transiency, parishioners do not know one another and cannot support one another as they once did. Baranowski further questions whether or not an adequate gospel lifestyle can be maintained by ordinary Catholics who only experience church for one hour per week. He concludes: "The parish as presently structured no longer brings us together to experience well what makes us Catholic Christians."[56]

Baranowski's plan for parish restructuring is a comprehensive one. It is founded on the vision of the parish being a "communion of small communities."[57] It does not simply entail the introduction of small groups for some parishioners who want them, but involves a pastoral commitment to move as many people as possible in this direction. "These small churches, therefore, are for all Catholic parishioners—not just the 'religious types.' They are intended to be permanent or semi-permanent and, eventually, to manifest all the activities of the larger church: worship, formation, service."[58]

---

[54] The idea of parish restructuring has been also receiving the attention of Canadian bishops. As a result of a recent three year study of Quebec parishes, a committee recommended to the bishops of Quebec that efforts to restructure the parish be not only endorsed but actively encouraged. In the formal report that was issued by this committee, positive mention was made of both *RENEW* and Art Baranowski's approaches to parish restructuring. Cf. Comité de recherche de l'assemblée des Évêques du Québec sur les communautés chrétiennes locales, *Risquer L'Avenir* (Montreal: Éditions Fides, 1992), pp. 25-31.

[55] Cf. Baranowski, *Creating Small Faith Communities*, p. 1.

[56] *Ibid.*, p. 4.

[57] *Ibid.*, p. 14.

[58] *Ibid.*, p. 16.

This vision is not realizable all at once. It is part of a gradual process. No one should be forced into an SCC, but nevertheless the goal is to get as many people as possible to join one. This vision should be the key organizing principle around which all other pastoral activity in a parish should flow (without neglecting other worthwhile and necessary pastoral activities and parish groups). Baranowski claims that after ten years of ministry in St. Elizabeth Seton parish, which has about 600 households, 250 people were involved in 34 SCCs. He estimates this figure of 250 people to represent about 25% of the parish's total population.[59] This means that 75% of the people were not as yet involved, nor might they ever be. Baranowski doesn't see this as being a failure or a problem. He says we must always respect people "where they are at." But the goal of trying to involve everyone in an SCC remains the same.

To reach this goal, Baranowski advocates the adoption of a three-phase process. The first phase is a "beginning experience" to introduce people in a general way to the dynamic of faith-sharing in small groups (8-12 people in size that meet once every two weeks). Baranowski says it doesn't matter what program is used at this stage. Any number of small group faith-sharing programs are available (i.e. *RENEW*, Genesis II, *The Parish Renewal Experience*, etc.). The second phase focuses on prayer in a more in-depth way. Baranowski has developed his own program for this stage, but says that any number of similar prayer-oriented programs would do just fine.[60] The third phase is entitled "Being Church for the Long Haul." It is at this point that the small groups reflect on whether or not they want to continue meeting on a regular basis. They will by this time have in place a trained "pastoral facilitator" who will act as a steward to the group and who will stay in regular contact with the parish priest.[61] "It is in phase three that we can really begin to speak of the small faith community as a 'base church.' There isn't any phase four because phase three is the mode for indefinitely continuing to live and renew one's Catholic Christianity."[62]

Baranowski doesn't see this plan as dividing the parish. According to him, the larger parish community and its pastoral leaders become important guarantors of this needed parish unity. The Sunday parish Eucharist remains the crucial unifying experience for small group members.

---

[59] *Ibid.*, p. 18.

[60] Cf. Arthur Baranowski, *Praying Alone and Together: An 11 Session Prayer Module for Small Faith Communities* (Cincinnati, Ohio: St. Anthony Messenger Press, 1988).

[61] Baranowski has also authored a companion volume dealing with the training of these pastoral facilitators. Cf. *Pastoring the 'Pastors': Resources for Training and Supporting Pastoral Facilitators for Small Faith Communities* (Cincinnati, Ohio: St. Anthony Messenger Press, 1988).

[62] Baranowski, *Creating Small Faith Communities*, p. 25.

What this plan does is redefine the role of the pastor and the people. It makes people more responsible for ministering to one another. This leads to a reduction in demands on the pastor's time by individuals, and frees him up to concentrate on pastoring the small group pastoral facilitators. He thus sees it as being an eminently practical plan.[63]

The rest of Baranowski's book is devoted to explaining how to go about launching this plan and motivating parishioners to join in a small group. The parish priest, working in unison with the parish council, is seen as being the key initiator of this whole process. While these and other pastoral details are interesting and important, they need not concern us further here. Neither are the specific features of an SCC meeting, which include the by now familiar elements of Scripture reflection, faith-sharing, and discussion of social justice issues that will hopefully lead to some form of committed service to the wider community outside of the group meeting.

3. Ecclesiological Reflection

Baranowski frequently uses the term "small basic Christian communities" (SBCCs) when referring to the fully evolved form of faith-sharing groups in the parish. He notes that this term resembles that of Latin American "basic communities." Indeed, his SBCCs are indebted to, and have much in common with, their Latin American counterparts. Curiously, however, he states that SBCCs are different from Latin American BCCs in that they are more closely related to the parish.[64] He does not elaborate on what is a mistaken claim, but he is perhaps alluding to the fact that some BCCs, as we have seen, operate or wish to operate with greater pastoral autonomy. The majority of Latin American BCCs, however, are very much parish-based and pastorally integrated affairs.

Much of the language Baranowski uses to describe SBCCs, especially their ecclesiological significance, seems to be influenced by certain Latin American motifs. For instance, he describes SBCCs as "a new way to be church," and says that they "become church at a new, more basic level."[65] His understanding of the church is that it is a communion which is realized in different ways and at different levels. The universal church is a

---

[63] Baranowski quotes the comments of a Fr. Dick Kelly, a pastor who has implemented this plan in his own parish: "What I like best about this parish restructuring plan is that it's possible for 'tired old ministers.' We are swamped by the day-to-day demands of ministry, often the demands of the moment. The restructuring does not just add more programs to get done and cause further burn-out. It gets away from having to relate directly to each person in the parish and gets people to relate to each other." (*Ibid.,* p. 34.)

[64] *Ibid.,* pp. vii-viii. In a later section Baranowski adds that his model for parish-based SBCCs is more directly inspired by the RCIA approach to the catechumenate (cf. pp. 5-6.).

[65] *Ibid.,* p. 13.

communion of dioceses, the diocese is a communion of parishes, and the parish is a communion of small communities. Thus:

> The Catholic Church, in fact, exists at many levels. It can be seen as a communion of different levels and expressions of church. The individual parishioner already belongs to the same church at various levels in different ways: the universal level, the diocesan level, and the parish level. The small, base church would constitute yet another level. (Recent popes and the American bishops have spoken of an even more basic experience of church: the "foundational church" of the family.)[66]

Furthermore, what links these various levels together is the designated leadership of pastors or pastoral agents at each level: from the Pope on the universal level, to the bishop on the local or diocesan level, to the priest on the parish level, to the pastoral facilitator on the SBCC level. This linkage is constitutive of what it means to be church. Therefore, without a direct pastoral connection of an SBCC to the parish priest, a group which engages in sharing and outreach activity may be a small group, but it isn't a "base church." Hence:

> We are Catholic—and not congregational—because of the way we are linked pastorally to every level of the church. Clearly, then, what makes this pastoral plan a restructuring of the parish church, and not only parishioners getting together in small support groups, is the pastoral linkage established between these small groups and the larger church. This pastoral link—the pastoral facilitator—is what keeps a small group from self-absorption, insulation, isolation, elitism.[67]

Given this requirement of pastoral linkage, Baranowski does not hesitate to call SBCCs "little churches" or "the church in miniature."[68] His reasons for explicitly referring to SBCCs in this manner are twofold. Theologically, he feels that because these small groups manifest many important elements of church (i.e. prayer, formation, service, etc.), they can be legitimately designated in this way. Pastorally, he feels it is important to

---

[66] *Ibid.*, p. 15.

[67] *Ibid.*, p. 17.

[68] *Ibid.*, p. vii and p. 74 respectively.

name them in this manner so that parishioners will take them seriously and understand that they are not just some optional activity, but are essential to the experience of parish life.[69]

From these statements it can be seen that Baranowski has attempted to offer a more detailed ecclesiology of SCCs than has for instance *RENEW*. While *RENEW* talks about parish restructuring and the importance of SCCs, Kleissler never really addresses these kinds of issues pertaining to their ecclesial identity or status. The question this naturally raises is whether or not Baranowski is justified from the point of view of official Catholic ecclesiology in making the kind of claim he does about SCCs. We shall attempt to answer this question in a more systematic fashion in the final chapter of this thesis.

D. St. Boniface Parish Cell System[70]

1. Emergence

Fr. Michael Eivers and Deacon Perry Vitale are the two people most responsible for spearheading the "Cell System" that is currently in place at St. Boniface parish in Pembroke Pines, Florida (Archdiocese of Miami). Both arrived at the parish in 1973 and became quite active in the Catholic Charismatic Renewal movement. At one time in the 1970s over 450 people were attending the weekly parish prayer meetings. By 1979, some 800 people had taken part in the *Life in the Spirit* seminars, which is a seven week program designed to help evangelize people and open them up to receive the charismatic gifts of the Holy Spirit.[71]

But despite this pastoral success, Eivers and Vitale became concerned about the large numbers of people who, after having gone through the *Life in the Spirit* seminars and attended the prayer meetings for awhile, would proceed to "drop out." The idea to form small communities, as a solution to this problem, occurred soon afterwards. In 1980, Eivers and Vitale attended a workshop on base communities which was led by José Marins. They immediately set to work training some 70 parishioners to

---

[69] "People make a different kind of commitment to a small community they perceive as church and not just a group of people they enjoy or even share faith with." *Ibid.*, p. 74.

[70] Principal sources for this section are: Robert Baldwin, "Think Small," *New Covenant* (Nov. 1991), pp. 7-12; Patrick Brennan, *Re-imagining the Parish* (New York: Crossroad, 1990); Tom Cooney, "Parish Cells," *Intercom* (Dec. 1990), pp. 14-15; and Michael Eivers and Perry Vitale *St. Boniface Parish Cell System: Leaders' Training Manual* (Pembroke Pines, Florida: St. Boniface Catholic Church, 1991).

[71] This and the following background information pertaining to the emergence of the St. Boniface Parish Cell System is taken from Tom Cooney, "Parish Cells," pp. 14-15.

launch base communities in the parish. But the project quickly fizzled out. As Eivers later explained, "we did not really know what we were doing."[72]

But they did not let the idea go away. Soon afterwards, they read about the enormous success that Paul Yonggi Cho, a pastor of an independent Protestant Evangelical church in Korea, was having with his system of "home cell groups."[73] They visited Cho's church in Korea and discovered it had 600,000 members in 50,000 cells. They also visited a nearby Protestant Evangelical church in Florida that had adopted Cho's approach.[74] Based on this home cell system, they proceeded to relaunch the program for small communities in St. Boniface parish in 1983. There are currently over 600 parishioners involved in about 50 cell groups (which Eivers reports represents about one-third of the total parish population). In addition, the parish hosts an annual workshop to explain the cell system to other interested pastors and pastoral workers. To date, over 700 people have attended these workshops. This has resulted in about 100 parishes formally adopting this system, mainly in the U.S. and Canada, but also elsewhere worldwide.[75]

2. Characteristics

The basis for the St. Boniface parish cell system is something called *Oikos Evangelization*. *Oikos*, as we have seen, is the biblical Greek word for household. Eivers and Vitale have broadened this biblical meaning of *Oikos* so as to define it as "that group of people whom you relate with on a regular basis."[76] This would include relatives, friends, neighbors, colleagues at work, etc. The idea being that this circle of acquaintances offers the most natural opportunities for evangelization. The *Oikos* strategy then is to focus evangelization efforts within already existing relationships.

The fundamental thrust behind organizing home cell groups is to promote this evangelization and discipleship effort in the broader parish community. Everyone is to be a missionary. Cell groups are organized by the parish, with trained leaders to oversee their development and act in

---

[72] Cited by Cooney, "Parish Cells," p. 14.

[73] Cf. Paul Yonggi Cho, *Successful Home Cell Groups* (Plainfield, N.J.: Logos International, 1981).

[74] Protestant churches, especially Evangelical and Pentecostal ones, have been very much in the forefront of small community development in North America. Thus, the impulse to form SCCs is not an exclusively Catholic phenomenon. This is understandable given the fact that North American Protestant congregations are facing the same social and cultural challenges to faith development as are their Catholic counterparts.

[75] Perry Vitale supplied this information to the author in a letter dated Jan. 30, 1992.

[76] Cf. Eivers and Vitale, *St. Boniface Parish Cell System: Leaders' Training Manual*, p. 4.

concert with the pastor. The cells are initially composed of about a dozen people each. Parishioners are encouraged to invite their inactive Catholic relatives, friends, and neighbors to these cell meetings with the hope that they might experience a spiritual reawakening and come back to the practice of the faith. This is how evangelization and cell growth takes place. As with biological cells, upon reaching a certain size, they are to divide so that the basic cell size averages twelve people. This is also how the cells multiply in the parish and overall church "growth" is achieved.[77]

The characteristic features of a home cell meeting are similar to what we have seen with other SCC programs. There is a time of prayer and recollection, faith-sharing, and a discussion of different Scripture-based teachings. The teaching or catechetical component is accomplished by means of a videotaped message by the pastor that is watched on a television in the home where the cell meeting takes place. Each week the cell leaders pick up a copy of the video cassette at the parish office along with some questions to help guide the discussion period. The emphasis of these teachings is on Christian discipleship. This approach has the added benefit of highlighting and strengthening the pastor's role as the overall leader of the parish community.[78] Finally, a commitment to outreach and ministry to the wider community is also stressed. But this is not organized by the cell groups themselves on an individual basis, but is accomplished by encouraging participants to join in any one of a large number of parish-coordinated ministry activities.

3. Ecclesiological Reflection

Eivers and Vitale do not focus a great deal on questions pertaining to the ecclesiology of these cell groups. The most direct comment they make on the matter is found in the following statement:

> The small group does not require throwing out the organized church. Small groups can be introduced without by-passing or undercutting the church, although the serious incorporation of small groups into the overall ministry of the church requires some adjustments and is bound to eventually raise questions about priorities. The small group is best seen as an essential component of the

---

[77] *Ibid.,* p. 81.

[78] *Ibid.,* p. 92.

church's structure and ministry, not as a replacement for the church.[79]

Furthermore, Eivers and Vitale describe the role of these cell groups as being that of "mediating communities." They are structures which help mediate an experience of church and Christian discipleship in a more personal and effective way to individuals and families within the parish. Although they do not use the term "restructuring," it is clear that they see such cell groups as reconstituting the parish experience, and becoming a newly normative feature of parish life in the process.

The overarching dynamic in the St. Boniface Cell System is evangelization. Being church, and being evangelistic, are seen as synonymous. So pronounced is this emphasis that one commentator reports that Eivers and Vitale have criticized some other small group efforts for being too static and self-nurturing in comparison.[80] What the Cell System does, in effect, is multiply the "doors" of entry to the parish, especially for people who have fallen away from the church and who need to be re-evangelized. By way of conclusion and summary, Eivers and Vitale state:

> It is questionable whether the institutional church can have a significant evangelistic ministry today through traditional methods. It may be able to build church and carry out programs, but it will never turn the world right side up. Most of today's methods are too big, too slow, too organized, too inflexible, too expensive and too professional ever to be truly dynamic in a fast-paced technological society. If the contemporary church would shake loose from plant and program, from institutionalism and inflexibility, and would return to the dynamic of the early church, it must seriously and self consciously build its ministry around the small group as its basic structure.[81]

---

[79] *Ibid.*, p. 90.

[80] This criticism was directed towards the Baranowski approach. Cited by Brennan, *Re-imagining the Parish*, p. 68.

[81] Eivers and Vitale, *St. Boniface Parish Cell System: Leaders' Training Manual*, p. 95.

E. Systematic Integral New Evangelization (SINE)[82]

1. Emergence

The Systematic Integral New Evangelization (SINE) program began in Mexico City in 1978. Alfonso Navarro, a priest of the Archdiocese of Mexico City, had been working for some time in a diocesan "Evangelization Center," directing a variety of local catechetical and evangelization efforts. He was eventually put in charge of a parish and was given permission to pilot a project he had formulated for parish renewal. Thus, was born the Systematic Integral New Evangelization program.[83]

Interest in the program led Navarro to begin hosting seminars for other priests and pastoral workers in Mexico and abroad. A SINE Office was opened in Mexico City to help respond to these enquiries and to disseminate the program literature. The program gradually spread northwards into the United States. In 1988 a U.S. SINE office, headed by Ernesto Elizondo, was first opened in San Antonio, Texas, and later moved to its new location in Rockford, Illinois. At present, there are some 80 parishes in the U.S. and Canada that have implemented SINE. Worldwide, the program is said to be in place in 14 different countries, involving a total of approximately 600 parishes.[84]

Although SINE arose in a Latin American context, it deliberately refrains from referring to the parish-based small groups it promotes as being base communities or BECs, preferring instead the terminology of "cells." Despite many similarities with other Latin American initiatives in the field, SINE sees itself as being somewhat different in its approach, and more explicitly parish-centered in its ecclesiology. Furthermore, although SINE has been influential in some predominately Hispanic parishes in the United States, it does not consider itself to be only an Hispanic entity.[85] Many Anglo parishes have also adopted its vision and system. Because of these facts, and because it has developed its own particular program literature, it

---

[82] Principal sources for this section are: SINE Team, *What Does SINE Really Mean?* (Rockford, Illinois: SINE National Office, n.d.); SINE Team, *An Overview of SINE* (Rockford, Illinois: SINE National Office, n.d.); SINE Team, *Basic Catechesis: People of God* (Rockford, Illinois: SINE National Office, n.d.); Bruce Nieli, "S.I.N.E." *National Council for Catholic Evangelization Newsletter* (Winter, 1990).

[83] SINE Team, *An Overview of SINE*, p. 1.

[84] *Ibid.*

[85] "The Pastoral Plan, which SINE presents, is not designed for a particular type of parish, rural or urban, rich or poor, nor for a particular country or culture or language. Since SINE presents the essential mission of the Church, the pastoral Plan it offers is for any parish in any continent or country. Though piloted in Mexico, it is not for Hispanics only." SINE Team, *What Does SINE Really Mean?* p. 3.

is being treated as a separate category here, rather than as a part of the earlier "Hispanic Ministry Initiatives" section.

2. Characteristics

As was the case with *RENEW*, and most of the other SCC initiatives we have looked at, SINE does not consider itself to be merely a method or a program, but sees itself as being a comprehensive process that results in a new pastoral model permanently taking root in the parish.[86] "SINE is a basic, organic and holistic pastoral model which seeks to transform the parish . . . [into] a missionary parish: an evangelizing community."[87] Although the SINE approach, like the St. Boniface Parish Cell System, has been very much influenced by the Catholic Charismatic Renewal, it does not see itself as being aligned to this or any other lay movement. Rather, it stresses its fundamental parochial nature, and the fact that it is intended for all parishioners. A major criticism SINE has of lay movements in general is that, despite their good work and good intentions, they tend to fragment efforts on the parish level aimed at achieving comprehensive renewal.[88]

SINE is implemented in a parish through a series of specific steps. Step one involves the presentation of the SINE vision and process to the pastor, staff, and lay leaders of the parish by means of a 4-day seminar given by the National SINE Office. Step two involves the participation of the above mentioned people in an initial "Evangelization Retreat," wherein they experience first-hand the small group faith-sharing dynamic. This is followed in step three by the training of a parish core group "Evangelization Team," who in turn will be the main implementors of the SINE program in the parish. In step four the parish Evangelization Team hosts an Evangelization Retreat for all interested parishioners. Step five involves the formation of permanent small communities for those who have made the retreat. Step six involves training small group participants to engage in parish ministry and evangelization outreach. The evangelization outreach leads in step seven to these participants doing home visitation in the parish to evangelize non-practising or alienated Catholics. They in turn are invited to participate in up-coming Evangelization Retreats that are intended to be regularly occurring parish events. Step eight involves ongoing "ministry and

---

[86] *Ibid.*, p. 1.

[87] *Ibid.*

[88] "The Church as a whole needs to be renewed. This renewal will not be fully accomplished by merely renewing individuals or groups in movements or organizations. We need to renew the Church itself as a living organism, and not just individual people in it. The renewal of the Church will be accomplished primarily through renewed parishes." *Ibid.*, p. 6.

discipleship" training for the small group participants, including training for social action.[89]

3. Ecclesiological Reflection

In describing the small communities which are formed as part of SINE's pastoral plan, their essential link to the parish is strongly insisted upon:

> The communities are united and integrated into the parish, and they are an integral part of the parish; guided, supervised and nurtured by the parish. Thus, the parish becomes what it ought to be: a communion of communities. The communities belong to the parish and are directly accountable to it. The ecclesial unit is the parish. The small communities are merely cells of the local body, the parish. Small ecclesial communities can be neither autonomous nor can they exist in isolation from the parish.[90]

SINE's small groups then are not treated as quasi-parishes. They do not have the same kind of liturgical role or sacramental responsibilities as do many of their Latin American BEC counterparts. Their basic function is to promote evangelization and discipleship. Because of this focus, and because it wants to avoid the problem of small groups acting in an autonomous manner, SINE actually ascribes less ecclesial "status" to them than many of the other SCC programs we have looked at. There is no talk of these small groups being "little churches." The basic ecclesial unit is seen as being the parish.

The basic features of the SINE small group meetings (prayer, Scripture reflection, faith-sharing, teaching/catechetical instruction and discussion) are similar to many other SCCs. So too is the training of group leaders who meet on a regular basis with the pastor for pastoral support and input. What is perhaps a little different, besides the door-to-door evangelization effort asked of the small groups, is the heavy emphasis on catechesis. Far from shying away from catechetical instruction, SINE provides a huge amount of detailed material for small group discussion in this area. This "basic" catechesis is intended to last for several years. As a result, participants are introduced or re-introduced in a very thorough and

---

[89] Cf. SINE Team, *An Overview of SINE*, p. 2.

[90] SINE Team, *What Does SINE Really Mean?* p. 5.

systematic manner to many of the major theological aspects of the faith, including a comprehensive account of Catholic ecclesiology.[91] Thus, the concerns we saw that the NCCB Committee on Doctrine initially had about the *RENEW* program would not seem to be as applicable to SINE.

F. Buena Vista[92]

1. Emergence

Buena Vista describes itself as "a national grassroots organization devoted to the formation of small Christian communities."[93] It is an umbrella organization which is made up of over 700 members to date (which includes individuals, parishes, diocesan offices, and other organizations). It espouses the development of SCCs, but does not promote any particular model or approach. Its main purpose is to provide a forum in which local SCC leaders and members can network with each other for the purpose of exchanging ideas and mutual support. To help accomplish this goal it has published a resource book, puts out a monthly newsletter, helps organize regional meetings for members, and also sponsors an annual National Convocation.

Buena Vista is a member of a special task force, along with the National Alliance of Parishes Restructuring Into Communities and the North American Forum for Small Christian Communities, that hopes to foster dialogue with the U.S. bishops about SCCs. These three organizations are also planning to sponsor joint national conferences in the near future. All three of these organizations have already collaborated with Bob Pelton of the University of Notre Dame's Institute of Pastoral and Social Ministry, having helped sponsor the 1990 National Consultation on Basic Christian Communities and the 1991 International Consultation on Basic Christian Communities.

Buena Vista traces its roots to Spirit of Christ parish in Arvada, Colorado. Mike Howard, a deacon at the parish, and his wife Barbara, had developed a small group program for the parish which they called *Journey*

---

[91] For example, in book three of SINE's "basic catechesis" series (*People of God*), there are some 23 different ecclesiological themes that are outlined for individual discussion. These themes, including treatment of the church as Mystery, Sacrament, Communion in the Spirit, as well as themes dealing with Royal Priesthood and Ministerial Priesthood, Catholicity, Magisterium, Ecumenism, Mary as Model, etc., seem to cover most of what is contained in *Lumen Gentium*.

[92] Principal sources for this section are: Barbara Howard, "Buena Vista History," (An unpublished paper presented at the fifth annual National Buena Vista Convocation, Estes Park, Colorado, Jan. 16-20, 1991), pp. 1-9; The official Buena Vista *Mission Statement* (featured in an article by Peg Bisgrove, "Is There a Place for Me in this Church?" *Today's Parish* (Sept. 1990), pp. 15-17; and various articles featured in the *Buena Vista Newsletter*.

[93] Howard, "Buena Vista History," p. 9.

(which eventually led to the establishment of over 50 SCCs in the parish). It was implemented there in the wake of the *RENEW* program beginning in 1984. As a result of the publicity that the *Journey* program and these parish SCCs received in the U.S. Catholic media, the Howards soon found themselves networking with other interested individuals and parishes. As a result of these contacts Buena Vista was formally begun in 1987.[94] Besides the Howards, other founding members included Peg Bisgrove, Barb Darling, and Bob Steininger.

2. Characteristics

The official *Mission Statement* of Buena Vista conveys its understanding of the general nature and significance of SCCs, as well as the raison d'etre of the organization:

We affirm the centrality of small Christian communities as the norm of a vital and healthy church.

We affirm that the basic elements of small Christian communities are sharing faith and life, prayer, ongoing learning, mutual support, belonging, and outreach in service.

We affirm that we are a church of diversity and that diversity should be reflected in our small Christian communities in manner of style, in membership, in levels of being and process of evolution.

We affirm the vision that the parish is a community of communities linked to the universal church.

We challenge ourselves to continue the formation of Christian communities; to provide opportunities, encourage participation, and foster the vision we believe is our inheritance from Jesus and as Roman Catholics.

We challenge ourselves to network for support, exchange of information, and encouragement.

We challenge ourselves to research and develop better ways to motivate and form facilitators for small Christian communities.

We challenge ourselves to minister to all God's people with love.

---

[94] *Ibid.,* p. 1. Buena Vista was chosen as the name of the organization for two reasons. First, it was the name of the small Colorado town in which the 1987 founding meeting took place. Second, the name means "beautiful vision" in spanish, and was seen by the participants as being a fitting description of their common vision regarding SCCs.

We challenge small Christian communities to develop structures that nourish service and commitment to the poor.[95]

3. Ecclesiological Reflection

All of the SCC programs and organizations we have reviewed to date stress the importance of the pastor in the overall effort to restructure the parish and promote the vision of small communities. Furthermore, most of them view this process as necessarily having to be *the* pastoral priority for the parish. SCCs are seen as being not just another parish activity, but as constituting a new norm for parish life. This understanding of SCCs and the parish is something that Buena Vista agrees with completely. But what makes Buena Vista different from these other efforts is that it also seeks to support SCCs which exist in parishes where there is no overall commitment to restructure, and where active pastoral support for them is sometimes lacking.

A case in point is outlined in a Buena Vista newsletter article about a California parish which has six SCCs.[96] These were established with the active help and support of the previous pastor. But the new pastor is not inclined to make SCCs a pastoral priority, although he's content to have them operate as parish groups. As a result, there is no real ongoing pastoral link with, nor input from, the pastor. Some groups are struggling as a result. In a later article, this kind of development is said to have taught the former pastor that "a high degree of autonomy was critical for the long-range health of SCCs."[97]

Other articles mention some parishes having only a single small community in existence. Some of these solitary SCCs were not established by the pastor or pastoral staff of the parish, but came into existence on their own initiative and sometimes operate in relative isolation. These developments raise the question then as to whether or not these groups can be properly called SCCs, and whether or not their ecclesiality is of the same kind as that of more explicitly parish-based SCCs. This issue of what constitutes and differentiates a *bona fide* SCC from other small groups has been an ongoing topic of reflection for Buena Vista.[98]

---

[95] This Buena Vista *Mission Statement* is featured in an article by Peg Bisgrove, "Is There a Place for Me in this Church?" *Today's Parish* (Sept. 1990), p. 16.

[96] Cf. Stephanie Pence, "My SCC Story," *Buena Vista Newsletter* (Sept. 1991), p. 2.

[97] This according to Stephanie Pence, in a summary of a recent Buena Vista Convocation workshop she gave dealing with the *Journey* program for SCCs, *Buena Vista Newsletter* (March 1992), p. 8.

[98] Cf. Howard, "Buena Vista History," p. 7.

Buena Vista is inclined to call an SCC any group which seeks to emulate the characteristic features of a typical small Christian community meeting and which has evolved a certain consciousness of being church. But without the concrete involvement of the pastor, nor active link to him in the form of a pastoral facilitator or other designated leader, is it not the case that from an ecclesiological point of view these kinds of SCCs have only the same comparable ecclesial status as that of a private lay association? We will leave this question for now, but will return again to this issue in the final chapter of this thesis.

G. North American Forum for Small Christian Communities (NAFSCC)[99]

1. Emergence

The North American Forum for Small Christian Communities (otherwise known as the NAFSCC or simply as the Forum) is a national organization intended for the support of diocesan personnel (clergy, lay, and religious) involved in local parish-based SCC promotion and development. As its name implies, it provides a forum wherein members can participate in ongoing discussion about SCC matters, share ideas and resources, as well as network and collaborate with other SCC programs and organizations. To help realize these objectives, the Forum holds an annual conference for its members and publishes a monthly newsletter.[100]

The Forum traces its roots to 1984-85, when some national *RENEW* leaders and a few diocesan *RENEW* personnel first met for the purpose of discussing ways to continue to support the small groups that had been formed in many parishes during the formal phase of the program. As we have seen when examining *RENEW*, many dioceses were asked to set up special diocesan offices to accommodate the initial coordination and training needed to implement the program for its three year duration. Because of the positive response generated by the *RENEW* small groups, many of whom continued to meet after the program had concluded, many dioceses decided to transform these temporary *RENEW* offices into

---

[99] Principal sources for this section are: NAFSCC, *Mission Statement and History* (Crookston, Minnesota: NAFSCC Office, 1991); Rosemary Blueher, "Creating Our Future: A Prophetic Way of Being Church," *Gifts* (Summer 1990), pp. 1-8; Rosemary Blueher, "A Response to a Paradigm Shift: The North American Forum for Small Christian Communities, *PACE* 21 (1991), pp. 115-118; Rosemary Blueher, "Shared Leadership as Experienced in Small Christian Communities," *The Catholic World* (July/August 1991), pp. 161-165; and various articles featured in the *NAFSCC Newsletter*.

[100] NAFSCC, *Mission Statement and History*, p. 1.

permanent ones overseeing SCC development and support. Hence the Forum was formed to support these diocesan personnel.

In 1986 it was decided that the Forum should not only encompass diocesan *RENEW* personnel, but people involved in any kind of diocesan SCC effort. With this broadening of its membership also came the decision to operate the NAFSCC as a separate entity from that of national *RENEW*. Further developments included a decision to collaborate more closely with both Buena Vista and the National Alliance of Parishes Restructuring Into Small Communities. At present, some 60 dioceses in the United States and Canada are members of the Forum.[101] Rosemary Blueher is the current chairperson of the NAFSCC.

2. Characteristics

The Forum is not committed to any specific type of SCC program. Rather, it is committed to the basic vision of SCCs being constitutive of a new "paradigm" of parish life.[102] The four essential elements of an SCC are said to be: (1) prayer/faith-sharing; (2) support; (3) continued learning; and (4) outreach or mission.[103] The optimum size of an SCC is said to be 8-12 people. Leadership or animation responsibilities within the groups are usually shared. If the SCC was established through the initiative of the pastor or pastoral staff, then there will naturally be more ongoing contact, recognition and support for these groups. If the SCC was started by the initiative of some of its own members, then it will usually have to assume its own leadership and animation responsibilities.

The Forum is of particular interest because it represents how prevalent dioceses have become in the effort to promote parish-based SCCs. More and more dioceses are opening special SCC offices or departments. A typical example is the Archdiocese of Milwaukee. Their SCC support effort is coordinated by the office for Adult and Family Ministry. As part of its work, it undertook a survey of SCCs in the diocese.[104] It discovered there were 26 groups in existence. No parish in the diocese had yet undertaken to restructure in a way advocated by some of the SCC programs we have

---

[101] *Ibid.*, p. 3.

[102] Cf. Blueher, "A Response to a Paradigm Shift: The North American Forum for Small Christian Communities," p. 115. Blueher describes this paradigm shift in the following way: "*Paradigm shift* is a term used to describe the drastic changes or transformations found in a culture or organization. . . . A paradigm shift calls for an examination and evaluation of our assumptions, beliefs, and 'ways of doing things'—our patterns of behaviour. . . . A movement that is growing throughout the U.S. church, the development of *small Christian communities*, has the potential of being a paradigm shift in parishes." (*Ibid.*)

[103] *Ibid.*

[104] Cf. Adult and Family Ministry Office, *Living the Vision* (Milwaukee: Diocesan Center, 1990).

looked at. Thus, the parishes that reported having SCCs, usually had only one or two of these small groups. What is striking about the survey is the diversity of these SCCs. They include post-*RENEW* groups, Hispanic groups, and a wide variety of other groups that make use of different program literature for continued support.

An example of a diocese having a greater amount of SCC activity is that of the Archdiocese of St. Paul-Minneapolis. Their Department of Small Faith Communities recently reported that 146 of its 223 parishes have some form of SCCs in operation, with nine of these parishes restructuring using the Baranowski model. The total number of people involved in these various kinds of SCC efforts is said to be approximately 10,000.[105]

The diocese which is said to have the most substantial diocesan-level commitment to SCCs is that of Hartford, Connecticut.[106] In the wake of the *RENEW* program, it set up a separate pastoral department for continued SCC support. Seventeen parishes are in the midst of formally restructuring, and over half the parishes have SCCs of one kind or another in existence. To support these efforts, they have published a special *Guidebook* to help explain the nature and purpose of SCCs, as well as the resources that are available for their continued operation. The goal of this Department, which flows out of the overall diocesan pastoral plan, is "to establish small Christian communities in each parish of the Archdiocese."[107]

What this kind of activity underscores is the fact that SCC efforts are not limited to the individual or even the parish levels, but are being supported at the diocesan and national levels as well. The vision of the parish being a community of communities, with special emphasis on SCCs, is appearing in more and more official diocesan pastoral plans. Thus, many bishops have taken an active interest in, and have provided leadership for, such SCC efforts.

For example, in a 1983 article Bishop William Weigand of Salt Lake City, Utah, reflected on his diocese's experience with BCCs.[108] Among the comments he makes is that BCCs help make the parish a community of communities. They become an effective parish outreach. The decentralization which BCCs help achieve in a parish is not necessarily of

---

[105] Cf. Department of Small Faith Communities, *Year End Report* (St. Paul-Minneapolis: Diocesan Center, 1991), p. 1.

[106] This according to the December 1991 NAFSCC Newsletter, p. 3.

[107] Department for Small Christian Communities, *Guidebook* (Hartford: Diocesan Center, 1989), p. 9.

[108] Cf. Bishop William Weigand (co-authored with Sr. Helen Marie Raycraft and Fr. Ralph Rogawski), "Basic Christian Communities: A New Hope," in *Basic Christian Communities: The United States Experience* (Chicago: NFPC, 1983), pp. 8-11.

a physical kind, leading to a multiplication of parish mission stations. Rather, it is of a ministerial kind, done to promote the pastoral effectiveness of various activities. "Some parishes decentralize their catechetical and social outreach programs through each community."[109]

In a 1990 Pastoral Letter to the Catholic faithful of the diocese of Brownsville, Texas, Bishop John Fitzpatrick explains his views about the growing proliferation of base communities in this diocese.[110] "The church is being reborn as small grassroots communities. Their rise is not only a dynamic response to impersonal times, but also a way of enacting the vision of Vatican Council II . . . Base communities are not a replacement for the parish, nor mere subdivisions of them. Rather, they are a fresh way of being church within the structured parish." He concludes his remarks by urging everyone in the diocese to become a member of a base community.

In another 1990 Pastoral Letter, Bishop James Timlin of the diocese of Scranton, Pennsylvania, refers to SCCs as being an important component of the diocese's overall pastoral plan dealing with the organizing of parish life.[111] He states in part that:

> The dynamic present in small Christian communities is the same as that found in the Rite of Christian Initiation of Adults. Both derive from the experience of the New Testament church. The same pastoral principles apply both to the process of initiation and to the life of the parish community: These communities share the good news, form Christian disciples, experience opportunities for spiritual renewal . . . .Undoubtedly, small communities will never engage all members of a parish. And, those in small communities need to balance this form of community with active participation in the larger, more inclusive parish liturgy and life. Small Christian communities by their very nature are in relationship and service to the broader church and the presence of these communities in the parish can significantly enhance the work of evangelization.[112]

---

[109] *Ibid.,* p. 10.

[110] Cf. Bishop John Fitzpatrick, "Base Communities of Faith," *A Pastoral Letter to the Catholic Faithful of the Diocese of Brownsville, Texas* (May 6, 1990).

[111] Cf. Bishop James Timlin, "The Welcoming Church: A Pastoral Vision," *Origins* 20/36 (1991), pp. 596-600.

[112] *Ibid.,* pp. 597-598.

3. Ecclesiological Reflection

At its 1989 conference, the NAFSCC produced a "theological reflection" on the nature and significance of SCCs. This reflection states in part that: "Small Christian communities are a prophetic way of being church—ecclesial communities in which the Word is lived out in sign and sacrament for the world. While an integral part of the larger church, the gift of small Christian communities is the experience of belonging, formation, worship and service at a more personal level."[113] This line of thinking is in essential continuity with much of the ecclesiological reflection we have already seen, and presents few theological or pastoral difficulties.

Somewhat more problematic is the following statement which is also found in the same *theological reflection* document: "Members of small Christian communities discern, develop, and commission the ministries of the individual and the community."[114] With no reference made to being under the ultimate authority of the pastor or parish, and no further explanation given, this statement can leave the impression that SCCs are relatively autonomous entities that totally organize and control their own affairs within a parish context. While the intent of the statement seems to be to encourage SCC members to take upon themselves the responsibilities for group leadership and outreach, which is especially apropos in those situations where SCCs do not enjoy active input and support from the pastor, it is still a statement lacking in balance.

For her part, Rosemary Blueher describes SCCs as being an important pastoral response to the cultural challenges faced by the church in North America. She also sees it as being an answer to the growing shortage of ordained leadership on the parish level. Lay people learn in SCCs how to pastor one another (relatively speaking). Thus, she sees the small Christian community movement as being "a Spirit-moved sign of the times—a paradigm shift—that serves a sociological occasion for the enablement and empowerment of the laity and a new way of being church."[115]

II. OTHER PARISH-BASED SCC PROGRAMS AND INITIATIVES

Although the North American parish-based SCC programs and organizations which have been highlighted in this chapter represent the major initiatives in the field to date, they do not collectively exhaust all that

---

[113] Cited by Blueher, "A Response to a Paradigm Shift: The North American Forum for Small Christian Communities," p. 116.

[114] *Ibid.*

[115] *Ibid.,* p. 118.

has been happening in this area. The purpose of this section is to draw attention to some of these other SCC initiatives. However, no attempt is being made to give a full account of their emergence, characteristics, or ecclesiology. This is because, at present, these other programs or initiatives have had less of an impact on the national level. This is not to say they are unimportant as a result. It is only to explain why they have not been chosen for closer scrutiny as were the previous seven.

The first of these other programs which is worth mentioning briefly is called Parish Neighborhood Renewal. In his book *Basic Communities: A Practical Guide for Renewing Neighborhood Churches,* Thomas Maney, a Maryknoll priest, explains the origins and nature of this program.[116] Maney had spent time as a missionary in South America in the 1960s and 70s and had encountered the phenomenon of basic communities while there. Upon his return to the United States in 1977 he obtained permission from the bishop of Duluth, Minnesota, to pioneer a similar type of small community program for U.S. parishes. He collaborated with Sr. Joan Gerads, OSA, who also had first-hand experience with Latin American BECs, in developing Parish Neighborhood Renewal.

Between 1978 and 1983, Maney estimates that over 300 SCCs were formed in parishes that had adopted this program (mainly in the Mid-West).[117] The basic features of Parish Neighborhood Renewal—small groups forming for the purpose of prayer, sharing, learning and outreach—are similar to what we have seen in other SCC initiatives. The method used to establish them involves hosting a parish mission and doing house-to-house visitation. There is a strong emphasis on the need for personal conversion to make SCCs work over the long haul. This approach necessitates the pastor's full cooperation and commitment to ongoing SCC support. From a ecclesiological-structural point of view, Maney sees SCCs as representing a new intermediary "level" (between that of family and parish) where the church is realized.[118]

In the mid-1980s Maney returned to full time missionary work in South America. With his departure, the Parish Neighborhood Renewal Ministry became virtually dormant. It is still in existence, but is operating on a much reduced scale.[119] It seems to have been effectively superseded by other SCC efforts in many areas where it first took root (i.e. *RENEW*). This

---

[116] Cf. Thomas Maney, *Basic Communities: A Practical Guide for Renewing Neighborhood Churches* (Minneapolis: Winston Press, 1984).

[117] *Ibid.,* p. 3.

[118] *Ibid.*

[119] This according to information obtained in a Aug. 27, 1992, telephone conversation with Anna Chernugal, who is a current member of the Parish Neighborhood Ministry Team.

development draws attention to the fact that it is difficult to ascertain what SCC programs at present are destined for any kind of longevity.

Another early effort was that of the *Koinonia* small groups developed by some Paulist Fathers in Boston. David Kilian, CSP, describes these groups as originating in response to a need some parishioners had voiced for a stronger experience of "community" in the Paulist Center Community in 1973.[120] From 10 the first year, these *Koinonia* groups grew to over 30 the following year. Kilian notes that these *Koinonia* small groups sought to emulate the Latin American BCC experience of Scripture reflection, faith-sharing, and outreach. In reflecting on their ecclesiological significance, Kilian states:

> My criteria for when a group becomes a BCC is when the members have a sense that "we are Church." It is when they take ownership and responsibility for the Church—when they accept their identity as Christians and call to share these values with others—that is when the group has matured. That is when it is truly an "*ecclesiola*" ("little church") in the larger "*ecclesia*" (Church). It is at that moment that the spirit of the early Church described in Acts is again alive and present in our world.[121]

It is not known how widespread the *Koinonia* program eventually became. But there is very little reference to it in recent literature on SCC development in North America. One may deduce from this that it too was probably superseded by other SCC programs like *RENEW* (which, incidently, Kilian endorsed as "the model we recommend most highly"[122]).

The Jesuits recently began a program in North America they call the Basic Church Community Project.[123] As its name implies, it takes its inspiration from the Latin American base community experience. The Project has been active in working with many post-*RENEW* groups who are endeavouring to continue meeting. It publishes a special leaflet entitled *The Word in Community* to help provide ongoing Scripture reflection and

---

[120] Cf. David Kilian, "How to Develop Basic Christian Communities in Your Parish or Diocese," in *Basic Christian Communities: The United States Experience* (Chicago: National Federation of Priest's Councils, 1983), p. 14.

[121] *Ibid.*, p. 17.

[122] *Ibid.*, p. 16.

[123] Cf. Jim Sheppard, "*The Word in Community* Begins to Fly," in *Small Christian Communities: Canada 1991*, ed. William O'Brien (Waterdown, Ontario: Canadian Office of *RENEW*, 1991), pp. 3-4.

discussion material for these and other SCCs. It is also helping to establish some full-fledged base communities in parishes on a number of Native People's reservations where the shortage of ordained clergy is more acute.

These efforts by the Maryknollers, Paulists, and Jesuits, indicate how much of an interest and role religious orders have taken in North American SCC development. Besides priests and brothers, many women religious have also been instrumental in parish and diocesan work in this area. Frequently, these efforts are inspired by and modelled after the Latin American experience (with adaptations). In addition to all this, there have also been many individual parish experiments with base communities/SCCs. These points are being stressed so that it does not appear that the only initiatives of consequence in North America have come about as a result of one of the higher profile programs we have chosen to examine in more detail.

III. SMALL CHRISTIAN COMMUNITIES AND THE RCIA

As we have already noted in passing, many SCC programs and organizations see these small groups as complementing the parish Rite of Christian Initiation for Adults (RCIA) program. It is worth examining this relationship more closely for a moment because it sheds further light on what has become yet another influence on SCC development in North America.

The RCIA is an officially mandated process/sacramental rite which was designed to help prepare adult catechumens for either baptism in, or full communion with, the Catholic church.[124] It represents the fruit of Vatican II's efforts to restore the ancient catechumenate.[125] It came into effect on Jan. 6, 1972 and has been vigorously promoted since then by many North American dioceses, although it is far from being a reality in every parish. Generally speaking, in those regions of the world where the vast majority of the populace are at least nominally Catholic, the RCIA has not been especially prominent because it has not been formally needed (other basic catechism programs are used for purposes of adult religious education). But in regions such as North America (except for Quebec), where there are people from many different Christian and non-Christian backgrounds living together, some of whom eventually desire to become Catholics, it is very much needed and utilized.

---

[124] Cf. Congregation for Divine Worship, *Ordo Initiationis Christianae Adultorum* (Vatican City: Typis Polyglottis, 1972).

[125] Cf. Aidan Kavanagh, *The Shape of Baptism: The Rite of Christian Initiation* (New York: Pueblo, 1978), p. 105.

The RCIA is comprised of four stages: (1) The Pre-Catechumenate (period of inquiry); (2) The Catechumenate (period of instruction in matters of church teaching and faith practice); (3) Enlightenment/Purification/ Illumination (Lenten period of spiritual recollection in preparation for Easter baptism or reception into full communion); and (4) Mystagogia (post-Easter period of assimilation and formation for ministry). Each of these stages is also marked by certain liturgical rites which are designed to highlight the wider parish and diocesan role in this process. But most of the catechetical activity in the RCIA is carried out in the context of small groups that are established for the duration of the program (which usually lasts from one to two years).[126]

After the RCIA is formally concluded for one group of catechumens, it usually begins again for another. It is thus intended to be a permanent fixture of parish life. It was originally envisioned that those who had become newly baptised members of the church, or in full communion with it, would naturally continue their faith growth and development by participating in the Eucharist and involving themselves in other parish programs and activities like other Catholics.

But interestingly enough, many people who worked as animators of RCIA groups discovered that many of their former catechumens felt "lost" in the parish crowd after the process was over. Many had benefitted so much from the small group meetings that they expressed a desire to see them continue. Another surprising reaction these animators encountered had to do with the many requests they received from ordinary Catholics wishing to participate in the RCIA for the purpose of further education and faith support. They were generally not allowed to do so because the RCIA's main focus had to be on catechumens.[127] Yet there was clearly a need for some kind of ongoing adult religious education program for ordinary Catholics that made use of these same small group dynamics.

One result of these developments was a request that the U.S. National Conference of Diocesan Directors of Religious Education made to Thomas Ivory for a study of the broader pastoral implications of the RCIA for parish life in general, and adult catechesis in particular. Ivory, who had collaborated with Kleissler in the original formation of the *RENEW* program, had since then become very active in both these fields of RCIA and adult religious education. He outlined his reflections in his book

---

[126] *Ibid.*, pp. 126-149.

[127] *Ibid.*, p. 189.

Conversion and Community: A Catechetical Model for Total Parish Formation.[128]

Ivory states that his book "has evolved from the original intuition that the *Rite of Christian Initiation of Adults* provides not only a framework for the formation of newly-initiated Catholic Christians, but a model for ministerial collaboration in the ongoing nurture and development of all the faithful."[129] What Ivory advocates is that the RCIA process, with its four stages, be seen as something necessary and normative for the entire parish community. This is because he sees each of the four RCIA stages as being representative of certain basic features of Christian discipleship. Thus, small faith-sharing groups which are established on a parish-wide basis can be theologically and pastorally explained as aiding in the process of ongoing discipleship and catechesis. He calls this a "catechetical model" for parish small groups.

Ivory sees the model he has developed as being an attempt "to integrate the development of small Christian communities with the pastoral principles of the catechumenate."[130] He also sees this as being the ideal post-*RENEW* strategy for small groups. He sees this approach to small group formation as having the further advantage of being clearly rooted in an already established, universally sanctioned church process. After all, the Synod of 1977 had affirmed that the "model of all catechesis" is the catechumenate.[131]

Building on Ivory's insights, Kleissler, in his latest book about small Christian communities, devotes an entire chapter to this idea of integrating SCCs and the RCIA.[132] In this chapter he makes reference to the success which Fr. Thomas Caroluzza has had with these types of RCIA-inspired SCCs in Holy Spirit parish in Virginia Beach, Virginia. However, it is important to note that the "catechumenal model" does not really represent a new program for SCCs, but rather an explanation of their long-term function and purpose in the parish community. Caroluzza found that his work promoting parish-wide awareness of the RCIA acted as a catalyst for subsequent SCC development for all parishioners.

What this development represents then is another important influence which is currently spurring the growth of SCCs in North American

---

[128] Thomas Ivory, *Conversion and Community: A Catechetical Model for Total Parish Formation* (New York/Mahwah: Paulist Press, 1988).

[129] *Ibid.,* p. 2.

[130] *Ibid.,* p. 126.

[131] Cf. 1977 Synod, "Message to the People of God," *La Documentation Catholique* 74 (1977), p. 1018 (#8).

[132] Cf Kleissler et al., *Small Christian Communities,* pp. 191-204.

parishes. Many of the SCC programs/organizations and we have examined in this chapter advocate SCCs as a natural follow up to the RCIA.[133] Not all of them would explain their major focus though as "catechetical." And yet, because of the emphasis on continued learning as being an important component of SCC activity, they do indeed fulfil a catechetical role in the church today. For all of these reasons, Ivory notes a consensus that is growing in the minds of many religious educators that small Christian communities offer the most holistic and propitious environment for adult faith development in the church today.[134]

IV. SUMMARY/PRELIMINARY CONCLUSIONS
A. Major Influences on North American SCC Development

In outlining the emergence and characteristics of the SCC programs and organizations which we have examined in this chapter, there was frequent mention made of important influences on their development. Although each specific SCC program and organization cited their own particular influences, and even those citing the same ones sometimes varied in the manner and degree to which they ascribed significance to them, it is nevertheless possible to list the major influences upon the North American experience as follows:

1) *The Latin American Experience with BECs*

Many groups appealed to the Latin American experience in the area of BEC development as being an inspiration for their efforts. However, due to differences in culture and pastoral exigencies, few groups attempted to pattern themselves in an exact fashion on this model.

2) *Parish Renewal Efforts*

The desire for postconciliar parish renewal led to many programs being implemented in parishes (i.e. Christ Renews His Parish, The Parish Renewal Experience, *RENEW)*. These efforts have had a great impact on parish life in general, and SCC formation in particular, by evangelizing parishioners and introducing many of them to the idea and practice of small faith-sharing groups.

---

[133] In addition to the remarks to this effect made above by both Ivory and Kleissler, for further evidence of this perceived link between SCCs and the RCIA see: Baranowski, "RCIA—A Model for Being Catholic," *Creating Small Faith Communities*, pp. 5-7; Brennan, "The RCIA as Model for Basic Christian Communities and Adult Faith Formation," *Re-imagining the Parish*, pp. 79-86; and Cooney, "Parish Cells," *Intercom* (Dec. 1990), p. 15.

[134] Cf. Ivory, *Conversion and Community*, p. 4.

3) *Lay Movements*

In a similar vein to what is noted above about parish renewal efforts, lay movements such as Cursillo, Marriage Encounter, and the Charismatic Renewal have also helped to evangelize many parishioners and introduce them to the idea and practice of small faith-sharing groups. This in turn has helped prepare parishioners to participate more readily in subsequent parish-based SCC initiatives. The influence then of lay movements on SCC programs may be indirect, but it is nevertheless significant.

4) *Vatican II*

All of the groups we have looked at cite the renewed ecclesiology of Vatican II as providing a theological rationale for SCCs. Also important in this connection is the renewed understanding of the laity's role in the life of the church.

5) *Scripture and The Early Church*

Many groups refer to the early house church phenomenon as being indicative of a more personally focused experience of Christian community which they are seeking to emulate. They also see in the Jesus-apostles relationship attested to in Scripture a type of small group discipleship dynamic at work which is influencing and legitimating their efforts to evangelize and disciple parishioners in a similar small group manner.

6) *Papal, Synodal, and other Episcopal Statements*

The various statements pertaining to BECs that have emanated from the Medellin and Puebla conferences of CELAM, plus Paul VI's *Evangelii Nuntiandi #58,* are the sources most frequently cited for the ecclesiological justification of SCCs. Also important are a variety of other Papal, Synodal, and North American Episcopal statements.[135]

7) *The RCIA*

The RCIA is not only seen as a process for catechumenal initiation, but also as a model for ongoing parish-wide catechesis and support. It has thus acted as an inspiration and catalyst for SCC formation.

---

[135] We will take a closer look at some of these statements in the next chapter. Although many groups made reference to such statements, it was decided not to dwell on them in this chapter, preferring instead to treat them together, and in a more systematic manner, later on.

8) *Modernity and Secularization*

These forces were often cited in a negative vein as being reasons for the pastoral necessity of SCCs. SCCs are portrayed as an excellent means for helping to meet the present day cultural challenges posed to Christian belief and church practice. In this sense, modernity and secularization can be seen as having influenced and spurred the development of SCCs.

9) *The Holy Spirit*

Because of the pastoral fruitfulness and widespread growth of the SCC phenomenon, not only in North America, but also around the world, many groups discern the inspiration of the Holy Spirit to be also at work influencing their development.

B. General Characteristics of North American SCCs

Although there were a wide variety of approaches advocated for the process of spearheading SCC development in the parish, and although different programs and organizations had different ecclesiological understandings of their role and significance in the church, it is nevertheless true that as regards the SCCs themselves, there was a remarkable similarity in basic structure and format. These common features can be explained under the following headings:

1) *Size*

Most groups saw 8-12 people as being the ideal number for SCCs. Anything larger was often seen as being counterproductive from the point of view of encouraging everyone to effectively participate in faith-sharing and discussion. Anything smaller was deemed potentially unstable and lacking in the diversity of charisms needed for ongoing group cohesion.

2) *Setting*

Most groups saw the home of fellow members as being the natural setting for SCC meetings. This was another reason for advocating that the group size be kept to a maximum of about twelve. That is about the number of people who can be seated comfortably in the living room or den of the average North American home.

3) *Frequency of Meeting*

The average recommended frequency of meetings was once every two weeks. Some groups advocated weekly meetings, while one group mentioned that meeting once every three weeks was allowable. But all groups stressed the importance of regularity.

4) *Format*

The standard features of an SCC meeting usually include three basic activities: (1) A period of prayer and/or Scripture reflection; (2) An extended period of personal faith-sharing based on the Scripture selection and/or life experiences; (3) Some form of teaching/catechesis for more general discussion.

5) *Commitment to Ministry Outside the Meeting*

Most groups saw the necessity of members participating in some form of wider social outreach or ministry. This was accomplished in one of two ways. Either members took it upon themselves to engage in some activity of this kind, or else they were encouraged to participate in an existing parish or diocesan initiative.

6) *Leadership and Animation*

Most programs and organizations stressed the shared responsibility which all SCC members have for the welfare of the group. No single person is considered the "leader" of the group in a formal pastoral sense. Those who are designated as pastoral facilitators have the role of helping to animate the meetings and liaise with the parish priest and/or staff.

7) *Connection to the Parish*

Because the focus of this study is on parish-based SCCs, it naturally follows that they have, or seek to have, some identifiable connection to the parish community. Usually this link was promoted by means of having the pastoral facilitators meet on a regular basis with the pastor and/or staff for input and formation, having a representative for SCCs on parish council, and having the SCCs make use of catechetical discussion material which either originates from the parish or is at least sanctioned by it.

C. Differences Between North American SCCs and Latin American BECs

As we have already seen, there are many similarities between the Latin American BEC experience and North American developments with SCCs. But there are also differences. These differences are important to take note of because they affect the assessment one makes of SCCs' ecclesiality and significance. While the major part of this ecclesiological analysis will be undertaken in the final chapter, a few summary remarks detailing these pastoral differences are in order here, so as to prepare for this later analysis. These differences are outlined in the following points:

1) *Liturgical Function*

Generally speaking, the majority of Latin American BECs function as quasi-parishes. North American SCCs do not. As a result, Latin American BECs often have responsibility for organizing and hosting the Sunday liturgies and engaging in other forms of sacramental preparation for the local Catholics in their area. North American SCCs do not have this same kind of liturgical role (except in a few cases).

2) *Size and Organizational Complexity*

Latin American BECs are larger on average than their North American counterparts. They are also more organizationally complex, usually having their own councils and sub-committees. This higher level of organization is needed in order to function properly as a quasi-parish.

3) *Political and Social Action*

Due to the extreme poverty and lack of available government assistance, many Latin American BECs have taken an active role in political and social action to help improve local conditions in the community. Because of a different political and social milieu, North American SCCs are generally not as active in the same way in these areas. Almost all North American SCCs are committed to ministry and outreach, but this takes a wide variety of forms.

4) *Pastoral Exigencies*

While BECs are pastorally justifiable for their own sake, it is also true that they and other forms of parish missions are a practical necessity in many regions of Latin America due to the large size of many parishes and the general shortage of clergy. North America is, relatively speaking, better off in this regard. Hence, the pastoral motivation for SCC development and parish restructuring is more exclusively linked to questions regarding the nature and functioning of parish community.

5) *Episcopal Sanctioning*

The Medellin, Puebla, and Santo Domingo statements of CELAM which pertain to BECs, in addition to a variety of National Pastoral Plans in such countries as Brazil which also promote BEC development, has lent a greater official impetus to Latin American BEC formation. Other than the U.S. NCCB's Pastoral Plan for Hispanic Ministry, there has been as of yet only minimal national episcopal sanctioning of SCC development in North America. However, as we have noted, many North American dioceses have opened SCC offices to encourage their growth, and we reported on a number of favorable statements made by individual bishops about local SCC development.

D. The Ecclesiality of North American SCCs

The question of how North American SCCs can be seen as functioning in an ecclesial manner, and what they are contributing to the vocation and mission of the parish church, will be addressed in greater detail in the final chapter. Before such an evaluation can be attempted though, more must be known about what "ecclesiality" theologically and practically entails. In the next chapter, we will outline some "criteria of ecclesiality" which have been gleaned from various papal and synodal documents which address specifically the issue of BECs/SCCs and/or lay groups. In the final chapter these criteria will be used to evaluate the essential ecclesiality of each the North American SCC programs/organizations studied here. Because of this approach there will be no listing here of the various "elements" of church which SCCs claim to help mediate in the parish community (this will occur in the final chapter).

What is listed in what follows are the various ways in which North American SCC programs/organizations have chosen to express or name their perceived ecclesial identity. This is an important indication of their perceived role within the parish community. We will return in the final chapter to an evaluation of the appropriateness of some of these names, and address the question of what kind of "recognition" should be accorded to SCC groups in the parish.

Since North American SCC programs/organizations are far from having a uniform position on this issue, this is one matter which is impossible to generalize. There seems to be a wide spectrum of opinions present. As we recall, at the 1991 International Consultation on BCCs it was stated that although all BCCs/SCCs can be said to represent 'a new way of being church,' "sometimes the emphasis is upon 'being church' and sometimes upon the 'new ways' of doing it."[136] This insight is especially apropos for the North American programs and organizations we have looked at. Their basic positions are briefly outlined in what follows so as to summarize the North American situation regarding this issue and prepare for this later assessment:

---

[136] 1991 International Consultation on Basic Christian Communities (Notre Dame University), *Final Statement*, p. 3.

1) *Hispanic Ministry Initiatives*

The 1987 NCCB Pastoral Plan for Hispanic Ministry referred to BECs as being a fundamental ecclesial nucleus, but also insisted that the parish is the basic organizational "unit" of the local church in North America. However, the NCCB's Secretariat for Hispanic Affairs, in a 1991 draft version of BEC guidelines, stated that nevertheless the BEC "is Church," though it is necessarily dependent on its pastoral link to the parish/diocese for this ecclesial identity.

2) *RENEW*

Although *RENEW* is based on certain convictions about what it means to be the church, and its small groups aim to make this a reality, *RENEW* does not really involve itself in the issue of "naming" the ecclesial identity of its post-*RENEW* SCCs. It simply states that small Christian communities are a "part" of the parish, and leaves it at that.

3) *National Alliance of Parishes Restructuring Into Communities (NAPRC)*

Baranowski clearly states that parish-based SCCs are "little churches" and represent "the church in miniature." SCCs are seen as constituting a new "level" wherein the reality of the church is realized in its parish setting.

4) *St. Boniface Parish Cell System*

Similar to *RENEW* in that the issue of the ecclesial identity of SCCs within the parish community is not really addressed. The preferred terminology is that of "cells." These cells are described as mediating communities within the parish structure.

5) *Systematic Integral New Evangelization (SINE)*

Similar to the St. Boniface System in that the terminology of cells is invoked to describe SCCs. The fundamental ecclesial "unit" is seen as being the parish. The small communities are seen as being cells of the parish body.

6) *Buena Vista*

Does not really attempt to address this issue either. Simply describes SCCs as being something which should be central to, and normative of, the parish church. Sees any SCC which is parish-based, regardless of whether or not there is a formal link to the pastor actively in place, as qualifying for the title of SCC.

7) *North American Forum for Small Christian Communities*

Describes SCCs as a prophetic way of "being church." Refers to them as being ecclesial communities. While seen as being an integral part of the parish church, SCCs are said to make present an experience of worship, formation, and service on a more personal "level."

Part Three:
Ecclesiological Analysis

CHAPTER SIX

Small Christian Community
and the Magisterium

This chapter will provide a synopsis of how the idea and practice of small Christian community has been addressed by the Magisterium of the church. The main focus will be on several papal and synodal statements wherein reference is made to this topic. The manner in which SCCs are treated and assessed in these documents sheds important light on their perceived pastoral and ecclesiological significance. After reviewing these statements, a conclusion will follow wherein the salient features of this assessment are highlighted. In the following chapter, many of these insights will form the basis for "criteria of ecclesiality" which are applicable to SCCs, and will be utilized in evaluating the North American experience in this area.

A. The 1974 Synod on Evangelization and Paul VI's 1975 Apostolic Exhortation *Evangelii Nuntiandi*

The 1974 Synod was devoted to the topic of evangelization. It sought to address the issue of how the church should best carry out its essential missionary task in the world today. Although it was recognized that Vatican II had extensively dealt with this same topic less than a decade previous, the question was asked as to why the church did not find herself better equipped as a result to proclaim the Gospel more effectively?[1] It was during these discussions that basic communities were strongly advocated as an evangelizing strategy by many Latin American bishops.

In the Apostolic Exhortation *Evangelii Nuntiandi* which followed this Synod, Paul VI directly addresses the topic of BECs in section #58. He notes that the Synod had "devoted considerable attention" to them and that they were "often talked about in the church today." He begins his comments

---

[1] Cf. *Evangelii Nuntiandi* 4.

by recognizing that most BECs develop within, and have solidarity with, the church and her pastors. He also notes that because of their capacity for being a means of evangelization, they are indeed a great "hope for the universal church."

This fact having been noted and appreciated, he then goes on to address some troubling aspects which seem to be characteristic of certain "other" kinds of base community. These communities are said to be marked by a spirit of pronounced criticism of the church, which they regard as too "institutional." In addition, some of these "hypercritical" communities have become ensnared by political entanglements and fashionable ideologies. As a result of their refusal to be subject to competent pastoral authority and supervision, these latter kind of base communities are said to be functioning as sociological entities, not as ecclesial ones.

In order for basic communities to be truly ecclesial entities, Paul VI articulates certain conditions or criteria which they must adhere to in their operations. They need: (1) to be nourished by the Word of God, and not become entrapped by political polarization or fashionable ideologies; (2) to avoid the temptation of systematic protest, hypercriticism, and the feigning of a true spirit of collaboration with the church; (3) to remain firmly attached to the local church in which they are inserted, and to the universal church, so as to avoid the danger of becoming isolated within themselves; (4) to be in sincere communion with their pastors; (5) to be aware of the need to constantly grow in missionary consciousness, fervor, commitment and zeal; (6) to be aware that they are not the only means whereby the church evangelizes people; and (7) to be universal in all things, and never sectarian. If they meet these criteria, then BECs will no doubt continue to bear good fruit in the church.[2]

The concerns that EN #58 raise about BECs are to be found in many other subsequent papal documents that addresses this topic. There is usually an insistent call for BECs to be always firmly rooted in the church and in communion with her pastors. BECs which ignore this call cannot consider themselves as ecclesial groups. This is a fundamental aspect then of what BEC ecclesiality practically entails.

B. The 1977 Synod on Catechesis and John Paul II's 1979 Apostolic Exhortation *Catechesi Tradendae*

The 1977 Synod focused on the topic of catechesis. The church has always considered catechesis one of her primary tasks.[3] It is inextricably

---

[2] The ecclesiology underpinning these criteria, as well as a more indepth account of their significance in the evaluation of BEC/SCC ecclesiality, will be a focus of the next chapter (cf. parts I and II).
[3] Cf. *Catechesi Tradendae* 1.

linked to the process of evangelization and the need for believers to continually deepen their awareness of the faith and the life of the church. As part of their deliberations on this topic, the bishops addressed different ways and means by which catechesis can be effectively imparted to people in the church today.

It was in the context of this discussion that reference was made to the phenomenon of small communities as being an effective means for catechesis. Despite recognizing that there were ongoing problems with some small communities manifesting hostility towards the church, and even engaging in illicit pastoral and liturgical activity, BECs were still seen as being an effective instrument for parish catechesis. Furthermore, the bishops saw in these small communities a great potential for overall parish renewal as well. They said it was becoming increasingly imperative "to renew the parish by making it a community of communities."[4]

In his Apostolic Exhortation *Catechesi Tradendae*, John Paul II mentions BECs (those that meet the criteria of EN #58) as being a suitable locus for catechesis (Cf. #47).[5] But little else of substance is said of them in the rest of the document. In section #67, the parish is described as the "pre-eminent place for catechesis." This statement is immediately followed by a dismissal of the assertion that "the parish should be considered old-fashioned, if not doomed to disappear, in favour of more pertinent and effective small communities." It is not indicated to whom this statement is directed. It does not seem to be a rebuff of the Synod's statement that the parish should be considered a community of communities. Rather, it seems to be addressed to those people (i.e. Leonardo Boff) who had called for the outright abolition of the parish in favour of BECs.[6] But as we have seen, most proponents of BECs/SCCs favour the restructuring of the parish, not its abolition or replacement.

C. The 1985 Extraordinary Synod of Bishops and *The Final Report*

As we have previously seen and noted, the 1985 Extraordinary Synod was convened by John Paul II in order to celebrate the 20th anniversary of Vatican II, and to reflect on and promote its role in the life of the church today.[7] The Synod produced two brief documents. One was a general *Message to the People of God*. The other was a *Final Report*,

---

[4] Cf. 1977 Synod, Proposition on the Parish, #8.

[5] This point was recently reaffirmed in the Vatican's International Council for Catechesis document *Adult Catechesis in the Christian Community: Some Principles and Guidelines* (Vatican City: Libreria Editrice Vaticana, 1990), #62.

[6] Cf. Chapter four, part II, section A § 3.

[7] Cf. Chapter two, part I, section A § 3, which dealt with "The Interpretation and Reception of the Council."

184 \ *Small Christian Communities and the Parish*

containing reflections on various themes in the Council's ecclesiology. In section C of this *Final Report*, dealing with the theme of the church as communion, the following statement is included: "Because the Church is communion, the new 'basic communities,' if they truly live in unity with the Church, are a true expression of communion and a means for the construction of a more profound communion. They are thus a cause for great hope for the life of the Church (*Evangelii Nuntiandi, 58*)."[8]

Given the fact that the Synod had affirmed that Vatican II's "ecclesiology of communion is the central and fundamental idea of the Council's documents," it is all the more noteworthy that they see in BECs a means for the construction of a more profound communion in the church.[9] That BECS/SCCs are even mentioned at all in such a brief document shows again the high regard that many bishops in the church have of them.

In reflecting on BECs, communion ecclesiology, and the role played by lay people in the church, Walter Kasper makes this interesting observation:

> Lay interest, and the preparedness of lay people to take a share of responsibility, is perhaps the most valuable and most important contribution of the post-conciliar period. It was not for nothing that in *Evangelii Nuntiandi* (58), Pope Paul VI termed the true basic communities a hope for the church universal; for communion ecclesiology means that there cannot be active members on the one side, and passive ones on the other. This ecclesiology puts an end to the pattern of a welfare church for looking after people.[10]

Kasper adds to this observation the comment that, unfortunately, there have been serious misunderstandings in the postconciliar period concerning what lay co-responsibility for the church practically entails. It does not mean that lay people can ignore the pastoral role played by ordained ministers in the church. For this too is what communion ecclesiology involves. Therefore, an important postconciliar challenge facing the church is the need to continue to work out the practical implications of this communion ecclesiology in all its dimensions. A balance must somehow be properly maintained between the need and right of lay

---

[8] Extraordinary Synod of Bishops, *A Message to the People of God* and *The Final Report* (Washington, D.C.: NCCB, 1985), II,C,#6.

[9] *Ibid.,* II, C, #1.

[10] Kasper, *Theology and Church* (London: SCM Press, 1989), p. 162.

people to get involved in the life and work of the church, and the need for pastoral supervision and accountability.[11] This topic was treated in a more indepth way in the following Synod.

D. The 1987 Synod on the Laity and John Paul II's 1988 Apostolic Exhortation *Christifideles Laici*

The 1987 Synod had as its topic the vocation and mission of the laity in the church and in the world today. The Synod discussions touched on a wide range of subjects relating to the laity and their role in both these spheres. In discussing what their role practically entails within the church, there was reference made to the parish. As part of their final series of propositions to the Holy Father a call for parish renewal was made (proposition #11). One sub-section of this proposition called for the fostering within the parish of "small basic or so-called 'living' communities, where the faithful can communicate the Word of God and express in service and love to one another; these communities are true expressions of ecclesial communion and centers of evangelization, in communion with their pastors."[12] This statement would later be directly quoted by John Paul II in his post-Synodal Apostolic Exhortation *Christifideles Laici* (#26).

Mention of basic ecclesial communities was also made briefly in the Synod's *Final Message to the People of God*. Of significance here is the reaffirmation of the concept of the parish being a community of communities. "We note with great satisfaction that the parish is becoming a dynamic community of communities, a centre where movements, basic ecclesial communities and other apostolic groups energize it and in turn are nourished."[13]

In an article commenting on the references made to BCCs in this particular Synod, Joseph Healey laments the fact that so few lines were devoted to the topic of BCCs in the Synod's two documents. He finds this somewhat surprising given the fact that there were 37 spoken and written interventions made on their behalf at the Synod, almost all of which were positive and supportive. He thus states: "while these statements on BCCs are very good, there is still the impression that BCCs are just one of many pastoral strategies along with various lay associations, Catholic Action movements and other apostolic groups. The uniqueness and the significance

---

[11] *Ibid.*, p. 163.

[12] The 1987 Synod on the Laity, "The Synod Propositions," *Origins* 17/29 (1987), p. 503.

[13] The 1987 Synod of Bishops, "Message to the People of God," Section #10, *Origins* 17/22 (1987), p. 388. Given the importance which the phrase "community of communities" has assumed in ecclesiological reflection on the nature of parish community, it is somewhat puzzling to note the absence of its mention in either of the two papal Apostolic Exhortations that followed the 1977 and 1987 Synods.

of Basic Christian Communities in the Church does not come through as forcefully in this final synodal statement as they did in the earlier interventions from the local churches."[14]

As noted earlier in this thesis, one of the great concerns that was expressed by this Synod was the need to devise criteria for use in formally discerning and recognizing lay groups and lay movements in the church. It was recognized that the laity have the right to form associations among themselves, but they also have the duty to be in true communion with the church. In responding to this concern, John Paul II in *ChL* #30 outlines what he calls "criteria of ecclesiality for lay groups." Although these criteria relate in general to lay groups, and not specifically to SCCs, they are valuable indicators nevertheless of what SCC "ecclesiality" constitutes.

These five criteria can be summarily listed as follows: (1) The call for lay members to manifest the fruits of holiness; (2) The responsibility of professing the Catholic faith and being in obedience to the Church's Magisterium; (3) The need to be in strong and authentic communion with the church and her legitimate pastors, especially the Pope and the local bishop; (4) Conformity to and participation in the Church's apostolic goals; and (5) A commitment to some form of social service to human society.[15] These criteria of *ChL* 30, as well as those of *Evangelii Nuntiandi* 58, can be effectively synthesized in order to provide us with some general criteria of SCC ecclesiality (this will follow in the next chapter).

E. John Paul II's 1990 Encyclical *Redemptoris Missio*

John Paul II's 1990 Encyclical *Redemptoris Missio* takes as its theme "the permanent validity of the church's missionary mandate." In reflecting on this mandate, John Paul II places great stress on the need for all Christians to play an active role in evangelization. He calls for a renewed commitment to evangelization on the part of all believers. Because of this stress, he sees this Encyclical as being very much in continuity with Vatican II's *Ad Gentes* document on missionary activity as well as Paul VI's *Evangelii Nuntiandi*.[16]

In chapter five of *Redemptoris Missio* John Paul II focuses on the "paths of mission." It is within the context of this chapter that he devotes an entire section (#51) to the subject of "ecclesial basic communities." This section states in part that:

---

[14] Joseph Healey, "BCCs in the 1987 Synod of Bishops' Documents," *AFER* 30 (1988), pp. 84-85.

[15] Cf. *Christifideles Laici* 30.

[16] Cf. *Redemptoris Missio* 2.

A rapidly growing phenomenon in the young churches—one sometimes fostered by the bishops and their Conferences as a pastoral priority—is that of "ecclesial basic communities" (also known by other names) which are proving to be good centers for Christian formation and missionary outreach. . . . These communities are a sign of vitality within the Church, an instrument of formation and evangelization, and a solid starting point for a new society based on a "civilization of love." These communities decentralize and organize the parish community, to which they always remain united. They take root in less privileged and rural areas, and become a leaven of Christian life, of care for the poor and neglected, and of commitment to the transformation of society.[17]

This section concludes with references to Paul VI's treatment of basic communities in EN #58, noting especially the need for these communities to be in communion with the church's pastors, and ends with a verbatim quote of what the 1985 Extraordinary Synod's *Final Report* had to say about them being a means for the construction of a more profound communion in the church (cf. section C above).

F. Other Papal Statements

In addition to the major documents examined above, the topic of BECs/SCCs has been featured in many other Papal statements. For instance, during John Paul's 1980 visit to Brazil, he issued a special "Message for Basic Christian Communities."[18] In the same year he also visited Kenya, and affirmed the work of establishing small Christian communities which was going on in much of Africa.[19] In 1986 the subject of BECs was again a focus in John Paul II's *Letter to the Brazilian Episcopal Conference*, which was issued in the wake of the Brazilian bishop's recent *Ad Limina* visit to Rome.[20]

There are other statements of a similar nature which could also be cited. But since much of the material in these statements repeats what is found in the major documents we have examined above, there is no

---

[17] *Ibid.,* #51.

[18] Cf. John Paul II, "Message for Basic Christian Communities," *Origins* 10/9 (1980), pp. 140-141.

[19] Cf. John Paul II, "The African Bishop's Challenge," *Origins* 29 (1980), pp. 28-30.

[20] Cf. John Paul II, *Letter to the Brazilian Episcopal Conference*, reprinted in the Appendix to Azevedo's *Basic Ecclesial Communities in Brazil*, pp. 257-267.

compelling reason to take a closer look at them. They are simply being mentioned here to give some idea of the overall extent of papal reflection on this topic.

G. Conclusion

What this survey of papal and synodal statements reveals is that the phenomenon of SCCs has indeed been officially recognized and encouraged by the Magisterium. From a pastoral or organizational point of view they are, therefore, considered to be an effective means of helping to physically decentralize the parish in order to help the church become a more localized reality. They are also recognized to be an instrument for deepening the communion that exists in the local church. In this task they can be seen as participating in the very sacramentality of the church, rendering the mystery of Christian communion more concrete and visible. The major pastoral concern which was often expressed is that they remain firmly attached to the local church and accountable to their legitimate pastors. This attachment and accountability is what ensures their fundamental ecclesiality.

Much more can be said about the significance of these papal and synodal statements, and the light they shed on our task at hand of evaluating the ecclesiological implications of the North American experience of SCCs. This will be done more thoroughly in the next and final chapter. The main purpose of this brief recounting of these papal and synodal statements in this chapter is to provide us with an overview of the development of magisterial teaching pertaining to this topic. Now that this review has been completed we are better able to synthesize some of these findings, integrate them with other insights about the nature of the parish which we have outlined in previous chapters, and utilize the result in our subsequent analysis and evaluation of parish-based SCCs.

CHAPTER SEVEN

An Evaluation of the Ecclesiality of North American Parish-Based SCCs

I. SCCs AND THE QUESTION OF ECCLESIALITY

A. Challenges Posed to an Evaluation of SCC Ecclesiality

As previously noted in our survey of the growth and development of small Christian communities around the world we took note of some of the ecclesiological reflection which their emergence has generated. An important issue which has arisen in many areas involves the question of how to assess and properly express the ecclesiality of BECs/SCCs. Aside from some attempts to ascribe an inordinate autonomy to BECs/SCCs, most advocates see them as being an integral part of the parish/local church.[1]

The need and desire for SCCs to be an integral part of the parish/local church is an ecclesiological stance which is generally characteristic of the North American experience in the area of parish-based SCCs.[2] At the outset of our study of the North American experience in this area we sought to explain how and why this type of parish-based SCC is different from similar kinds of small groups and communities which are affiliated with various lay movements, and from those which operate for all intents and purposes as purely private associations.[3]

After our analysis of the major programs/organizations which are promoting parish-based SCCs, we saw that despite the great influence of the Latin American experience on North American attitudes and SCC

---

[1] For evidence of this see the *Ecclesiological Reflection* sections of chapter four, wherein these issues are briefly looked at in the context of the Latin American and African experiences with BECs/SCCs (chapter four, part II, sections A § 3 and B § 3).

[2] See the *Ecclesiological Reflection* sections of chapter five, wherein the ecclesial orientation and self-understanding of seven North American SCC programs/organizations are examined (cf. Chapter five, part I, sections A-G).

[3] See chapter four, part III, section B, which outlines: "A Typological Classification of North American SCCs."

development, some important differences are to be found as well.[4] One major difference has to do with how SCCs pastorally function within the wider parish community. Due to pastoral necessity many Latin American (and African and Asian) parishes have needed to physically decentralize in order to benefit the apostolate. In such cases many of these BECs are really operating as quasi-parishes in the canonical sense of the term.[5] They are a locus for the celebration of the eucharist and other sacramental activity in addition to the other characteristic features of BEC life. In general, North American parishes are not yet faced with the same pastoral exigencies, and so the presence and possible reorganization effected by SCC development is of a different kind. We have surmised that this difference has a definite impact on how the issue of North American SCC ecclesiality is understood and addressed.

Because North American parish-based SCCs, for the most part, do not function liturgically as quasi-parishes in the canonical sense of the term, they would seem to have less of an immediate theological claim to ecclesial recognition or identity as a basic "unit" of the church. For instance, in reference to Latin American BECs Karl Rahner once stated that "when living Christian communities are formed by Christians themselves, when they possess and attain a certain structure, solidity and permanence, they have just as much right as a territorial parish to be recognized as a basic element of the Church, as a Church of the bishop's Church and of the whole Church."[6] In a similar vein T. Howland Sanks claims that BECs are:

> . . . analogous to other forms of church in historical
> experience. They are a community (*koinonia*) gathered in
> the name of Jesus (*memoria domini*) in service to one
> another and the rest of the world (*diakonia*). The fact that
> they are small in size, participatory in operation, and led
> by lay men and women makes for differences from some
> other forms of church, but these need not deny them the
> title of "church."[7]

---

[4] See chapter five, part IV, section C, which outlines in summary fashion: "Differences Between North American SCCs and Latin American BECs."

[5] The significance of the category of "quasi-parish," as a canonical term, was outlined in chapter two, part II, dealing with: "The Parish in the New Code of Canon Law."

[6] Karl Rahner, *The Shape of the Church to Come*, trans. Edward Quinn (New York: Seabury Press, 1974), p. 109.

[7] T. Howland Sanks, "Forms of Ecclesiality: The Analogical Church," *Theological Studies* 49 (1988), pp. 703-704.

Sanks understands BECs to be indicative of a broadening of the notion of what being church means on the local level. He refers to such groups as representing an "emerging form of ecclesiality" in the church today.[8]

Leaving aside the question of the theological merit of these kinds of explanations regarding BEC ecclesiality, it is obvious that such characterizations (i.e. that BECs are "a Church of the bishop's Church" [Rahner], or that they are deserving "the title of church" [Sanks]) seem out of place when applied to the North American situation of parish-based SCCs. Most of the North American SCC programs/organizations we have reviewed do not even make the question of whether or not they are "church" a real issue. They perceive SCCs to be of vital pastoral importance, but seem content to view the parish as being the basic unit of the local church. However, some advocates of parish-based SCCs invoke the language of "little churches" and "the church in miniature" to describe their ecclesial significance.[9] Even those programs/organizations which do not use this terminology frequently refer to SCCs as being a new "level" or "cell" of the parish church community.[10]

A question that arises therefore is how to evaluate and properly express the ecclesial character of North American parish-based SCCs. Is it ecclesiologically appropriate to speak of them as forming some kind of new level or cellular entity within the structure of the parish church? If so, do they warrant some kind of enhanced recognition as a unit of the church which is different from that accorded to other existing kinds of parish groups and associations? Seen in this light the North American experience seems to present a different set of challenges to how the issue of SCC ecclesiality is addressed and understood.

In many ways reflection on the ecclesiality of SCCs has certain parallels with the earlier *ecclesiola* debate about the theological nature and ecclesial identity of the parish community within the diocesan church.[11] Because the parish had been viewed for many years in mainly juridical-sociological terms, the question of its "theological" identity was a relatively new issue. As we recall, it was Wintersig who had described the parish as

---

[8] *Ibid.,* p. 696.

[9] These terms were used by Art Baranowski in his explanation of the significance of parish-based SCCs. Cf. Baranowski, *Creating Small Faith Communities* (Cincinatti: St. Anthony Messenger Press, 1988), pp. vii and 74 respectively.

[10] The idea of SCCs being "cells" of the parish is a prominent feature of both *SINE* and the St. Boniface Parish Cell System. The idea that SCCs somehow constitute a new "level" of the parish church was mentioned in the ecclesiological explanations of the NCCB's Secretariat for Hispanic Affairs, [Draft] *Guidelines for Small Church-Based Communities* (Washington, D.C: NCCB, 1991), pp. 49-50 and Baranowski's National Alliance of Parishes Restructuring Into Communities, *Creating Small Faith Communities*, p. 15.

[11] See chapter one, part III, section A, wherein "The Ecclesiola Debate" is outlined.

being a cell of the Body of Christ, a place where the church becomes concrete for ordinary Christians. Building on this insight, other liturgists such as Parsch were to describe the parish as being, in effect, the church in miniature. Echoing this phrase, Schurr used the term *ecclesiola* to describe the parish, claiming furthermore that it was just as much of a supernatural reality as was the universal church. This *ecclesiola* idea was not invoked to claim that the parish could exist in a self-sufficient manner, or that it was ecclesiastically complete in and of itself. It was really intended to invest the parish with a greater theological weight than it had heretofore been given.

Other theologians and canonists objected to this line of thinking on the grounds that it unduly exaggerated the theological nature and identity of the parish. Siemar argued that, for historical and theological reasons, it was the diocese which was the essential unit of the local church. He saw the *ecclesiola* thesis as being the result of fallacious reasoning. It is not true, he said, to simply claim that as regards the church what is true of the whole must be true of the parts. He also saw this claim as being dangerous because it could be misinterpreted as according a certain theoretical independence to the ecclesial role of the parish. Although this debate remained unresolved, it contributed important insights that later theologians would utilize in their efforts to articulate a more comprehensive theology of parish.[12] In a similar fashion the question today of SCC ecclesiality is a relatively new issue which is being discussed in the church because SCCs are a largely postconciliar phenomenon. They are precipitating a rethinking in how the pastoral structure and theology of parish is viewed. This reflection, as we have noted, has resulted in quite a variety of terms and images being invoked to explain their ecclesiality and the nature of the parish-SCC relationship. For instance, we have seen how some advocates state that SCCs function as an *ecclesiola* within the parish church.[13] Some prefer the image of cells. Others have described them as being a portion of the parish in the same way that the parish is a portion of the diocese and the diocese is a portion of the universal church.[14] Others still have invoked the idea that having an ecclesial consciousness or intention to be the church suffices as a basis for their ecclesiality.[15] Most of these explanations are not being

---

[12] We noted in particular the contributions of Yves Congar and Karl Rahner to the task of articulating a more comprehensive theology of parish in the years before Vatican II. See chapter one, part III, sections B § 1-2.

[13] Cf. Note #9 above.

[14] This was an explanation found in the NCCB's Secretariat for Hispanic Affairs [Draft] *Guidelines for Small Church-Based Communities*, pp. 49-50.

[15] Cf. David Kilian, "How to Develop Basic Christian Communities in Your Parish or Diocese," in *Basic Christian Communities: The United States Experience* (Chicago: National Federation of Priest's Councils, 1983), p. 14.

advanced to lay claim to any kind of autonomous ecclesial existence for SCCs, but to better promote their role and importance within the parish community.

Therefore, an initial challenge to our analysis of the question of SCC ecclesiality is that of determining how best to approach this issue given the diversity of ways and means with which the case for SCC ecclesiality has been presented by their advocates. It is helpful to recall that, despite this terminological diversity, we are really dealing with a similar basic phenomenon. Our analysis of North American parish-based SCCs has shown that there is a fundamental similarity in the size, setting, frequency, format, and ways in which SCCs meet and carry out their affairs.[16] This fact would seem to justify treating the North American experience in a generic fashion for the purposes of this evaluation of SCC ecclesiality.[17]

But before attempting such an evaluation what is needed at the outset is an explanation and clarification of what is meant by the idea of *ecclesiality*. Just what does ecclesiality comprise and entail in terms of Catholic ecclesiology? We need to briefly review what it means to be the church and identify criteria of some kind in order to provide a suitable foundation for our subsequent evaluation of this issue as it pertains to SCCs. Given this task, the process of evaluation for the remainder of this thesis will be organized around the answers to three fundamental questions: (1) What is ecclesiality? (2) How can criteria of ecclesiality be found which are applicable to an assessment of SCCs? (3) How can one best explain the ecclesiological nature of the parish-SCC relationship?

B. Defining Ecclesiality

1) Introduction

At the beginning of this thesis we made reference to how the word *ekklēsia* came to be used by the early Christians as a way of naming or designating their communities.[18] In addition to being used in reference to local churches, it had, or came to have, a universal connotation as well.[19] In

---

[16] See chapter five, part IV, section B, which summarizes the "General Characteristics of North American SCCs."

[17] For the sake of greater clarity a review of each of the North American SCC programs/organizations will be undertaken in connection with our analysis of how each of them embody the so-called "criteria of SCC ecclesiality." Once it has been established that they meet these criteria individually, then they will be treated generically for the purpose of evaluating how this type of parish-based SCC is impacting on our understanding of the vocation, mission, and theology of the parish church.

[18] See chapter one, part I, section B § 1 wherein the original meaning of *ekklēsia* is explained.

[19] Cf. Pontifical Biblical Commission, *Unity and Diversity in the Church* (Vatican City: Liberia Editrice Vaticana, 1991), p. 24.

regards to our study of the house churches of the Pauline mission we noted how they were not isolated islands but were established and nourished upon a wider ecclesial foundation.[20] The later Apostle's Creed gives further expression to the perceived nature of the entire Christian community when faith is professed in the "one, holy, catholic, and apostolic church."

From one perspective the adjective *ecclesial* can be seen therefore as simply referring to anything which is expressive of what it means to be the church of Christ. The word *ecclesiality*, which is a noun, can be seen in a similar light. It pertains to the quality or character of being the church. For someone to be able to undertake an ecclesial activity necessitates their being fully a part of, related to, in communion with, inserted in, and oriented towards this totality. However, before one can say what ecclesiality entails, one has to know what it means to be the church. This of course is a vast subject encompassing all of what the study of ecclesiology represents. Each of the documents of Vatican II in their own way address various aspects of what it means to be the Catholic church.

Our overview of *Lumen Gentium* revealed that the essential nature of the church can be expressed in a number of mutually related ways (i.e. Divine Mystery, Sacrament of Salvation, The Body of Christ, People of God).[21] These images are expressive of both the vertical and horizontal dimensions inherent in the *koinōnia* of the church. But not to be separated from the essential nature of the church is its visible structure. The visible structure and spiritual communion inherent in what it means to be the church together form one complex, interrelated reality (LG 8).

The structure of the church, involving its hierarchical organization, pastoral leadership, sacramental ministry, teaching authority, and so forth, is part of the concrete form in which the essence of the church is said to reside. These institutional features of ecclesial *koinōnia* are of crucial importance for helping to maintain the spiritual welfare, unity, and catholicity of the Body. Therefore, any definition of what ecclesiality entails is naturally grounded in the totality of what it means to be the church.

2) Ecclesiality in the Context of Ecumenism

If one is looking for further insight into the issue of what ecclesiality concretely entails, then an awareness of how the church defines itself in relation to the other Christian churches will shed more light on this topic. We mentioned earlier that in *Lumen Gentium* 8 it is asserted that the

---

[20] Cf. Robert Banks, *Paul's Idea of Community: The House Churches in Their Historical Setting* (Grand Rapids, Michigan: Eerdmans, 1980), p. 41.

[21] See chapter two, part I, section A § 2.

sole church of Christ "subsists in" the Roman Catholic church.[22] Also in LG 8, and found immediately following this assertion, is the statement that in regards to the Roman Catholic church "many elements of sanctification and of truth are found outside its visible confines." Commenting on the implications of these statements Aloys Grillmeier says that "it brings up the question of the 'ecclesiality' of the Churches and communities apart from the Catholic."[23]

Instead of employing the term *subsistit*, the original draft of Vatican II's Constitution on the Church had simply equated the Catholic church with the Body of Christ in an exclusive fashion.[24] But after hearing criticism of this point during the first Council session a redrafted version which appeared for debate the following year added the admission that "many elements of sanctification can be found outside its total structure."[25] However, now the question was asked about the consistency of maintaining on the one hand that the church of Christ was simply identical with the Roman Catholic church, and yet admitting that there were "ecclesial elements" to be found outside it.[26] The solution which was arrived at was to also change the original statement from saying that the church of Christ *is* the Catholic church, to saying that it *subsists in it*.[27]

According to Francis Sullivan, "practically all commentators have seen in this change of wording a significant opening toward the recognition of ecclesial reality in the non-Catholic world."[28] However, problems remain in understanding what *subsistit* exactly means in this context. It was never defined in any precise way.[29] What is clear though is the underlying idea

---

[22] This point was mentioned in passing in our overview of *Lumen Gentium* in chapter two, part I, section A § 2.

[23] Aloys Grillmeier, "The Mystery of the Church," in *Commentary on the Documents of Vatican II*, Vol. I, ed. Herbert Vorgrimler (New York: Herder, 1967), p. 150.

[24] "The Roman Catholic Church is the Mystical Body of Christ . . . and only the one that is Roman Catholic has the right to be called church." *Acta Synodalia Concilii Vaticani II*, 1/4, 15.

[25] For an overview of these developments during Vatican II, and for a more detailed discussion of what "subsists in" means, see Francis Sullivan, *The Church We Believe In* (New York/Mahwah: Paulist Press, 1988), pp. 23-33.

[26] Reference to what some of these ecclesial elements are finds expression in *Unitatis Redintegratio* 3: "Moreover some, even very many, of the most significant elements or endowments which together go to build up and give life to the Church herself can exist outside the visible boundaries of the Catholic Church: the written word of God; the life of grace; faith, hope and charity, along with the other interior gifts of the Holy Spirit and visible elements. All of these, which come from Christ and lead back to him, belong by right to the one Church of Christ."

[27] *Ibid.*, p. 24.

[28] *Ibid.*, p. 25.

[29] Sullivan notes that the Congregation for the Doctrine of the Faith, in response to Leonardo Boff's assertion that the church of Christ can be seen as subsisting in other Christian churches (a claim he makes in *Church, Charism and Power*), states that the Council "had chosen the word

196 \ *Small Christian Communities and the Parish*

this statement is trying to express, namely, that there is only one essential Body of Christ. It is theologically impossible for there to be two Mystical Bodies of Christ.[30] Thus, "we believe that the unity which Christ from the beginning endowed his church is something it cannot lose; it subsists in the Catholic Church, and we hope that it will continue to increase until the end of time" (UR 4).

Vatican II made the restoration of unity among all Christians one of its principal concerns (UR 1). The fact that there are divisions in the essential unity of the Body of Christ is a scandal to the world and a cause for remorse among all Christians. The work of the ecumenical movement in trying to restore unity was affirmed and said to be inspired by the Holy Spirit (UR 1). Thus, the church wanted to encourage ecumenical dialogue and cooperation among all churches and Christian communities. To help guide this process *Unitatis Redintegratio* articulates a number of specific "Catholic Principles on Ecumenism."[31]

In the context of explaining what these ecumenical principles are, UR 2 gives a succinct presentation of what it sees as the kind of unity which Christ gave to the church. This also makes for a good description of ecclesiality. Hence, the church is said to be a communion of faith, hope, and love, whose principle cause is the Holy Spirit. The church was given an essential unity by Christ. It is intended to be visibly united in the profession of the same faith, the celebration of the sacraments, and in the fraternal concord of the one people of God. In order to bring about and maintain such unity, Christ endowed his church with a threefold ministry of word, sacraments, and leadership. This threefold ministry was first entrusted to the apostles, with Peter at their head, and then continued in the college of bishops under the Pope.

The essential unity which Christ willed to his church was sadly ruptured over the course of the centuries as "serious dissentions appeared and large communities became separated from full communion with the Catholic Church" (UR 3). So how does the Roman Catholic church view its relationship to these separated brethren? One text which is worth quoting at length directly addresses this question, and in the process sheds further light on the question of ecclesiality and ecclesial elements. LG 15 states:

---

subsistit precisely to make it clear that there exists only one subsistence of the true Church, whereas outside of its visible structure there exist only elements of Church which, being elements of the church itself, tend and lead toward the Catholic Church (LG 8)." [*AAS* 71 (1985), pp. 758-759] Cited in Sullivan, *The Church We Believe In*, p. 29.

[30] Cf. Michael Schmaus, *The Church: Its Origin and Structure*, Vol. IV (London: Sheed and Ward, 1972), p. 83.

[31] This is in fact the title given to chapter one of UR, comprising sections 2-4.

> The Church knows that she is joined in many ways to the baptized who are honored by the name of Christian, but who do not however profess the Catholic faith in its entirety or have not preserved unity or communion under the successor of Peter. For there are many who hold sacred scripture in honor as a rule of faith and of life, who have a sincere religious zeal, who lovingly believe in God the Father Almighty and in Christ, the Son of God and the Saviour, who are sealed by baptism which unites them to Christ, and who indeed recognize and receive other sacraments in their own Churches or ecclesiastical communities. Many of them possess the episcopate, celebrate the holy Eucharist and cultivate devotion of the Virgin Mother of God. There is furthermore a sharing in prayer and spiritual benefits; these Christians are indeed in some real way joined to us in the Holy Spirit for, by his gifts and graces, his sanctifying power is also active in them and he has strengthened some of them even to the shedding of their blood.

The distinction referred to above in LG 15 between "Churches and ecclesiastical communities" is an important one. It is also touched upon in UR chapter three. The details of this analysis in UR chapter three need not detain us here. But what is important to recognize is that the church views the ecclesial status of Eastern/Western Churches in a manner different from that of Eastern/Western ecclesiastical communities. Generally speaking, the Catholic church has always recognized the ecclesiality of the so-called Eastern Churches.[32] In terms of the West, it is not specified which churches are considered to be "Churches" and which "ecclesial communities."[33] But commenting on this distinction Sullivan states that it "is based on what may be called a principle of 'eucharistic ecclesiology': i.e., there is not the full

---

[32] The Eastern Orthodox Churches should be kept distinct from the Eastern Catholic or Uniate Churches. These latter churches are treated in Vatican II's Decree on the Catholic Eastern Churches (*Orientalium Ecclesiarum*).

[33] According to Schmaus, the term "Churches" in the West would seem to refer to those churches which have preserved a form of eucharistic celebration and the episcopate (such as certain Lutheran and Anglican groups). But lacking such important ecclesial elements, the rest would seem to merit only the status of "ecclesial communities." Cf. Schmaus, *The Church: Its Origin and Structure*, p. 99.

reality of church where there is not the full reality of the Eucharist. However, the very term 'ecclesial' suggests a recognition that these communities have an ecclesial, that is, churchly character."[34]

Thus, far our analysis of the meaning of ecclesiality, as can be gleaned from some suggestive passages of Vatican II, has revealed a number of important criteria which can be utilized in our efforts to understand and assess the ecclesiality of small Christian communities. One can see that much of what we have just reviewed forms the broader ecclesiological foundation upon which Paul VI bases his instructions for the necessary ecclesial conditions which BECs/SCCs are to observe in *Evangelii Nuntiandi* 58, and the "criteria of ecclesiality for lay groups" which John Paul II articulated in *Christifideles Laici* 30.[35] Shortly, we will be synthesising these papal conditions and criteria to provide a comprehensive set of criteria of ecclesiality which are specifically applicable to BECs/SCCs. These we will then apply to an evaluation of North American SCCs.

3) Ecclesiality and Ecclesial Elements

By way of concluding this reflection on the essential meaning of ecclesiality a few preliminary comments should be made about the appropriateness of appealing to the idea of "ecclesial elements" as a justification for BEC/SCC ecclesial recognition. We have seen that in the above analysis, although the focus was on the ecumenical recognition of ecclesiality, it was clearly seen why the mere presence of some ecclesial elements, as important and as worthwhile as they may be, was not seen as being a sufficient cause to extend to some communities the designation "Churches." This is because they lacked certain other decisive elements such as eucharist, ordained ministry, and so forth.

It seems all the more remarkable therefore when one finds some Roman Catholics trying to argue, on the basis of Catholic ecclesiology, that BECs/SCCs which are not regular centers of eucharist, and which either lack or do not want the presence or input of ordained ministry, nonetheless can be equated with church in the same manner as a duly constituted parish community. This conclusion is said to be justified because these BECs/SCCs are said to embody other kinds of important ecclesial elements and furthermore they have a "consciousness" of being church. In essence, this

---

[34] Sullivan, *The Church We Believe In*, p. 32.

[35] See chapter six, sections A and D.

seems to be the argument we noted earlier that Leonardo Boff makes in his book *Ecclesiogenesis*.[36]

What Boff seeks to address in this section of his book is what he calls "the theological problem of the ecclesial character of the basic community."[37] Thus, his question: "Are these communities themselves actually church, or do they merely contain elements of church?"[38] Boff's review of the elements of church present in BECs (i.e. faith, worship, love, service) leads him to conclude that such elements are important conditions for ecclesiality. Not wanting to ascribe to BECs a totally independent ecclesial identity, he grounds their local/universal link to the wider church on the thinking that since these groups are serving "the cause" of the universal church, they are thus "in communion" with it and the parish/diocesan church.

The fact then that some of these BECs do not have ordained ministers attached to them or the eucharist celebrated there on a regular basis (due to clergy shortages) should, in Boff's opinion, not be held against them. "Are we now going to tell these people that they are not church, that they have certain 'ecclesial elements,' but that these do not actually constitute the essence of church?"[39] Boff's conclusion, reached after ruminating over Vatican II's idea of the church being the sacrament of salvation, is to claim that "the basic church community truly constitutes church-as-sacrament. . . . In their own particular way, the basic ecclesial communities incarnate this experience of salvation. Therefore, they are indeed authentic universal church become reality at the grassroots."[40]

Given our review of what Catholic ecclesiality entails, and our earlier analysis of the nature of the universal/local character of the church, it becomes apparent that Boff's analysis "from below" is lacking in balance. Earlier, we noted that Azevedo simply dismissed Boff's analysis because it was not consistent with a holistic understanding of Roman Catholic ecclesiology.[41] The fact that BECs/SCCs possess some worthwhile ecclesial elements and engage in certain beneficial activities does not suffice for these groups to be considered automatically as authentic "church" entities. Neither is the possessing of an "ecclesial consciousness" a sufficient reason.

---

[36] Cf. Leonardo Boff, *Ecclesiogenesis: The Base Communities Reinvent the Church*, trans. Robert Barr (Maryknoll, N.Y.: Orbis, 1986), pp. 10-22. His argument was referred to earlier in chapter four, part II, section A § 3.

[37] *Ibid.*, p. 13

[38] *Ibid.*, p. 11.

[39] *Ibid.*, p. 13.

[40] *Ibid.*, p. 22.

[41] Cf. Marcello de Carvalho Azevedo, *Basic Ecclesial Communities In Brazil* (Washington, D.C.: Georgetown University Press, 1987), p. 206.

It is unfortunate that Boff's argument seems to tarnish the legitimate use which can be made of ecclesial elements in building a case for a qualified and integrated understanding of SCC ecclesiality. It seems also to be indicative of a certain thinking that exists in some quarters of the church today; which in turn has made this question of BEC/SCC ecclesiality somewhat of a polemical issue.[42] Often times compounding this problem on the popular level is the poor or insufficient grasp which some lay people have of Roman Catholic ecclesiology. Hence some people lack a proper "ecclesial sense" of what it means to be the church in all its dimensions, and can thus fall prey to erroneous or incomplete depictions of what being the church entails both essentially and structurally.[43]

So in the light of what we have observed in this section to be the fundamental aspects of what Roman Catholic ecclesiality practically entails, let us turn now and see how these concepts underpin the papal criteria for BEC/SCC ecclesiality which have been recently enunciated.

II. SCCs AND THE CRITERIA OF ECCLESIALITY

A. Criteria Applicable to the Issue of SCC Ecclesiality

In our earlier exposition of the papal and synodal documents which have addressed the phenomenon of BECs/SCCs we have noted that in addition to praise for their work there have been a number of cautions sounded and conditions laid down to ensure they remain in genuine communion with the church.[44] These exhortations, conditions, and caveats can be seen as providing some criteria of ecclesiality which apply to BECs/SCCs.[45] What follows is a synthesized listing of these criteria which have been gleaned from the various documents we have reviewed (the most pertinent of which are the statements found in Paul VI's *Evangelii Nuntiandi* 58 and in John Paul II's *Christifideles Laici* 30).

The reason these criteria are being presented in a synthesized format is because many of the cautions/conditions/ criteria which are to be found in these documents often times repeat or reiterate what previous statements have said, or else offer similar remarks about a particular facet of BEC/SCC ecclesial existence. In listing these remarks in a thematic

---

[42] *Ibid.*, p. 13.

[43] This was the observation we noted that A. Kalonji Ntekesha made regarding the situation of some SCCs in Africa. Cf. *Les communautés de base: Foyers d'un Christianisme Africain?* (Rome: Gregorian University Doctoral dissertation, 1983), p. 45.

[44] See chapter six, sections A—F.

[45] In *Catechesi Tradendae* 47, John Paul II refers to BECs as being a good locus for catechetical activity, "insofar as they [BECs] correspond to the criteria laid down in the Apostolic Exhortation *Evangelii Nuntiandi*" (with a footnote to section 58).

manner it will also be possible to see more clearly the basic ecclesiological assumptions which underpin them (which we have explained in general in part I above). Once this list is compiled and commented upon (and it is by no means exhaustive of what BEC/SCC ecclesiality entails), it will be used in the next section to measure and evaluate the ecclesiality of the North American parish-based SCC programs and organizations we have featured earlier in chapter five. What we designate as "the papal criteria of SCC ecclesiality" can be listed as follows:

1) Remain attached to the local/universal church.

In *Evangelii Nuntiandi* 58 Paul VI stated that BECs will be a hope for the church to the extent that "they remain firmly attached to the local Church in which they are inserted, and to the universal Church, thus avoiding the very real danger of becoming isolated islands." Being firmly attached to the church is also described in EN 58 as necessitating "solidarity with her life" and "being nourished by her teaching."

Being attached to the local/universal church and in active solidarity with her is also said to preclude certain negative behaviour. Elsewhere in EN 58 the following attitudes and stances are said to be inappropriate and unacceptable: (1) fostering a spirit of radical opposition to the church; (2) systematic protest and hypercriticism of the church, (3) hostility towards the hierarchy; (4) seeing oneself or one's group as being free from institutional structures and accountability; (5) feigning a spirit of collaboration with the church; (6) acting in a sectarian manner; and (7) becoming ensnared by political polarization and fashionable ideologies.

Communities which engage in these types of activities and inculcate these types of attitudes are said to "wound the unity of the church." In reality they have cut themselves off from communion with the church and are BECs in a sociological sense only, for they are not functioning as "ecclesial" communities.

2) Maintain a sincere communion with the church's pastors.

EN 58 states that BECs must "maintain a sincere communion with the pastors whom the Lord gives to His Church." This means having an active sense of communion with the Pope, who is the visible center of unity for the universal church, and with one's local bishop, who is visible center of unity in the diocesan church.[46] For SCCs and lay groups specifically associated with the parish, communion with the church's pastors also entails communion with the parish priest. For "the parish is a community of faith and an organic community that is constituted by the ordained ministers and

---

[46] Cf. *Christifideles Laici* 30.

other Christians, in which the pastor—who represents the bishop—is the hierarchical bond with the entire particular church."[47]

John Paul II recognizes that there are many forms of lay associations and expressions of the lay apostolate which do not have the parish for their setting.[48] He says that Vatican II recognized the right of lay people to associate in a variety of ways and encouraged them to engage freely and fully in the mission of the church.[49] Nevertheless, it must be remembered that "it is a question of a freedom that is to be acknowledged and guaranteed by ecclesial authority and always and only to be exercised in Church communion. Consequently, the right of lay people to form groups is essentially in relation to the Church's life of communion and to her mission."[50]

Thus, all SCCs come under the legitimate pastoral authority of the church in some way, shape or form. They are pastorally accountable and answerable for their activities. This is all part of what good order and communion practically entails in the church. This takes nothing away from the fact that the laity can and do share in the leadership of such groups and exercise their own personal charisms in the process.[51] But a visible pastoral link with the ordained leadership of the church must be actively and sincerely maintained. In this way, according to John Paul II, the distinction between the exercise of the common priesthood of all the faithful and role of the ministerial priesthood is not forgotten or glossed over.[52]

3) Profess and teach the Catholic faith.

In outlining the criteria of lay group ecclesiality, John Paul II states that they have "the responsibility of professing the Catholic faith, embracing and proclaiming the truth about Christ, the Church and humanity, in obedience to the Church's Magisterium as the Church interprets it. For this

---

[47] *Ibid.*, #26.

[48] *Ibid.*

[49] *Apostolicam Actuositem* 18-19 outlines the variety of forms which "group apostolate" for laity can take. In AA 23-27 a call is made for all lay groups and associations to observe proper pastoral order in the church. "In the Church are to be found, in fact, very many apostolic enterprises owing their origin to the free choice of the laity and run at their own discretion. . . . But no enterprise must lay claim to the name *Catholic* if it has not the approval of legitimate pastoral authority" (AA 24).

[50] *Christifideles Laici* 29.

[51] As important as the exercise of charisms are to life of the church, in *ChL* 24 it is stated that "no charism dispenses a person from reference and submission to the *Pastors of the Church*. The Council clearly states: 'Judgment as to their [charisms'] genuineness and proper use belongs to those who preside over the Church, and to whose special competence it belongs, not indeed to extinguish the Spirit, but to test all things and hold fast to what is good (cf. 1 Thes 5:12 and 19-21)." [Vatican II reference is to *Lumen Gentium* 12].

[52] *Christifideles Laici* 23.

reason every association of the lay faithful must be a *forum* where the faith is proclaimed as well as taught in its total content."[53] This means that in the catechetical component of SCC meetings care must be taken that any presentation of the message of the Gospel, or doctrine of the church, be in conformity with the teaching of the Magisterium. This is because an SCC meeting is a semi-public or semi-official "forum" wherein the faith is being proclaimed and taught. Teachings and discussions undertaken in this context are not private matters.

4) *Conform to the church's apostolic goals.*

The church's essential apostolic goals were described by Vatican II as being "the evangelizing and sanctification of humanity and the Christian formation of people's conscience, so as to enable them to infuse the spirit of the Gospel into the various communities and spheres of life."[54] Commenting on this text John Paul II says that "from this perspective, everyone of the group forms of the lay faithful is asked to have a missionary zeal which will increase their effectiveness as participants in a re-evangelization."[55] Resembling this criterion is Paul VI's reference to BECs needing to "constantly grow in missionary consciousness, fervor, commitment, and zeal."[56] He also notes elsewhere in *Evangelii Nuntiandi* (#60) that "evangelization is for no one an individual and isolated act; it is deeply ecclesial."

5) *Avoid the spirit of elitism.*

Paul VI warned BECs not to think of themselves "as the sole beneficiaries or sole agents of evangelization—or even the only depositories of the Gospel—but, being aware that the Church is much more vast and diversified, accept the fact that this Church becomes incarnate in other ways than through themselves."[57] Elsewhere in EN 58, BECs are warned not to believe themselves to be "the only authentic Church of Christ." Hence, they are to avoid condemning other ecclesial communities or group apostolates for being supposedly inferior. Having such respect is an important dimension of what it means to maintain unity and catholicity in the church.

---

[53] *Ibid.*, #30.

[54] *Apostolicam Actuositatem* 20.

[55] *Christifideles Laici* 30.

[56] *Evangelii Nuntiandi* 58.

[57] *Ibid.*

6) Manifest the fruits of holiness.

Vatican II says that every Christian has a vocation to holiness, and so they need to witness to this call by bearing "the fruits of grace which the spirit produces" in their lives and thus continue to grow in the ways of Christian love and perfection.[58] Commenting on this text John Paul II says that "in this sense whatever association of the lay faithful there might be, it is always called to holiness in the Church, through fostering and promoting 'a more intimate unity between the everyday life of its members and their faith'."[59]

7) Manifest solidarity with and service to society.

In elaborating on a further criterion of ecclesiality John Paul II states that Christian service to society must be seen in the light of the church's overall social doctrine. "Therefore, associations of the lay faithful must become fruitful outlets for participation and solidarity in bringing about conditions that are more just and loving within society."[60] In *Redemptoris Missio* 51 the Pope recognizes that the social outreach work which is characteristic of many BECs/SCCs, makes them become "a leaven of Christian life, of care for the poor and neglected, and of transformation of society."

One can see in this listing of what we have called the papal criteria of ecclesiality certain parallels with the classic "marks" of the church (i.e. one, holy, catholic, and apostolic), and with Vatican II's ecclesiology of communion. This is not all that unexpected given the fact that these criteria seek to provide a solid ecclesial foundation for BECs and other lay groups to gauge their activity by, and to base their community life on.

There are perhaps other criteria which could be found and added to this list, for it is by no means exhaustive. But it does accurately reflect most of the major insights which recent popes themselves have articulated about the subject of the fundamental ecclesial criteria which are applicable to BECs and other lay groups. It may be noticed that there has been little mention yet of the activities which BECs/SCCs carry out (i.e. prayer, Scripture reflection, faith-sharing, catechesis, evangelization, ministry, and so forth). The ecclesial significance of these particular activities or elements, as they pertain to the parish-SCC relationship, will be addressed later. They are not included in the present list because they are activities which only have real meaning if these foundational criteria of ecclesiality

---

[58] Cf. *Lumen Gentium* 39-40.

[59] *Christifideles Laici* 30. Citation in the text is a reference to AA 19.

[60] *Ibid.*

are first in place. This will be explained more clearly in the analysis which follows.

B. A Preliminary Assessment of North American Parish-Based SCCs in the Light of the Papal Criteria of Ecclesiality

The time has come to make a preliminary assessment of the ecclesiality of the North American SCC programs/organizations we have highlighted in our study in chapter five. The question being asked is whether or not each of these groups meets all of the papal criteria of SCC ecclesiality we have outlined above. In the literature with which these groups have sought to explain their own programs and the nature of the parish/SCC relationship, it can be determined how they measure up. Do they comply with all of the criteria? Are some criteria perhaps being neglected or overlooked? The answers to these questions will not conclude our evaluation of SCC ecclesiality. But a positive assessment will provide us with a reason for being able to continue our investigation in good faith, confident that we are not dealing with an ecclesiologically flawed or problematic study group. Our final task will be to assess the ecclesial nature of the contribution which these types of SCCs are said to be making to the life and mission of the North American parish church, and to pass judgment on whether or not it is theologically appropriate to accord them an enhanced form of ecclesial recognition for this role.

This latter assessment will not require the same degree of individual scrutiny if it can be established that these groups are each fundamentally sound in their ecclesial outlook and orientation. Then we will be able to generalize about this study group as a whole based on the fact that they have similar basic characteristics (meeting size, setting, frequency, format, commitment to outreach, animation and leadership). But first to the task at hand. The groups will be reviewed in the same order with which we examined them in chapter five.

i) Hispanic Ministry Initiatives

As we saw earlier in our overview of Hispanic initiatives in the area of BEC development in the United States, this category does not represent one specific program/organization, but a variety of local/diocesan efforts that are underway and which are loosely coordinated and supported by the NCCB's Secretariat for Hispanic Affairs. We saw that there were some problems reported with a few individual Hispanic BECs who were not willing to be pastorally accountable for their activities because they thought of themselves as being private associations. But this was not a characteristic feature of the majority of Hispanic BECs.[61]

In the deliberations of Hispanic Ministry leaders during the various national *Encuentro* meetings a more representative picture of Hispanic BEC activity emerged. As a result of the input received at these *Encuentros* the Secretariat of Hispanic Affairs helped draft a set of BEC guidelines which gave expression to how their ecclesiality was perceived.[62] A study of the pastoral attitudes and ecclesiology inherent in these guidelines reveals that their perception of BEC ecclesiality is in essential harmony with the seven papal criteria of SCC ecclesiality we have identified (i.e. they are attached to the local/universal church, in sincere communion with the church's pastors, profess and teach the Catholic faith, conform to the church's apostolic goals, avoid the spirit of elitism, manifest the fruits of holiness, and manifest solidarity with and service to society).

The only problematic aspect in the ecclesiology articulated in these guidelines is the reference to the idea that "theologically, the BEC is a PORTION of the Church and, at the same time, the whole Church. It is a portion because it is small; the parish is a PORTION of the diocese, which is a PORTION of the Church in every country and of the universal Church. Each of these levels is the whole Church because it contains all the elements, in smaller or greater portion, of the Church of Jesus."[63] This claim is not being made to promote the idea of BEC autonomy in the church, but to explain the idea that they have a real ecclesial nature.

As we noted at the time this explanation is not sufficiently balanced or theologically nuanced. It seems reminiscent of the terminology and theories of Leonardo Boff. It is not ecclesiologically acceptable to speak in terms of being both "a portion" and also "the whole" of the church. One can certainly be a portion of the church, but it seems an exaggeration to say that one is therefore also the whole church.[64] What they are perhaps trying to

---

[61] Cf. Allan Deck, *Hispanic Ministry in the United States* (Rome: Gregorian University Doctoral Dissertation, 1988), p. 45.

[62] Cf. NCCB's Secretariat for Hispanic Affairs, [Draft] *Guidelines for Small Church-Based Communities* (Washington, D.C.: NCCB, 1991). These draft guidelines do not explicitly refer to the "ecclesiality" of BECs, but they do seek to address the question of their "ecclesiology" (p. 4).

[63] *Ibid.*, pp. 49-50.

[64] As we recall, in the *ecclesiola* debate about the theological nature and identity of the parish community vis à vis the diocese and the universal church, L. Siemar had argued that it was fallacious to reason that what was true of the whole, must be true of the parts (cf. chapter one, part III, section A). In a similar vein, we noted in our review of recent thinking about the local church that it was not the case that the diocese functions in a manner identical to that of the universal church. For instance, certain properties of the church such as indefectibility, the ability to define dogma, and so on, are accorded to the universal church as a whole, and not to the local churches (cf. chapter two, part I, section B § 1).

express is the idea that although BECs are only a small ecclesial group, they are nevertheless an authentic manifestation of the church. However, in lacking such nuance they run the risk of undermining their attachment to the local/universal church (criterion #1).

It should be remembered that the Secretariat's Guidelines exist only in draft form. This text could well be edited out by the time the final version is officially released. It seems unlikely that the NCCB would want to promote a vision of SCC ecclesiality which was at odds with the papal criteria we have identified. At any rate, given the pastoral soundness of the rest of these Guidelines, and their conformity with these criteria, one can confidently say that the major part of the Hispanic experience in BEC development in the United States is in full compliance with them.

ii) RENEW

We mentioned at the time of our examination of the *RENEW* program that it had sought to be a very Catholic and mainstream instrument of parish renewal. Nevertheless, it had initially run into some criticism from the NCCB Committee on Doctrine.[65] The NCCB Committee, while being on the whole very positive about its assessment of *RENEW*, also saw the need for greater doctrinal balance and completeness in the program. Initially, Kleissler and the other authors had not seen *RENEW* in terms of being a typical catechetical or adult education program. The focus was on helping to engender personal conversion as a part of what parish renewal entails.[66] But in response to the NCCB recommendations, changes were made to add more doctrinal material. As Kleissler now recognizes in terms of post-*RENEW* SCCs, there is actually an abundance of time with which to cover doctrinal material because these groups are ongoing.[67]

This development underscores the importance of the third criterion of SCC ecclesiality, which is the need to profess and teach the Catholic faith in its entirety. This is because an SCC becomes, in the words of John Paul II, "a forum where the faith is proclaimed." Catechesis and evangelization carried out in the name of the church are not just private affairs.

In terms of the rest of Kleissler's views regarding the ecclesiality of SCCs, they can be seen as being in full conformity with the papal criteria we have listed. He makes a point of stressing the need for SCCs to be in true

---

[65] Cf. NCCB Committee on Doctrine, "The *RENEW* Process: Strengths and Areas for Improvement," pp. 547-549.

[66] Cf. National Office of *RENEW*, *RENEW: An Overview* (New York/ Mahwah: Paulist Press, 1988), p. 23.

[67] Cf. Thomas Kleissler et al., *Small Christian Communities: A Vision of Hope* (New York/Mahwah: Paulist Press, 1991), p. 104.

communion with the pastor and the rest of the parish community. This is made abundantly clear in the following statement:

> Small Christian communities are part of the parish. Small community leaders are clear that as leaders they are a necessary link to the larger parish. Leaders know that these small communities exist in order to be at the service of the parish, the larger church, and the world. . . . [Thus,] small community leaders are always encouraged to have respect for the teaching authority of the church and to recognize that through the body of the entire church that truths are revealed. To be pastoral means to look to the church for guidance.[68]

Given the fact that *RENEW* has been successfully implemented in so many dioceses in North America, the bishops have welcomed the ecclesial role it envisions for post-*RENEW* SCCs. As we also noted at the time, one of the strengths or advantages of *RENEW*'s pastor-supervised approach to SCC formation is that the "process defuses fears about small faith-sharing groups becoming parallel or underground churches."[69] The same thing could be said of any SCC program which is implemented with the active support and supervision of the pastor.

iii) National Alliance of Parishes Restructuring Into Communities (NAPRC)

Art Baranowski and the NAPRC desire to see parishes become a "communion of small communities."[70] Thus, they believe in the value of parish restructuring efforts which actively promote SCC formation that is instigated and coordinated by the pastor in conjunction with the parish pastoral team. Group facilitators who are in regular contact with the parish priest and/or pastoral team are said to help ensure that communion with the broader parish community is effectively fostered and maintained. "This pastoral link—the parish facilitator—is what keeps a small group from self-absorption, insulation, isolation, elitism."[71]

A review of Baranowski's book *Creating Small Faith Communities* shows that in its essentials, his plan meets all of the papal criteria of ecclesiality for SCCs (i.e. remain attached to the local/universal church,

---

[68] *Ibid.,* p. 166.

[69] Deck, *Hispanic Ministry in the United States*, p. 47.

[70] Cf. Baranowski, *Creating Small Faith Communities*, p. 14.

[71] *Ibid.,* p. 17,

maintain a sincere communion with the church's pastors, profess and teach the Catholic faith, conform to the church's apostolic goals, avoid a spirit of elitism, manifest the fruits of holiness, and manifest solidarity with and service to society).

The only problematic area lies in his approach to "naming" what SCCs ecclesiologically represent. Given the idea that SCCs are an integral part of the parish pastoral structure, and derive their ecclesiality from this link, he does not hesitate in this context to refer to them as being "little churches" or "the church in miniature."[72] He also sees them as constituting a new ecclesial "level" in the parish/diocesan church structure.[73] His desire to refer to them in this manner is motivated in part by the thought that such a title would give the SCC concept more respectability, and help ensure pastoral acceptance by parishioners.[74] He also thinks that it helps people realize the distinctiveness of what SCCs represent. They are not simply another parish group.

We will leave for later an answer to this question of what kind of ecclesial recognition should be accorded parish-based SCCs. In our review of the papal and synodal documents relative to the issue of BECs/SCCs, we did not come across any endorsement of, or prohibition against, using such terminology per se. What was strenuously objected to was any inference that BECs/SCCs could enjoy some kind of ecclesial existence apart from proper pastoral supervision and full communion with the church and all that such communion practically entails. Thus, the insistence in the first and second criteria for SCCs to remain attached to the local/universal church and remain in sincere communion with one's pastors.

iv) St. Boniface Parish Cell System

As its name implies, the St. Boniface Parish Cell System sees SCCs functioning as cells of the parish church Body. Great stress is placed on their potential for evangelization and discipleship. In fact, Michael Eivers and Perry Vitale have referred to the home cell system as being an instrument of "*oikos* evangelization."[75] The pastor and pastoral team are seen as playing a major role in helping to coordinate SCCs and ensure their viability over the long haul. In addition to helping to pastor the cell leaders, the pastor has further direct input into the groups by means of the video teachings he prepares for the catechetical component of the cell meetings.

---

[72] *Ibid.*, p. vii and p. 74 respectively.

[73] *Ibid.*, p. 15.

[74] *Ibid.*, p. 74.

[75] Cf. Michael Eivers and Perry Vitale, *St. Boniface Cell System: Leaders' Training Manual* (Pembroke Pines, Florida: St. Boniface Catholic Church, 1991), p. 4.

A review of the *St. Boniface Parish Cell System: Leaders Training Manual* reveals that the vision of SCCs it promotes meets all of the papal criteria of ecclesiality. The cells are firmly rooted in the parish community and as such remain attached to the local/universal church. The cells are coordinated by leaders who are in ongoing contact and communion with the pastor. The cells strive to profess and teach the Catholic faith. They conform to the church's apostolic goals, especially with the stress placed on evangelization. They avoid the spirit of elitism. They manifest the fruits of holiness. They manifest solidarity with and service to society.

Therefore, there are no obvious problem areas. The only possible concern one might have is whether or not the cell groups are getting a sufficiently comprehensive and balanced presentation of church doctrine in the teaching component of the meetings. With such great stress placed on personal faith sharing and scripture reflection, there is always the possibility that such balance might be missing. However, as was the case with *RENEW*, this can be easily rectified if need be.

v) Systematic Integral New Evangelization (SINE)

If one were to single out one SCC program that best fulfilled the letter and spirit of all the papal criteria for ecclesiality, then the choice would have to be Alfonso Navarro's Systematic Integral New Evangelization approach. As we noted at the time of our review of SINE, its approach was defined somewhat in reaction to the perceived ecclesial failings inherent in some Latin American BEC undertakings. Thus, SINE stresses its fundamental parochial identity and nature:

> The communities are integrated into the parish, and they are an integral part of the parish; guided, supervised and nurtured by the parish. Thus, the parish becomes what it ought to be: a communion of communities. The communities belong to the parish and are directly accountable to it. The ecclesial unit is the parish. The small communities are merely cells of the local body, the parish. Small ecclesial communities can be neither autonomous nor can they exist in isolation from the parish.[76]

---

[76] SINE Team, *What Does SINE Really Mean?* (Rockford, Illinois: SINE National Office, n.d.), p. 5.

SINE also places a great stress on comprehensive catechesis, as well as on evangelization. Its approach to both these activities is indeed "systematic" and "integral."

vi) Buena Vista

Buena Vista is a national "grassroots" organization devoted to promoting and supporting the formation of small Christian communities in the parish church. It supports a variety of SCC efforts and programs. As such, it does not have its own specific Buena Vista plan. But it does have its own philosophy, which is articulated in its official "Mission Statement."[77] This Mission Statement reveals that the ecclesiality which Buena Vista sees as being inherent in SCCs, as well as the pastoral principles which should guide their development, indicate that it is in basic conformity with what we have called the papal criteria of SCC ecclesiality (i.e. remain attached to the local/universal church, be in communion with the church's pastors, profess and teach the Catholic faith, conform to the church's apostolic goals, avoid the spirit of elitism, manifest the fruits of holiness, and manifest solidarity with and service to society).

Buena Vista, being a broad-based umbrella organization, includes not only parishes which are restructuring or having their SCC development coordinated by the pastor/pastoral team, but also SCCs which have arisen due to individual lay initiative. As we have seen in our review of their Newsletter articles, sometimes these groups exist in relative pastoral isolation within the parish.[78]

The question that arises is whether or not these latter kinds of groups are in concrete communion with the pastors of the church, as outlined in criterion number two. They certainly consider themselves to be parish SCC groups, and we have noted that sometimes the lack of pastoral input is more the result of some priests not understanding or caring what they are trying to be all about. But due to this lack of active pastoral supervision and accountability, with no pastor-SCC liaison link in place, are these groups not operating simply as any other kind of private lay association? It is certainly not ecclesially inappropriate to be a private lay association. But given this situation should these kinds of SCCs be accorded the same kind of "recognition" as parochial groups or units of the church in the manner which someone like Baranowski is seeking for his SCCs (i.e. to refer to them as "little churches")?

---

[77] Cf. Buena Vista *Mission Statement*, printed in the context of an article by Peg Bisgrove, "Is There a Place for Me in This Church?" *Today's Parish* (Sept. 1990), p. 16.

[78] See the two quotes to this effect cited in chapter five, part I, section F § 3.

212 \ *Small Christian Communities and the Parish*

We will return to this question later for it is an important issue. But for now it must be stressed that this situation of isolation is not characteristic of most Buena Vista SCCs. Therefore, it should not skewer the fact that the vision is fundamentally sound and in accord with the papal criteria of SCC ecclesiality.

vii) North American Forum for Small Christian Communities

The North American Forum for Small Christian Communities (NAFSCC) is a national organization intended for the support of diocesan personnel involved in parish-based SCC promotion. Through its Newsletter and annual conferences it provides diocesan personnel with a forum in which to network together and reflect on SCC matters.[79] Although the NAFSCC was an outgrowth of *RENEW*, it is no longer directly affiliated with this particular SCC program. Like Buena Vista, it is supportive of any program that seeks to renew parishes by means of SCC development. As we mentioned in our review of the NAFSCC, it is indicative of the growing involvement of diocesan offices in the promotion of parish-based SCCs.

Given this fact of diocesan membership, it is difficult to evaluate the significance with which the NAFSCC's understanding of SCC ecclesiality is actually held in different dioceses. It can be assumed that diocesan offices, operating under the supervision of their local bishop, would not be likely to promote a vision of parish-based SCCs which was antithetical to our suggested papal criteria of SCC ecclesiality. But aside from Newsletter articles and a brief theological reflection, there is very little official written material available to scrutinize. Its *Mission Statement* does not present any major difficulties vis-à-vis these criteria.

As we referred to earlier, the only problematic aspect which was found in the theological reflection was the following statement: "Members of small Christian communities discern, develop, and commission the ministries of the individual and the community."[80] Commenting on this statement, we pointed out that it was probably meant to affirm the idea that members of SCCs use their personal gifts and talents in taking an active role in running the internal affairs of their groups. However, the "ministerial" language with which this idea is expressed, without any reference to the role of pastor or bishop mentioned in connection with the process of discernment and commissioning, could lead one to the conclusion that SCCs can usurp or disregard the role of the ordained ministers. This would be a

---

[79] Cf. NAFSCC, *NAFSCC Mission Statement and History* (Crookston, Minnesota: NAFSCC Office, 1991), p. 94.

[80] Cited by Rosemary Blueher in "A Response to a Paradigm Shift: The North America Forum for Small Christian Communities," *PACE* 21 (1991), p. 116.

misinterpretation of the "charisms" lay people can and should be exercising in such groups.

This is not mere quibbling over a minor point. This pertains to the very essence of what the ecclesiality of SCCs is said to entail in criterion number two. This is not to say that SCCs need to consult and get the approval of their pastor for every little matter. But surely as a minimum, the pastor needs to know who the group's leader or facilitator is, have some form of regular contact with him or her, have an awareness of what sources the group uses in its teaching/discussion time, and approve of any major ministerial activities which the group desires to undertake in the name of the church. Groups which feel threatened or insulted by the prospect of such an arrangement are not exhibiting one of the fundamental characteristics of ecclesiality (i.e. the realization of effective and sincere communion with the pastors of the church). By way of conclusion it can be seen how the North American experience of parish-based SCCs, as a whole, is in essential harmony with, and fulfilment of, what we have called the seven papal criteria of ecclesiality (i.e. remain attached to the local/universal church, be in sincere communion with the church's pastors, profess and teach the Catholic faith, conform to the church's apostolic goals, avoid the spirit of elitism, manifest the fruits of holiness, and manifest solidarity with and service to society).

This means at the very least that these types of North American SCCs generally pose no danger to the church. They can be recognized as being fundamentally sound entities within the church which enjoy a certain "ecclesiality" to the extent that they possess and express those ecclesial qualities we have delineated on the basis of papal teaching about small Christian community as "criteria for ecclesiality." Having established this fact, it is now possible to move onto the final stage in our evaluation and attempt to see how the parish-SCC relationship can best be understood and expressed from an ecclesiological point of view.

III. THE PARISH/SCC RELATIONSHIP: AN ECCLESIOLOGICAL ASSESSMENT

A. The History and Theology of Parish: Context for Understanding the Ecclesial Role of SCCs.

In chapter one of this thesis we surveyed some of the major developments in the life of the early church which helped to shape its theological understanding of itself and its organizational structure.[81] We saw how Christian *koinōnia,* and the Kingdom of God ethos, became embodied and expressed in the idea of *ekklēsia.* These early communities

---

[81] See chapter one, parts I and II.

214 \ *Small Christian Communities and the Parish*

also saw themselves as being a type of *paroikía*—a group of foreigners living in the midst of a world which is not their ultimate homeland. The Christian community is thus said to exist both as an *ekklēsia* (relative to God), and as a *paroikía* (relative to the world).[82] In conjunction with this countercultural perception of itself, we have noted that many SCC advocates see a need in the church today to recover this "contrast society" sense of what it means to be a church community.[83]

In our brief look at the emergence of the early church we also took particular note of the phenomenon of the house churches, focusing on those of the Pauline mission. These house churches served as important bases for liturgy, catechesis, and fellowship in the local Christian community. We observed how many advocates of SCCs see in the house church phenomenon an experience of a more comprehensive and supportive environment for Christian community, one which they seek to emulate in some way today.[84] They speak of SCCs as being a new locus or base for fellowship and ministry in the parish church.

With the development of a more regularized church order in post-apostolic times, the local church came to have a definite episcopal identity in terms of its leadership and pastoral organization. The bishops were seen to be carrying on the role and ministry of the apostles. These communities would gather with their bishop for the celebration of eucharist, baptism, and other ecclesial activities. There were also presbyters and deacons who would assist in ministry to the community.[85]

With the spread of Christianity into the countryside it became increasingly difficult to have the Christians of a given locale physically gather every Sunday with their bishop for eucharist. There was a similar problem in the bigger cities. We saw that in the case of Rome, many titular churches existed which served as a locus for pastoral ministry and liturgical celebration. The presbyters and deacons would go to these titular churches, and to outlying places in rural settings, in order to carry out the ministry of the church. This decentralization of pastoral ministry did not seem to

---

[82] Cf. K.L. and M.L. Schmidt, "*Pároikos/Paroikía/Paroikéō*" in *Theological Dictionary of the New Testament*, pp. 788-790.

[83] Cf. Baranowski, *Creating Small Faith Communities*, p. 4. The nature and extent of North American cultural challenges affecting Christian belief and faith practice were briefly outlined in chapter three, part II, sections A and B.

[84] Cf. 1991 International Consultation on Basic Christian Communities (University of Notre Dame), *Final Statement*, p. 1.

[85] Cf. Raymond E. Brown, "Church in the New Testament," in *The New Jerome Biblical Commentary*, eds. Raymond E. Brown et al. (London: Geoffrey Chapman, 1989), pp. 1339-1346.

adversely affect the unity of the local church.[86] The practice of permanently stationing priests in outlying rural churches of the local community did not seem to begin until the fourth or fifth century. This practice is said to mark the early beginnings of the diocesan "parish system" as we know it today. In this sense then the parish, as Yves Congar described it, "was born of pastoral convenience."[87] But this also means that pastoral need has been an important criterion which has guided the structural development of church organization. It was just such a need that was behind Trent's attempts to reorganize the parish system for the church in that era. For similar reasons a pastoral "need" is said to be spurring the growth and development of BECs/SCCs in the parish church of today.[88] They decentralize the parish for the sake of the apostolate, in a manner similar to how and why the early parishes decentralized the diocesan church.

Given the pastoral context in which the parish arose as an institution of the local church, its origin is said to be of a *de jure humano* nature, not *de jure divino*. The same thing is said today about SCCs. No one is claiming SCCs are an ecclesial structure mandated by divine revelation. Yet recognizing this fact does not mean that neither the parish nor the SCC has no claim to a theological identity. It simply means that they both derive their ecclesiality from being rooted in the diocesan church, which is the fundamental ecclesiological "unit" of the universal church.[89]

If the diocese can be described as a means for making the mystery and communion of the universal church visible and concrete in a given locale, theologians have come to recognize that in an analogous way this is the role the parish plays vis-à-vis the diocese.[90] In our review of what Vatican II had to say about the ecclesiality of the parish community, much of this thinking finds expression. *Lumen Gentium* 26 states that "in these communities, though they may often be small and poor, or existing in the diaspora, Christ is present through whose power and influence the One, Holy, Catholic, and Apostolic Church is constituted." LG 28 mentions that the ministry of parish priests helps "render the universal Church visible in their locality and contributes efficaciously towards building up the whole

---

[86] Cf. W. Croce, "A History of the Parish," in *The Parish: From Theology to Practice*, ed. Hugo Rahner (Westminster, Maryland, The Newman Press), p. 11.

[87] Cf. Yves Congar, "Mission de la Paroisse," in *Structures sociale et pastorale paroissiale* (Paris: Union des Oevres Catholiques de France, 1949), p. 51.

[88] We have noted Paul VI's observation in EN 58 that BECs/SCCs "spring from the need to live the Church's life more intensely, or from a desire and quest for a more human dimension such as larger ecclesial communities can only offer with difficulty."

[89] The universal/local nature of the church was outlined in chapter two, part I, section B § 1.

[90] Cf. Karl Rahner, "Theology of Parish," pp. 28-29.

body of Christ."[91] In a similar vein the SCC can be described as a grouping which helps to make the parish church more visible, thus helping to build up the parochial Body of Christ.

Another similarity between Vatican II's description of the parish, and SCC depictions of themselves, can be found in some of the other images of parish which are used in the documents. In *Apostolicam Actuositatem* 10 the parish is said to be an "ecclesial family," a "kind of cell" of the diocese, and as a place which provides an outstanding field for the exercise of the apostolate of the laity. We have seen how some SCCs refer to themselves as "cells" of the parish community, and consider themselves to be special places for the exercise of lay ministry in the parish.

Elsewhere in Vatican II mention of the parish is often made in connection with the celebration of the eucharist. In *Presbyterorum Ordinis* 5 the celebration of parish eucharist is said to be the "center of the assembly of the faithful" and a means by which the faithful are helped to be more "fully incorporated in the Body of Christ." The parish then is a eucharistic community of the local church. Hence it can be considered from a theological point of view as a unit or "church" of the diocesan church.[92]

Given the importance which eucharist plays in the overall understanding of what makes a parish a "church" of the diocese, it becomes evident that North American parish-based SCCs would seem to be lacking a vital element to the extent that North American SCCs do not usually have a eucharistic celebration which is proper to their own particular group and setting. Does not this lack of eucharist make it inappropriate for these types of SCCs to describe themselves as "little churches" of the parish?[93]

The answer to this question would seem to be yes. It seems inappropriate to refer to North American parish-based SCCs as "churches" given the specific connotation this term has in Roman Catholic ecclesiology. But this is not to imply that SCCs and parish eucharist are totally unrelated.[94] And it still leaves unresolved the question of whether or not

---

[91] In a similar vein SC 42 instructs bishops to establish parishes where needed so that "they may represent the visible church constituted throughout the world."

[92] Cf. Karl Rahner, "Theology of Parish," pp. 28-29.

[93] There is a certain parallel here with how we saw earlier in this chapter the principle of "eucharistic ecclesiology" being used in the context of ecumenical analysis. Commenting on the significance of UR 22, Francis Sullivan concluded that "there is not the full reality of the church where there is not the full reality of the eucharist." Cf. *The Church We Believe In*, p. 32.

[94] For instance, John C. Haughey makes the argument that parish eucharist and SCCs are vitally interrelated. He says that the presence of SCCs in North American parishes is helping to lend authenticity and credibility to the claim that the eucharist makes the church. SCCs, as embodiments of Christian *communio*, are helping the whole parish realize and live out the "praxis" of what eucharist entails better than parishes wherein an authentic experience of community is lacking. Cf. "The Eucharist and Intentional Communities," in *Alternative Futures for Worship, Vol. 3*. Ed.

SCCs qualify for consideration as newly identifiable units of the church from an ecclesiological point of view. For instance, the family unit is often referred to as being a kind of "domestic church" even though it is not a usual locus for the celebration of the eucharist (LG 11). Before addressing this question, and the related question of what kind of ecclesial recognition North American SCCs should be accorded on the parish scene, it is first necessary to examine more carefully what their role fully encompasses (this will follow immediately in the next section).

North American parish-based SCCs are obviously different then from Pauline house churches and from contemporary quasi-parishes in the sense of lacking a celebration of the eucharist which is proper to their own gathering. As a result, it is true that they will never have the same kind of formal ecclesiological status as that accorded the parish community as a whole. This may appear to some as a limitation, but it is also a pastoral safeguard.[95] This also means that it is somewhat inaccurate to refer to SCCs as being a portion or level of the parish church in the same way that a parish is a portion of the diocesan church. The analogy does not fully hold. The difference between the ecclesiality of the parish and that of the SCC is not simply a matter of degree, but also of kind (i.e. the sacraments are not celebrated in SCCs). Therefore, caution is needed if one is to avoid describing the ecclesiality of SCCs in too facile a manner.

However, our analysis in this section has revealed that the parish and the SCC share many similar pastoral aims. Our review of the history and theology of the parish provides us with the necessary point of departure and context for understanding the ecclesiological nature of the parish-SCC relationship. What is needed next is a more careful look at how the SCC is helping in the vocation of the parish church.

Bernard Lee (Collegeville, Minnesota: The Liturgical Press, 1987), pp. 49-84.

In a similar vein, Thomas Sweetser speculates that the celebration of parish eucharist would be possibly enhanced if the liturgy was restructured to take into account the participation of SCCs. He envisions SCCs meeting together on Sunday mornings at the church and incorporating their meetings into the liturgy of the Word segment of the Eucharist. This would lead to a prolonged celebration at one of the parish's scheduled Masses. People not participating in an SCC would be directed to attend a more "regular" Mass. Regardless of how one views the merits of such a proposal, Sweetser's speculation is indicative how SCCs can be seen as revitalizing parish eucharist. Cf. "The Parish of the Future: Beyond Programs," *America* (March 10, 1990), pp. 238-240.

[95] Many advocates of parish-based small communities welcome this so-called limitation to the understanding of SCC ecclesiality. They see the emphasis on eucharist in Roman Catholic ecclesiology as being pastorally beneficial in helping to prevent SCCs from lapsing into elitism, exclusivity, and isolation in the church. Cf. Raymond Collins, "Small Groups: An Experience of Church," *Louvain Studies* 13 (1988), pp. 133-134.

B. The Contribution of SCCs to the Vocation and Mission of the Parish Community

1) The Ecclesial Elements/Activities of SCCs Re-examined

Given what we know of the pastoral purpose and theological identity of the parish community, let us now turn and assess the manner in which SCCs can be said to be contributing to, and sharing in, its vocation and mission in the local church. This evaluation needs to be focused first on the characteristics of SCC meetings and activities. Because there was an essential similarity in the organizational traits and activities of North American SCCs, we are justified in treating them in a generic manner for the purpose of this assessment.[96] By reviewing these activities it will be made clearer exactly what aspects of parish life SCCs are rendering more visible and how this is contributing to the building up of the local Body of Christ. These SCC activities are listed here as follows:

i) Communal Prayer

SCCs are gatherings in which communal prayer occurs. Although they are not prayer meetings, in that this is not the central or exclusive activity of the group, the fact that some worship and intercession takes place is important. This prayer is not of an official liturgical kind as that found in the context of parish celebrations. Yet it is nonetheless an expression of *leitourgia* in the church.[97] It does not have simply a private character. It is prayer which is undertaken as a cell group of the parish. This regular prayer thus takes on public significance for the group itself and for the wider parish community.

The fact that SCCs are an important locus for prayer in the church was recognized and affirmed by Paul VI in *Evangelii Nuntiandi* 58, when he stated that "such communities can quite simply be in their own way an extension on the spiritual and religious level [of] worship, deepening of faith, fraternal charity, prayer. . . . " Because of such activity, Christ is present to the group in a special way, for "wherever two or three are gathered in my name, I am there" (Mt 18:20).

ii) Scripture Reflection

Most SCCs incorporate a reading from Scripture and a time of reflection/discussion on its meaning and significance. "They gather people

---

[96] See chapter five, part I, sections A § 2—G § 2, wherein the "Characteristics" of North American SCCs are outlined. These characteristics are summarized in part IV, section B of this same chapter.

[97] This is according to Bernard Lee and Michael Cowan, *Dangerous Memories: House Churches and Our American Story* (Kansas City: Sheed and Ward, 1986), p. 27.

for the purpose of listening to and meditating on the Word."[98] Although SCCs are not Bible studies, in that this is not the exclusive activity of the group, the fact that God's Word is a prominent feature of the gathering mirrors the prominence Scripture has in parish liturgies and in the overall life of the church. Thus, they are a place where the Gospel *kerygma* is proclaimed and meditated upon. In this process they are helping people deepen their awareness of biblical spirituality.[99] Furthermore, reflection on the Scripture in BECs/SCCs is seen as helping the faithful to "communicate the Word of God and express it in service and love to one another."[100]

iii) Faith Sharing

The personal sharing of life experiences in the light of faith that occurs during an SCC meeting is usually a major activity of the group. Whether this is done in the context of the Scripture reflection period, or as a separate activity, it contributes immensely to the support and encouragement members feel they receive in their quest to live out the Gospel as disciples of Christ. This kind of sharing is something which is not possible to do with the wider parish community as a whole. It is also not a common feature of regular parish life. But this SCC activity, along with all the others, helps create a stronger bond of *koinonia* in the group.

In experiencing *koinonia* at this level, many SCC members report that it enhances the *koinonia* they feel with the wider parish church as a whole. As John Paul II recognizes: "within them, the individual Christian experiences community and therefore senses that he or she is playing an active role and is encouraged to share in the common task."[101] SCCs provide people then with a more personally focused sense of ecclesial community. As Paul VI recognized, "they spring from the need to live the Church's life more intensely, or from a quest for a more human dimension such as larger ecclesial communities can only offer with difficulty" (EN 58). In this way SCCs are indeed "a means for the construction of a more profound communion" in the church.[102]

---

[98] *Evangelii Nuntiandi* 58.

[99] The idea that SCCs help deepen biblical spirituality was a point singled out for special attention in the statement made by the 1991 International Consultation on Basic Christian Communities (University of Notre Dame). Cf. *Final Statement*, p. 4.

[100] *Christifideles Laici* 26.

[101] *Redemptoris Missio* 51.

[102] Cf. The 1985 Extraordinary Synod, *The Final Report*, part II, section C § 6. Repeated by John Paul II in *Redemptoris Missio* 51.

iv) Evangelization and Catechesis

SCCs are evangelistic by nature. This point was repeatedly stressed in the comments made by SCC program organizers. The work of evangelization is reflected in all of its activities. In this connection, *katechesis* is an important dimension of what it means to evangelize. We have noted that many SCCs incorporate a teaching or catechetical component into their meetings. This can take many forms. The result of this activity is that continued growth in knowledge about the faith occurs. This all contributes in a very beneficial way to the promotion of ongoing Christian formation.

For these reasons Paul VI referred to these communities as a special "place of evangelization" (EN 58). John Paul II referred to them as a "force for evangelization" and as "good centers for Christian formation and missionary outreach."[103] John Paul II also said they were a suitable locus for catechesis.[104] These activities are thus helping the parish community as a whole realize its apostolic goals and mission in these areas.

v) Outreach/Service

All SCCs stress the crucial importance of outreach or ministry beyond the confines of the group. Regardless of the form this takes, and whether or not it is directly related to parish efforts, it is being undertaken for the sake of the Gospel. It is thus promoting a key aspect of what it means to be a Christian and to be a member of a parish. This outreach or service is a concrete expression of *diakonia* in the church and for the world. The laity are using their charisms in a special manner in this task. Because of this service, SCCs are able to "become a leaven of Christian life . . . and a source of new ministries" in the parish.[105]

It can be seen then that SCCs, in their own way, partake of many of the same activities as does the parish as a whole. These activities in turn help promote *leitourgia, koinonia, katechesis, diakonia,* and the proclamation of the *kerygma*; all of which are important aspects of what it means to be the church. It can said then that, in a manner dependent on the parish, SCCs embody ecclesial elements. But what is important to note is not just the question of *what* they embody, but *how* they convey it in relation to the parish community. Understanding the "how" sheds more light on the ecclesiological nature of the parish/SCC relationship.

---

[103] Cf. *Redemptoris Missio* 51.

[104] Cf. *Catechesi Tradendae* 47.

[105] John Paul II, *Redemptoris Missio* 51.

In one sense SCCs can be said to be helping to mediate these aspects of being the church. They are ecclesial "mediating structures" in the parish community. In their book *Dangerous Memories: House Churches and Our American Story,* Lee and Cowan explain what is meant by a mediating structure. They borrow this insight from sociology, wherein mediating structures are described as "those institutions standing between the individual in his private life and the large institutions of public life."[106] They see this insight as being applicable to the parish/SCC relationship.[107] From a sociological point of view, this is because many parishes have become in fact large institutions in the church today. There is a need in the church for a smaller intermediary structure wherein the private faith life of the individual or family can be better supported and integrated into the public ecclesial life of the parish community.

This idea of SCCs functioning as a mediating structure in the parish community is a very good way of explaining their pastoral role in the church. Clearly, in functioning in this role SCCs are not only fulfilling a sociological purpose but an ecclesial purpose as well. They are a structural response to the pastoral exigencies of our day. They are providing a new locus within the parish where ministry and community can occur. Although the vocation and mission of the parish is not directly or exclusively dependent on SCCs, their presence contributes to this vocation and mission. Thus, SCCs not only have an ecclesiality which is proper to their own groups, but they strengthen the ecclesiality of the parish community as well.

2) SCCs as Instruments of Subsidiarity, Decentralization, and Lay Co-responsibility in the Parish Church

Besides the concept of mediating structures, another means by which the parish/SCC relationship has been expressed is in reference to the principles of subsidiarity, decentralization, and lay co-responsibility. To begin with, the general concept of subsidiarity is a relatively simple one. Avery Dulles defines its basic meaning as follows: "higher authority is to be seen as a *subsidium* (support) for the lower when the latter is incapable of handling a given problem by its own resources."[108] However simple this principle may appear to be in the abstract, determining how it applies to the functioning of the church is a complex matter.

---

[106] Peter Berger and John Neuhaus, *To Empower People: The Role of Mediating Structures in Public Policy* (Washington, D.C.: American Enterprise Institute for Public Policy Research, 1977), p. 2.

[107] Cf. Lee and Cowan, *Dangerous Memories*, p. 19.

[108] Dulles, "The Reception of Vatican II at the Extraordinary Synod of 1985," in *The Reception of Vatican II*, eds. G. Albergio et al. (Washington, D.C.: Catholic University of America, 1987), p. 360.

Vatican II affirmed a qualified understanding of subsidiarity when it described the nature of the rights and responsibilities of local bishops vis-à-vis the Holy See (CD 8). This principle is also echoed in the understanding of a priest's rights and duties vis-à-vis his local bishop (PO 6). But this principle seems to be restricted to making judgments regarding pastoral matters. It does not apply to doctrinal issues. In this latter case the proper ecclesiastical competence to judge and formulate doctrine is a matter for the magisterium of the universal church to decide.[109]

Since Vatican II the principle of subsidiarity has been discussed further at several subsequent Synods. At the 1969 Extraordinary Synod of bishops, in an interview given on its eve, Cardinal Julius Döpfner of Munich gave a carefully worded formulation of how he saw this principle as applying to the whole church:

> Subsidiarity—an important principle of Christian social doctrine, which holds equally for the Church—signifies that the higher instances and organisms must respect the capacities, competencies, and tasks of individuals and communities, in theory and in practice. In this way a healthy and vigorous life, adapted to different situations, can develop. This holds also for the Church as a whole, for the pope and his curia, for the bishop and his ministers, for the pastor and the government of his parish. On this point much remains to be done on all levels.[110]

At the 1985 Extraordinary Synod the principle of subsidiarity was once again a topic of discussion.[111] It was recognized as an important and helpful ecclesiological principle, but one which was problematic as well. For instance, one discussion group cautioned against trying to extend the conditions under which this principle can be invoked by bishops on the grounds that may imply that local churches could be more independent from the primacy of Rome. Another group felt it was inappropriate to extend it on the grounds that it did not really apply to the sacramental or liturgical life of the church. Dulles quotes Cardinal Hamer as saying in an plenary meeting immediately before the Synod that subsidiarity does not really apply at all

---

[109] *Ibid.,* p. 361.

[110] Cardinal Julius Döpfner, Interview in *La Documentation Catholique* 66/1546 (Sept. 7, 1969), p. 789.

[111] Cf. Dulles, "The Reception of Vatican II at the Extraordinary Synod of 1985," p. 361.

to the church "because the universal church is not a mere support (*subsidium*) for the particular church."[112]

Reflecting the general trend of the bishops' discussions, the *Final Report* of the 1985 Synod recommended further study in order to determine how and to what degree the principle of subsidiarity should be understood as applying to the actual functioning of the church.[113] In response to this request, John Paul II noted that this issue was indeed a complex one and that its manifold implications needed to be studied more thoroughly. Dulles says that "in his personal reflections the pope seemed to suggest that, because of the unique nature of the ecclesial society, the principle of subsidiarity as generally understood could not be applied to the Church without being modified."[114]

Given the fact that the question of subsidiarity in pastoral practice has not been fully resolved, it may seem somewhat premature to be applying the principle of subsidiarity to the relationship of SCCs to the parish. Yet, some SCC advocates appeal to this principle in a non-juridical or non-technical way to explain in general terms how they see the nature of the parish-SCC relationship. For instance, in an African context, this is the argument that Eugène Lapointe makes in his assessment of the ecclesiological significance of SCCs in rural parishes in Lesotho.[115] Lapointe is really using the idea of subsidiarity as a way of describing how SCCs have taken over certain functions of the parish church at the village or outstation level. This in turn is a consequence of parish decentralization. Furthermore, he sees subsidiarity as being intimately linked to the principle of lay co-responsibility for the church.

But in Lapointe's description of SCCs in Lesotho it becomes clear that they are really functioning as quasi-parishes. They are said to be responsible for hosting Sunday liturgies, organizing catechetical instruction in the outstation school, sacramental preparation, social activities, and so on. Many of the day-to-day pastoral decisions affecting the life of the outstation are undertaken by the laity who are on the outstation/SCC council. They do so in communion with and under the ultimate direction of the pastor. However, since the pastor is not always on the scene or easily consulted, many practical decisions on various matters are carried out by the laity. Lapointe believes this to be an example of subsidiarity in action, and a

---

[112] *Ibid.*, p. 362.

[113] Cf. 1985 Synod, *Final Report* (part 2, section C § 8).

[114] Dulles, "The Reception of Vatican II at the Extraordinary Synod of 1985," p. 362.

[115] Cf. Lapointe, *Une expérience pastorale en afrique australe* (Paris: Editions L'Harmattan, 1985), pp. 229-230.

healthy sign of the laity exercising a pastoral co-responsibility for the welfare of the church.[116]

In a similar vein, and in a Latin American context, Azevedo sees the idea of decentralization and lay co-responsibility as being marked features of Brazilian BECs, and as going together hand-in-hand. Without losing sight of the necessary pastoral role provided by the parish priest, he states that day-to-day life in the BEC community "does not rest upon the initiative of the clergy and even less on the need for its constant involvement or required approval."[117] The exercise of ordained pastoral leadership is not meant to stifle or oppress the character and quality of lay participation in BECs.

One of the consequences then of BEC/SCC decentralization in the parish is a growing collaboration in the exercise of pastoral leadership. The ability of lay men and women to freely and fully participate in the operation of a BEC/SCC is creating a new dynamic in how pastoral leadership on the local scene is being exercised. The need remains though to strike a proper balance between the exercise of lay charisms in ministry and leadership and the institutional charisms of ordained pastoral ministry.[118] But the upshot of this new dynamic does not mean that the pastor has no business in overseeing the affairs of SCCs in the parish. SCCs are contributing to a redefining of the pastor's role, they are not however replacing or by-passing it altogether.[119]

The question that arises is how do the issues of subsidiarity, decentralization, and co-responsibility apply to the situation of North American parish-based SCCs? To begin with, we have seen that all of the SCC programs and organizations we have examined stress the idea that the laity need to take more of an active role in, and responsibility for, the task of being the church. The growth of SCCs, lay movements, and lay ministry in the postconciliar church in North America is a sign that Vatican II's call for more active lay involvement in the church has indeed been heeded by

---

[116] *Ibid.,* p. 231.

[117] Azevedo, "Basic Ecclesial Communities: A Meeting Point of Ecclesiologies," *Theological Studies* 46 (1985), p. 603.

[118] Dulles notes that the various *theologies of ministry* that have blossomed after Vatican II have had an important bearing on ecclesiology. "In these theologies the hierarchical stratification of the Church into classes is being offset, to some degree, by a *theology of interrelated gifts and callings.* Authority is perceived as depending *less on office and power* than on *charism and service."* Cf. Dulles, "Catholic Ecclesiology Since Vatican II," *Concilium* 188 (1986), pp. 10-11.

[119] We have seen how some commentators have spoken of the parish priest as needing to act more like a bishop in the parish church, engaged in delegating and coordinating lay ministries, rather than being the one who does all the ministry himself.

many Catholics in this region of the world.[120] In his address to the 1987 Synod on the Laity, Archbishop John May described the U.S. experience of lay involvement (including reference to SCCs) as being a positive manifestation of "co-discipleship for the mission of the church in the world."[121]

So the idea of co-responsibility for the church is a major factor in the promotion and operation of North American SCCs. However, opinions differ as to the manner and degree to which this co-responsibility should be practically exercised. Some programs and organizations we have seen stress the need for SCCs to have a certain pastoral autonomy in arranging and managing their own internal affairs.[122] They are not usually, however, making any kind of claim for outright ecclesial autonomy. They see themselves as being parish groups that are under the ultimate authority of their pastor. But they do not regard the pastor's role, as important as it is, as having much practical bearing on their activities. Sometimes, this is a consequence of the pastor's lack of interest in or support for their welfare. Thus, they see SCCs as needing to be relatively self-sufficient in order to survive.

But most of the SCC programs and organizations we have seen stress the active role of the pastor as being something which is essential to the group's ecclesial existence. The pastor, via his dealings with the group animators, takes a direct interest in promoting the welfare of each group. His efforts are often times connected to some form of overall plan to restructure the parish. Because of this active pastor/animator link, the idea and practice of subsidiarity is more clearly established and properly safeguarded in these kinds of SCCs. This also explains why this type of SCC which is actively linked to the pastoral apparatus of the parish has a more defined parochial identity than those SCC groups which exist in relative pastoral isolation.[123]

Leaving aside the issue of how and to what degree direct input from the pastor should be exercised in SCCs, it is clear that SCCs are manifesting the fundamental dynamic of lay co-responsibility. The SCC meetings in themselves are essentially an exercise in peer ministry. The laity are utilizing their own charisms in this process. Members are described as

---

[120] For evidence of this, see the results of the Notre Dame Study of Parish Life that were outlined in chapter three, part I, section B § 2.

[121] May, "Parishes in the Laity's Life," *Origins* 17/20 (1987), p. 354.

[122] We found this sentiment expressed by certain members of *Buena Vista*. Cf. Chapter five, part I, section F § 3 (note #97).

[123] This is the answer then to question raised earlier about the ecclesiality of certain Buena Vista SCCs. See this chapter, part II, section B above.

sharing in the responsibility for each other's ongoing formation.[124] They are the ones who usually take the initiative in inviting new people to the meeting in the hopes of having them share in the SCC evangelization and discipleship process. They often determine where and how they should be involved as individuals or even as a group in outreach activities. Through this activity they are said to be changing, not undermining, the role of the pastor. What they are doing is revalorizing the role of the laity. Thus, SCCs of whatever orientation are promoting a new dynamic of shared pastoral responsibility in the church today.

SCCs are a means then of decentralizing and multiplying ministerial activity within the parish church. We noted earlier in this thesis that the Pauline house churches served as a basis for liturgy, catechesis and fellowship for Christians in a given area. While North American SCCs are not usually a setting for formal liturgy, they are a base for catechesis, fellowship, and other ministry. They decentralize some of these parish activities not for reasons of physical necessity but for the sake of greater pastoral effectiveness.[125]

The need to physically decentralize for the sake of the apostolate was, as we have seen, a major factor in the historical emergence of the parish system in the local church. It is also part of what is spurring BEC/SCC development in places like Africa, Asia, and Latin America. But in North America the idea of parish decentralization by means of SCCs is stressed not for reasons of physical necessity, but mainly for reasons of greater pastoral effectiveness in promoting the overall vocation and mission of the parish church.

3) SCCs as an Expression of the Discipleship Model of Church

Although the North American programs and organizations we have examined differ somewhat in regards to the issue of how best to characterize SCC ecclesiality, they are in fundamental agreement when it comes to the importance of their role and purpose in the parish community. One image which was used repeatedly to describe this purpose was that of engendering

---

[124] For instance, in Kelly's evaluation of *RENEW* he claims that "*RENEW* directly engages the laity in sharing responsibility for spiritual formation." Cf. Kelly, "Does the *RENEW* Program Really Renew?" *America* (March 7, 1987), p. 198.

[125] This point was affirmed by Bishop Weigand of Salt Lake City when, reflecting on his diocese's experience with BECs, he noted that it wasn't due to physical necessity but pastoral effectiveness that some parishes had chosen to decentralize various activities like catechetical and social outreach programs through these groups. Cf. Bishop William Weigand (co-authored with Sr. Helen Marie Raycraft and Fr. Ralph Rogawski), "Basic Christian Communities: A New Hope," in *Basic Christian Communities: The United States Experience* (Chicago: NFPC, 1983), p. 10.

discipleship.[126] Like the family, SCCs are seen as being an ideal forum in which the process of Christian discipleship can be both fostered and effectively realized.

Because of this emphasis on discipleship, there have been some observers who have made the comment that SCCs are an expression of the "discipleship model" of church which Avery Dulles has described in the expanded version of his famous work *Models of the Church*.[127] In fact in this book Dulles himself makes reference to basic ecclesial communities as being able "to best promote discipleship in its full range."[128] Since the concepts of "discipleship" and "model of the church" possibly have an important bearing on our task of evaluating the ecclesiological significance of the parish/SCC relationship, it is worthwhile to take a closer look at some of Dulles' insights as a further way of assessing the nature of the North American SCC experience.[129]

Dulles begins his book by explaining how the concept of scientific models can be adapted and applied as a valuable methodological tool for use in understanding ecclesiology.[130] He sees models being used as an exploratory and heuristic device to deepen the theoretical understanding of a reality. They are not formal definitions. In the area of ecclesiology they function in a manner similar to the images and metaphors that Scripture employs to describe the mystery of the church. Models are thus a limited but nonetheless helpful means for synthesising and expressing the important ideas and images that are inherent in the church's ecclesiology.

Because the mystery of the church is a complex divine-human reality, which involves many different aspects of Christian faith and practice, a certain plurality of models is to be expected in ecclesiology. No single model or image has the expressive power to do justice to the full range of what being church encompasses. In his original book Dulles

---

[126] There was reference to discipleship in nearly all of the SCC programs/organizations we reviewed. For evidence of this see: National Office of *RENEW*, *RENEW: An Overview*, p. 62; Baranowski, *Creating Small Faith Communities*, p. 1; Eivers and Vitale, *St. Boniface Parish Cell System: Leaders' Training Manual*, p. 143; and Sine Team, *What Does SINE Really Mean?*, p. 3.

[127] See for instance the comments to this effect made by Denise and John Carmody, *Bonded in Christ's Love: An Introduction to Ecclesiology* (New York/Mahwah: Paulist Press, 1986), pp. 112-113. See also Brennan, *Re-imagining the Parish*, pp. 13-15.

[128] Cf. Avery Dulles, *Models of the Church* (New York: Doubleday, 1987 Expanded Edition), p. 218.

[129] These insights are taken from his expanded *Models of the Church* book, but they also received treatment in *A Church to Believe In: Discipleship and the Dynamics of Freedom* (New York: Crossroad, 1982). In this latter book, Dulles makes the point that ordinary believers can benefit from a suitable "guiding vision" of the church that a good image can provide (cf. p. 1).

[130] Cf. *Ibid.*, Chap. 1.

identifies five dominant models that, taken together, account for most of the major themes in Catholic ecclesiology today. These are: church as institution; church as mystical communion; church as sacrament; church as herald; and church as servant.

There is no need to describe the features of these five models in any detail. They correspond to major themes we have already noted in our earlier review of Vatican II's ecclesiology. Since the publication of *Models of the Church*, there have been other theologians who have further explored Dulles' way of approaching the church in terms of models. For example, we have noted in passing that Azevedo applies Dulles' models to BECs in an effort to show how they incarnate these dimensions of being church.[131] In a similar manner, Kilian uses a Dulles-inspired models approach in his exposition of the theology of the parish.[132]

In his evaluation of these ecclesiological models, besides noting their strengths, Dulles also points out the limitations of each of them when taken to certain extremes or when seen only in isolation. He stresses that in the lived experience of being the church these models do not exist in isolation from one another. They are always interrelated and integrated into the whole of the mystery. He therefore rejects attempts to exalt one or more models as primary and somehow denigrate the rest. They are all important, and need to be harmonized with one another in order to maintain a holistic and balanced ecclesiology.[133]

Because of this fact, no one "supermodel" exists which has the expressive power as an image to do full justice to all these aspects of the church simultaneously. Dulles states that:

> The Church, as a mystery, transcends all creaturely analogies and defies reduction to a single theological paradigm. Members know the Church primarily through a kind of existential affinity or familiarity, of which images and concepts are rather crude objectifications. No one set of categories can capture in their full richness the manifold dimensions of the Church. Various models can complement one another and compensate for one another's shortcomings.[134]

---

[131] Cf. Azevedo, *Basic Ecclesial Communities in Brazil*, pp. 208-244.

[132] Cf. Sabbas Kilian, *Theological Models for the Parish* (New York: Alba House, 1977), chap. III.

[133] Cf. Dulles, *Models of the Church*, p. 196.

[134] *Ibid.*, p. 206.

Having stressed this point, Dulles still felt it was possible and necessary to attempt to find an image that would somehow integrate and harmonize the five basic models, without being thought of as a supermodel. In a later essay written after the original 1974 publication of *Models of the Church*, he seized on a remark made by John Paul II suggesting the idea of church as being a "community of disciples."[135] This essay was subsequently adapted and included as a new final chapter to *Models of the Church* in the 1987 expanded version of the book.

Dulles sees the concept of church as a community of disciples as being a variant of the communion model. An advantage it has over this communion model taken in isolation is that it precludes any possible misguided impression that ecclesial communion exists merely for the sake of mutual gratification and support. It calls attention to the ongoing relationship of the church to Christ, who is continuing to direct it through the Spirit. This image also acts as a bridge to the other models. It illuminates the institutional and sacramental aspects of the church and provides a context within which the functions of evangelization and service that are central to the herald and servant models can be understood. He concludes: "the notion of 'community of disciples' is thus a broadly inclusive one. Without being adequate to the full reality of the Church, it has . . . potentialities as a basis for a comprehensive ecclesiology."[136]

What does this community of disciples model encompass and image? For one thing, the original disciples of Jesus constituted a group of believers who were very committed to his message and mission. Because of their decision to adopt a new way of life as a result of this relationship with Jesus and with one another, they thus constituted a "contrast society" that prefigured what a renewed Israel should look like.[137] After the death/ resurrection of Jesus, the early church understood itself as being commissioned to go out and "make disciples of all the nations" (Mt 28:19) in a similar manner.

Throughout the early centuries membership in the church retained many of the demands of discipleship. Christians endeavoured to maintain a critical distance from pagan society, and many were willing to face martyrdom for the faith. But with the conversion of Constantine and the official adoption of Christianity as the established religion of the empire that soon followed, the situation of the church was radically changed. The concept of discipleship was not lost altogether as a result of this change, but

---

[135] Cf. *Redemptor Hominis* 21.

[136] Dulles, *Models of the Church*, p. 207.

[137] *Ibid.*, p. 209.

what happened was that the more radical features of what it entailed began to be identified more with formal religious life.[138]

This did not mean that lay believers stopped actively living out the gospel. Indeed, they were urged to practice a kind of interior discipleship in their efforts to be followers of Jesus. But as a result of different factors and influences, many of the original features of what discipleship and being a contrast society meant became obscured or compromised in the church at large. However at Vatican II, the idea that discipleship is a part of every Christian's vocation, not just priests' and religious, was once again clearly reaffirmed.[139]

Dulles feels that this recovery of a holistic understanding of what discipleship entails, and to whom it applies, has significant pastoral implications for the church today, especially in the area of faith transmission and support:

> For the successful transmission of Christian faith, it is highly important for the neophyte to find a welcoming community with responsible leaders who are mature disciples, formed in the ways of the Lord. . . . Faith is most successfully passed on by trusting masters in a network of interpersonal relations resembling the community life of Jesus with the Twelve.[140]

As concrete examples of where one can find loci of this kind of discipleship in the church today, Dulles points to the family unit, various lay movement groups, and to the experience of Latin American BECs. He seems to think that for many other Catholics lacking such group support, even those who are faithful to their religious obligations, they "rarely experience Church as a community of mutual support and stimulation. Although they may accept the teachings of the Church, they find it hard to relate the Church to their daily life, which is lived out in a very secular environment."[141]

In his own evaluation of the adequacy of the concept of church as a community of disciples, Dulles notes certain objections that could be raised. One possible objection is that an over emphasis on the idea of church as a contrast society can lead to a sect-like mentality taking root. Rather than engaging the world in dialogue, the church would seem to be retreating from

---

[138] *Ibid.,* p. 213.
[139] See for example: LG 40; AA 10; and PO 9.
[140] Dulles, *Models of the Church,* p. 218.
[141] *Ibid.,* pp. 218-219.

it. In answer to this, Dulles says that given the state of today's society and its values, the church must take a strong countercultural position and actively strive to call attention to the necessity for believers to make a radical break with worldly values for the sake of fidelity to the message and person of Christ. Being a disciple is not a simple or easy task. He paraphrases a key insight that Dietrich Bonhoeffer makes in his famous work *The Cost of Discipleship*: "Christ's grace is not cheap, but demanding."[142]

Another possible objection flows from this conception of discipleship. In proposing such an arduous style of Christianity, does not the discipleship model make excessive demands on the average believer? Is not this a form of elitism? Dulles does not think so. The demands inherent in discipleship are the ones Christ himself made. If discipleship is for all believers, and not just for a select few, then the church should be setting high standards in what it expects from members. We will always be a church of sinners, and so compassion must always be exercised, but this does fact not alter the nature of discipleship.

In conclusion, Dulles reiterates that this model is not intended to take the place of all the other images and descriptions found in Scripture or expounded upon in the documents of Vatican II. Many of these images, such as People of God, Body of Christ, etc., retain their validity. They even surpass the community of disciples image in expressing the theological basis for the church. Nevertheless, he thinks that given the need in the church today to once again visualize itself and function as a contrast society, the image of the community of disciples "has the advantages of being closer to our experience and of suggesting directions for appropriate renewal."[143]

In Dulles' reflection about the church as a community of disciples we find a concern not only for theological reflection, but for concrete means by which to help engender this dynamic. That is why he specifically mentions BECs/SCCs, as well as other types of small groups, as being effective instruments in this process.[144] If this is the case, one can see how and why SCCs are expressing a vital dimension of what it means to be church. For engendering discipleship is an inherently ecclesial task. They are not merely a means for personal faith support and development.

We have seen that because the parish was born historically out of pastoral convenience, one can generally suppose that much of its organizational structure is not *de iure divino*. As such, these structures by

---

[142] *Ibid.,* p. 225.

[143] *Ibid.,* p. 222.

[144] Dulles sees lay people in the church today as needing an experience of Christian community that would be analogous to the religious novitiate. This idea of a permanent form of "lay novitiate" can be seen as another way of characterizing the SCC dynamic. *Ibid.,* p. 219.

and large can and should continue to evolve so that the parish can remain faithful and effective in carrying out its mission in the local church.[145] An SCC can be seen as a new type of parish entity which helps meet the need for a more personally focused and participatory experience of community and discipleship. It is thus a valuable complement to the liturgical activity of the wider parish community that is carried out on Sundays. Fostering discipleship should always be a necessary activity in the church.

Discipleship is one way then of succinctly characterizing what the sum total of SCC activities aims at promoting. The SCC is really serving in a subsidiary capacity the parish effort as a whole to foster discipleship. Therefore, because of its size and function, the SCC is effectively able to help the parish realize its vocation and mission as a community of disciples.

Not only can it be seen that the theology of parish has a bearing on the evaluation of SCCs, but it can also be seen that SCCs are having a bearing on the theology of parish. Having seen how the relationship of SCC to parish can be ecclesiologically characterized (i.e. mediating structure; instrument of subsidiarity, decentralization, co-responsibility; means of promoting discipleship), let us now turn and determine whether or not this role gives a special or enhanced quality or status to the ecclesiality of parish-based SCCs.

C. SCCs and the Idea of Being an Ecclesial Unit of the Parish Church

1) SCCs and the Domestic Church

During his 1987 visit to the United States John Paul II gave an address in San Antonio, Texas, wherein he referred to the parish as being a "family of families." In this address he stated that "the family in fact is the basic unit of society and of the church. It is the 'domestic church.' Families are those living cells which come together to form the very substance of parish life."[146]

The idea of the family being a kind of "domestic church," was a phrase used at Vatican II (LG 11) and also repeated in John Paul II's 1981 post-Synodal Apostolic Exhortation *Familiaris Consortio* (#51). This image of the domestic church indicates how highly regarded and important the family is to the life of the church. Because family life is grounded in a sacramental reality (matrimony), it is thus recognized to be an eminently "ecclesial" entity (FC 49). Families share in the life and mission of the church in many ways (ie. prayer, the witness of Christian love and reconciliation, evangelization and catechesis of children). Because of these

---

[145] See the quote from Sabbas Kilian to this effect. Cited in chapter two, part I, section C. (Kilian, *Theological Models for the Parish*, pp. 17-18.)

[146] John Paul II, "The Parish: Family of Families," *Origins* 17/17 (1987), p. 289.

ecclesial activities, and since Christ promised to be present wherever two or three are gathered in his name (Mt 18:20), some theologians have come to describe the family as constituting a "privileged locus of the church."[147]

Many advocates of SCCs see a need in the church today to support family life. They do not see SCCs as replacing or usurping the family's purpose and role, but rather as helping it in its mission. This is especially needed today because family life is under increasing social pressures which are undermining its ability to be an effective community.[148] In fact, the desirability of having families join together in various groups for mutual support, and so to aid in the lay apostolate, was something Vatican II had also affirmed.[149]

But although SCCs partake of many of the same kinds of ecclesial activities in the parish as do families, and can seen as an effective means of support for them, they are not constituted sacramentally in quite the same manner. Because of this fact, the designation "domestic church" cannot be uncritically transferred or broadened to include the idea of SCC ecclesiality. Families constitute a unique ecclesial reality within the church. They have "a specific and original ecclesial role."[150]

However, the fact that families are accorded a special recognition as being fundamental ecclesial units of the parish church invites an investigation as to whether SCCs can perhaps be looked upon in a similar or analogous fashion. Like the family, SCCs have been referred to as being important "cells" of the parish church. They are both settings wherein the life and mission of the parish is fostered. SCCs have also been described as playing a mediating role in helping to link or integrate individuals and families more effectively into the communion of the parish.

---

[147] Cf. Normand Provencher, "The Family as Domestic Church," *Theology Digest* 30/2 (1982), p. 149.

[148] "Two or three generations ago it would have been the 'norm' to have families living in the same town or neighborhood for many years. Families supported one another in many of their daily and crisis needs because they were 'just next door.' This is not true today. [Thus] . . . with the 'many faces of family' and the growing change in the nuclear family, small Christian communities not only enhance family life, but offer increased support to strong as well as struggling families." Kleissler et al., *Small Christian Communities*, p. 208.

[149] "To attain the ends of their apostolate more easily it can be of advantage for families to organize themselves into groups." *Apostolicam Actuositatem* 11.

[150] Cf. *Familiaris Consortio* 50.

2) SCCs and the Emerging "Community of Communities" Image of the Parish

Due to the postconciliar increase in the number and variety of lay groups that have grown to be associated with the parish, a new conception of parish as being a "community of communities" has risen to prominence in the church today. This was the phrase we saw used in two previous Synods by the bishops to describe both what the parish already is and what it should become further.[151] Although this phrase does not just refer to the presence of BEC/SCC groups in the parish, it is an expression which many proponents of SCCs have utilized in their explanations of parish restructuring efforts.[152] This image seems to represent a new awareness in the church today as to the valuable ecclesial role played by small parish groups and communities of all types.

In one sense the phrase seems to be a variation of the traditional idea that the parish is a community of families. The importance of families for parish life still holds true (as we noted above). But what the image of *community of communities* seems to recognize is that the family is not the only form of smaller Christian community with which the parish is comprised. There are other groups, like SCCs, which are manifestations of authentic communion and places wherein the mission of the parish is carried out. And so far from dividing the parish, the role of families and other small communities is seen as strengthening it.

The intent of the *community of communities* image of parish is not to replace the parish with a series of smaller communities, but to help integrate these smaller communities into the parish structure. In fact, the situation of North American parish-based SCCs makes nonsense of the idea of doing away with the parish. The parish is a vitally needed center for liturgical and sacramental activity, as well as for pastoral support and supervision. It does not become a merely administrative office or outpost of the local church. SCCs, as wonderful as they are said to be, do not have all

---

[151] Cf. The 1977 and 1987 Synods (quotes cited in chapter six, sections B and D). In using this *community of communities* image the bishops did not explain its full ecclesiological implications. But there is little justification for seeing in this image any reference to these communities somehow functioning as "levels" of the parish church. The idea of levels of the church is a useful way of expressing, in one form, its hierarchical structure (i.e. universal-local-parish). However, its usefulness as a means of explaining the structure of parochial communion is questionable. It is better to express the communio of the parish in more organic terms, which the *community of communities* image seems to imply.

[152] This *community of communities* image of parish was specifically cited by at least four of the SCC programs/ organizations we surveyed: NCCB, *The Hispanic Presence: Challenge and Commitment*, p. 60; Baranowski, *Creating Small Faith Communities*, p. 14; SINE Team, *What Does SINE Really Mean?*, p. 5; and *The Buena Vista Mission Statement* (cf. Peg Bisgrove, "Is There a Place for Me in This Church?" *Today's Parish* (Sept. 1990), p. 16.

the gifts needed to fully and effectively be the church in a given neighborhood.

So it can be seen then that the *community of communities* image of parish both validates the SCC experience and valorizes their ecclesial role. However, it does not tell us whether or not SCCs are deserving of a special kind of ecclesial recognition in the parish community. No distinctions are made between SCCs and other parish groups and organizations. In the absence then of any kind of magisterial or canonical statement on this question as it applies to the North American situation of SCCs, we are left therefore to draw our own tentative conclusion about this question for now. This we shall endeavour to do in the conclusion which follows.

3) Conclusion

In our study of North American SCC programs/organizations we repeatedly came across the claim that SCCs were different from most other types of parish groups and parish renewal programs.[153] Unlike many parish renewal programs which are only of a temporary duration, SCCs are described as being an on-going evangelization and discipleship process which results in parish groups of a more permanent nature being established. They are intended to be a permanent fixture on the parish scene. Because of this specific parish focus and orientation, parish-based SCCs are also said to be different from so-called movement-based SCCs.[154]

In regards to other kinds of parish groups which meet on a regular basis, SCCs see themselves as being different in that they are multi-dimensional in scope. For instance, they are not single-issue therapy or support groups (i.e. Alcoholics Anonymous, Separated and Divorced Catholic Support Groups). They are not ministry planning groups (i.e. the liturgy committee, the social justice committee). They are not just an adult education group, prayer group, bible-study group, and so forth.

While they share some similar characteristics with these other kinds of parish groups, many SCC proponents claim that what sets them apart is their more holistic ecclesial focus and purpose. Advocates of SCCs are not trying to claim that because of this difference, they are somehow "more" ecclesial than these other parish groups and organizations. All parish groups, organizations, committees, and programs play an important role in

---

[153] Reference to SCCs being different and/or ecclesially distinct from other types of parish groups and/or renewal programs was specifically cited by at least four of the SCC programs/organizations we studied. See chapter five, part I, sections: C § 2; D § 3; E § 2; and F § 3.

[154] The differences between parish-based and movement-based SCCs was addressed in chapter four, part III, section B: "A Typological Classification of North American SCCs."

their own way in contributing to the life of the parish community. SCCs are not seen as being a replacement for all of them.

We have already explained why it is not really appropriate to refer to North American SCCs as "churches" of the local or parish church. They do not generally stand poised, as do parish missions or so-called quasi-parishes, to become potentially full-fledged parochial assemblies of their own. But our study has shown that the small Christian community has indeed become a newly identifiable "ecclesial locus" in a growing number of North American parishes. They are redefining the pastoral structure of the parish and what it means to participate in it. They are obviously not changing the ontological status of the parish as church. But they represent more than mere structural tinkering of a purely sociological kind. If this is so, should not more ecclesiological "weight" be accorded to SCCs which are part of a comprehensive parish restructuring effort?

This thesis has demonstrated that SCCs exhibit a certain number of ecclesial traits, to the extent that they can be truly said to enjoy a certain ecclesiality. Those SCCs which foster the full activation of what it means to be a parish must be acknowledged as sharing to that extent in the ecclesiality of the parishes in which they exist and whose effectiveness and welfare they promote. Thus, the answer suggested by the findings of this thesis to the above question is "yes they should." They are distinctive enough to warrant the conclusion that they are newly identifiable "units" of the parish church. At this stage in their historical emergence and development they are really only beginning to take on an institutionalized presence within the pastoral framework of the North American parish church. It will take time and more pastoral experimentation and theological reflection to shed further light on the full implications inherent in their ecclesiality. Hopefully this thesis has made some contribution to this task.

Having made this assessment, a question remains as to how such recognition as units of the church might be best expressed or articulated from a theological point of view. Some SCC programs/organizations have used the image of "cell" to express and name their ecclesiality and identity. This image has the advantage over the "little church" image in that it clearly implies that the SCC is integrally a part of and dependent on the Body of the parish for its ecclesial existence. It is also an organic image that gets away from the problematic idea of "levels" in the parish church. It corresponds with the *community of communities* paradigm quite well, and it echoes the cellular identity granted the family in the parish community too. For these reasons the image of cell would seem a very appropriate means with which to express and delineate their theological identity as ecclesial units of the parish community.

Thus, it can be seen that even though SCCs are only a small part of the ecclesial body of the parish, they are deserving of honour and recognition as being a specialized unit of the church. In the final analysis the words of St. Paul regarding the nature of the church as "body" seem especially apropos in this context:

> As it is, there are many members yet one body. The eye cannot say to the hand, "I have no need of you," nor again the head to the feet, "I have no need of you." On the contrary, the members of the body that seem to be weaker are indispensable, and those members of the body that we think less honorable we clothe with greater honor, and our less respectable members are treated with greater respect; whereas our more respectable members do not need this. But God has so arranged the body, giving the greater honor to the inferior member, that there may be no dissension within the body, but the members may have the same care for one another.[155]

---

[155] I Cor 12:20-25.

General Conclusion

This thesis has sought to examine the ecclesiological underpinnings and implications of the small Christian community phenomenon as it is currently being experienced in the North American parish context. We have highlighted the emergence, characteristics, and ecclesiological reflection of seven major SCC programs/organizations in an effort to comprehend the general nature of the North American experience. We have taken particular note of the major issues which the emergence of SCCs have been raising vis-à-vis the vocation, mission, and theology of the parish church.

In order to effectively comprehend these issues, and be able to evaluate the contribution SCCs are said to be making, it was necessary to begin this thesis with a brief study of the early church and an overview of the emergence of the parish system; including an analysis of the parish's traditional theological identity and status. This was followed by a review of the major ecclesiological themes inherent in Vatican II's depiction of the church. Special attention was paid to the theology of local church and the place of the parish community within it.

We also took brief note of the pastoral significance of the parish for church life in North America, and examined its current standing. Because this examination had revealed that the ability of parishioners to be supported in their parochial faith practice had been undermined to some degree in the postconciliar era by a radically altered cultural climate, mention was also made of the challenges posed to the church by the forces of modernity and secularization. As a response to these challenges, we took note of the pastoral strategy employed by various lay movements, associations, and parish renewal programs in the church today. This in turn provided a context for understanding the relatively recent growth and development of small Christian communities in the church. We explored the situation of BECs/SCCs in other regions of the world in order to understand how their emergence, characteristics, and ecclesiological self-perception compares with that of the North American experience. To finally set the stage for our North American analysis of the SCC phenomenon, we distinguished different "types" of small group communities so as to make clear the reason for focusing on the parish-based variety.

After having examined the North American situation, we then reviewed the mention which has been made of SCCs in recent papal and synodal documents. We gleaned from these documents what we have referred to as the papal criteria for SCC ecclesiality. After further exploring the nature of ecclesiality, these criteria were subsequently utilized in an evaluation of the North American SCC programs/organizations. We concluded that these various SCC programs/organizations embodied a fundamentally sound ecclesial outlook and practice.

We developed this analysis further by reflecting on how the parish-SCC relationship could be best construed from an ecclesiological point of view. The ecclesial elements or aspects which SCCs help mediate were scrutinized in the light of the vocation and mission of the parish. SCCs were described as being an expression of subsidiarity, decentralization, lay co-responsibility, and discipleship in the church today. Given the fact then that these SCCs possess a number of important ecclesial traits, and given there important ecclesial function in the parish, it was concluded that these types of SCCs are special units of the church and thus enjoy a certain enhanced ecclesial status when compared to other parish groupings.

North American parish-based SCCs are therefore deserving of a similar kind of ecclesiological status as that accorded to the BEC/SCC phenomenon in many other regions of the world. They would thus benefit from some kind of enhanced official recognition by the bishops of North America. While they do not enjoy, and perhaps do not require, any kind of explicit canonical recognition, as do for instance quasi-parish communities, their continued growth and development would nevertheless benefit from an official statement to the effect that they are a significant ecclesial locus in the church today. Also important would be a clear endorsement of parish restructuring efforts which are striving to help make the parish a more effective "community of communities."

In postulating the need for and legitimacy of this kind of enhanced recognition, we are not attempting to canonize the SCC movement. Much work remains to be done in examining and evaluating the pastoral and theological issues which their emergence have been generating in the church at large. Hopefully, this thesis has made a contribution to the on-going task of attempting to understand their essential nature, and the impact they are having on our understanding of the vocation, mission, and theology of the parish. In the final analysis, it is realized that their continued fruitfulness and ultimate validation is dependent always on the abiding presence and ministry of the Holy Spirit, who continually helps the church in her mission of "proclaiming the kingdom of God and teaching about the Lord Jesus Christ in all boldness" (Acts 28:31).

Appendix

Office Addresses of North American Small Christian Community Programs/Organizations

I. HISPANIC MINISTRY INITIATIVES
National Conference of Catholic Bishops
Secretariat for Hispanic Affairs
1312 Massachusetts Ave. N.W.
Washington, D.C. 20005, U.S.A.

II. RENEW
International Office of *RENEW*
1232 George St.
Plainfield, NJ 07062, U.S.A.

III. NATIONAL ALLIANCE OF PARISHES RESTRUCTURING INTO COMMUNITIES
National Alliance of Parishes Restructuring into Communities
P.O. Box 1152
Troy, Michigan 48099, U.S.A

IV. ST. BONIFACE PARISH CELL SYSTEM
St. Boniface Catholic Church
8330 Johnson St.
Pembroke Pines, Florida 33024, U.S.A.

V. SYSTEMATIC INTEGRAL NEW EVANGELIZATION (SINE)
SINE National Office
4401 Highcrest Rd.
Rockford, Illinois 61107, U.S.A.

VI. BUENA VISTA
Buena Vista
P.O. Box 5474
Arvada, Colorado 80005-0475, U.S.A.

VII. NORTH AMERICAN FORUM FOR SMALL CHRISTIAN COMMUNITIES
The North American Forum for Small Christian Communities
Office of the Word
430 N. Center St.
Crookston, Minnesota 56716, U.S.A.

Bibliography

PART ONE: THE PARISH

I. EARLY CHURCH—HISTORY OF THE PARISH—20TH CENTURY PRECONCILIAR REFLECTION ON THE THEOLOGY OF THE PARISH

Aguirre, Rafael. "Early Christian House Churches." *Theology Digest* 32/2 (1985), 151-155.

Arnold, F.X. *Glaubensverkündigung und Glaubensgemeinschaft*. Dusseldorf, Germany, 1955.

Banks, Robert. *Paul's Idea of Community: The Early House Churches in Their Historical Setting*. Grand Rapids: Eerdmans, 1980.

Blöchlinger, Alex. *The Modern Parish Community*. Trans. Geoffrey Stevens. New York: P.J. Kenedy, 1965.

Brown, Raymond E. *The Churches the Apostles Left Behind*. New York/Mahwah: Paulist Press, 1984.

_____. *Biblical Exegesis and Church Doctrine*. New York/Mahwah: Paulist Press, 1985.

_____. "Church in the New Testament." In *The New Jerome Biblical Commentary*, Eds. Raymond E. Brown, Joseph A. Fitzmyer, and Roland E. Murphy. London: Geoffrey Chapman, 1989, 1339-1346.

Congar, Yves. "Mission de la paroisse." In *Structures sociale et pastorale paroissiale*. Paris: Union des Oevres Catholiques de France, 1949, 48-65.

Croce, W. "The History of the Parish." In *The Parish: From Theology to Practice*, Ed. Hugo Rahner. Trans. Robert Kress. Westminster, Md.: The Newman Press, 1958, 23-35.

Cwiekowski, Frederick J. *The Beginnings of the Church*. New York/Mahwah: Paulist Press, 1988.

Delespesse, Max. *The Church Community: Leaven and Life Style*. Ottawa: St. Paul University, 1969.

Floristan, Casiano. *The Parish: Eucharistic Community*. Trans. John Byrne. London: Sheed and Ward, 1965.

Gómez, Felipe. "Notes on the History of the Parish." *East Asian Pastoral Review* 3 (1988), 242-248.

Grasso, D. "Observazioni sulla teologia della parrocchia." *Gregorianum* 40 (1959), pp. 297-314.

241

Kahlefeld, H. "Community Life in the New Testament." In *The Parish: From Theology to Practice,* Ed. Hugo Rahner. Trans. Robert Kress. Westminster, Md.: The Newman Press, 1958, 36-63.

Kilian, Sabbas J. *Theological Models for the Parish.* New York: Alba House, 1977.

Kittel, Gerhard, and Gerhard Friedrich, eds. *Theological Dictionary of the New Testament—Abridged One Vol. Edition.* Trans. G. Bromiley. Grand Rapids, Michigan: Eerdmans, 1985.

Klauck, Hans-Josef. "The House-Church as Way of Life." *Theology Digest* 30/2 (1982), 153-157.

Lohfink, Gerhard. *Jesus and Community: The Social Dimension of Christian Faith.* Trans. J. Gavin. New York/Mahwah: Paulist Press, 1984.

Meeks, Wayne A. *The First Urban Christians.* New Haven: Yale University Press, 1983.

Meyer, Ben. "The Initial Self-Understanding of the Church." *Catholic Biblical Quarterly* 27 (1965), 35-42.

Michiels, R. "The Model of Church in the First Christian Community of Jerusalem." *Louvain Studies* 10 (1985), 303-323.

Minear, Paul S. *Images of the Church in the New Testament.* Philadelphia: Westminster Press, 1960.

Nell-Breuning, Oswald von. "Pfarrgemeinde, Pfarrfamilie, Pfarrprinzip." *Trier Theologische Zeitschrift* 56 (1947), 258-275.

Parsch, Pius. "Die Pfarre als Mysterium." In *Die Lebendige Pfarregemeinde.* The Vienna Congress of 1933: Seelsorger-Sonderheft, 1934, 13-33.

Pontifical Biblical Commission. *Unity and Diversity in the Church.* Vatican City: Libreria Editrice Vaticana, 1991.

Rahner, Karl. "Theology of the Parish." in *The Parish: From Theology to Practice.* Ed. Hugo Rahner. Trans. R. Kress. Westminster, MD.: The Newman Press, 1958, 23-35.

_____. "Peaceful Reflections on the Parochial Principle." *Theological Investigations.* Vol. II. Trans. Edward Quinn. New York: Seabury Press, 1963, 283-318.

_____. "Structural Change in the Church of the Future." *Theological Investigations.* Vol. XX. Trans. Edward Quinn. London: Darton, Longman and Todd, 1981, 115-132.

Schnackenburg, Rudolf. *The Church in the New Testament.* Trans. W. J. O'Hara. New York: Herder and Herder, 1965.

Schroeder, H. J. *Canons and Decrees of the Council of Trent.* St. Louis, MO.: B. Herder, 1960.

Schurr, Maurice. "Die Uebernatürliche Wirklichkeit der Pfarrei." *Benediktinische Monatsschrift* 19 (1937), 81-106.

Schweizer, Eduard. *Church Order in the New Testament.* Trans. Frank Clarke. London: SCM Press, 1961.

Siemar, L. "Pfarregemeinde und *Ecclesiola.*" *Die Neue Ordnung* 3 (1949), 37-51.

Theissen, Gerd. *The Social Setting of Pauline Christianity.* Philadelphia: Fortress Press, 1982.

White, Allan. "Seeking a Theology of Parish." *Priests and People* 5/4 (1991), 130-133.

Wintersig, Athanasius. "Le réalisme mystique de la paroisse." *La Maison Dieu* 8 (1936), 15-26.

II. VATICAN II ECCLESIOLOGY—THEOLOGY OF LOCAL CHURCH—THE PARISH IN CANON LAW

Abbot, Walter M., ed. *The Documents of Vatican II.* New York: America Press, 1966.

Acerbi, Antonio. *Due ecclesiologie: Ecclesiologia giuridica ed ecclesiologia di communione nella "Lumen gentium".* Bologna: Dehoniane, 1975.

Alberigo, Giuseppe, ed. *Les Églises après Vatican II.* Beauchesne, 1981.

Alberigo, Giuseppe, Jean-Pierre Jossua, and Joseph Komonchak, eds.*The Reception of Vatican II.* Trans. Matthew O'Connell. Washington, D.C.: Catholic University of America, 1987.

Antón, Angel. "Postconciliar Ecclesiology." in *Vatican II: Assessment and Perspectives.* Vol.I. Ed. René Latourelle. Trans. Louis-Bertrand Raymond and Edward Hughes. New York: Paulist Press, 1988, 407-38.

_____. "Iglesia Local/Regional: Reflexion Sistematica." Paper Presented at the *2nd International Colloquium on Catholicity and Local Churches,* Salamanca, April 1-7, 1991, 1-59.

Baum, Gregory. "The Church as Movement." In *Readings in the Theology of Church.* Ed. E. Dirkswater. Englewood Cliffs, N.J.: Prentice-Hall, 1970, 239-57.

Brambilla, F.G. "La Parrocchia nella Chiesa: Riflesione Fondamentale." *Theologia* 13 (1988), 18-44.

Burghardt, Walter, and William Thompson, eds. *Why the Church?* New York/Ramsey: Paulist Press, 1977.

Callahan, Daniel. "Creating a Community." In *The Postconciliar Parish,* Ed. James O'Gara. New York: P.J. Kenedy, 1967, 105-121.

Carlen, Claudia, ed. *The Papal Encyclicals.* 7 Vols. Raleigh: The Pierian Press, 1990.

Carlson, Robert J. "The Parish According to the Revised Law." *Studia Canonica* 19 (1985), 5-16.

Carmody, Denise L. and John T. Carmody. *Bonded in Christ's Love: An Introduction to Ecclesiology* New York/Mahwah: Paulist Press, 1986.

Cobble, jr., James F. *The Church and the Powers: A Theology of Church Structure.* Mass.: Hendrickson Publishers, 1988.

Colombo, Giuseppe. "La teologia della Chiesa locale." in *La Chiesa locale.* Bologne: Dehoniane, 1969, 17-38.

Congar, Yves. "L'Église une, sainte, catholique, et apostolique." In *Mysterium Salutis*, Vol. IV/I. Eds. J. Feiner and M. Löhrer. Einsiedeln: Benziger, 1972, 357-599.

_____. *Diversity and Communion*. Trans. John Bowden. London: SCM Press, 1984.

_____. *Lay People in the Church*. Trans. D. Attwater. London: Geoffrey Chapman, 1985 Revised Edition.

_____. "Moving Towards a Pilgrim Church" and "A Last Look at the Council." in *Vatican II: By Those Who Were There*. Ed. Alberic Stacpoole. London: Geoffrey Chapman, 1986, 129-152; and 337-358.

Congregation for the Doctrine of the Faith. *Mysterium Ecclesiae*. AAS 65 (1973), 396-408. Trans.: "Declaration in Defense of the Catholic Doctrine on the Church against Certain Errors of the Present." *Catholic Mind* 71 (1973), 54-64.

Corecco, Eugenio. "Ecclesiological Bases of the Code." *Concilium* 185 (1986), 3-13.

Coriden, James A., Green, Thomas J., Heintschel, Donald E., eds. *The Code of Canon Law: A Text and Commentary*. New York/Mahwah: Paulist Press, 1985.

Daniélou, Jean. *Why the Church?* Trans. M. De Lange. Chicago: Franciscan Herald Press, 1975.

Davis, Charles. "The Parish and Theology." *The Clergy Review* 49 (1964), 265-290.

Delhaye, Philippe, et al, eds. *Concilium Vaticanum II: Concordance, index, listes de fréquence, tables comparatives*. Louvain: Cetedoc, 1974.

Donovan, Daniel. *The Church as Idea and Fact*. Wilmington, Del.: Michael Glazier, 1988.

Doohan, Leonard. *Laity's Mission in the Local Church*. San Francisco: Harper and Row, 1986.

Dulles, Avery. *The Resilient Church*. Garden City, N.Y.: Doubleday and Company, 1977.

_____. *A Church to Believe In*. New York: Crossroad, 1982.

_____. "The Church: Sacrament and Ground of Faith." In *Problems and Perspectives of Fundamental Theology*, Eds. R. Latourelle and G. O'Collins. New York: Paulist Press, 1982.

_____. "The Signs of the Times in the Church." *The Canadian Catholic Review* 2/3 (1984), 83-88.

_____. "Catholic Ecclesiology Since Vatican II." *Concilium* 188 (1986), 3-13.

_____. *Models of the Church*. (Expanded edition.) New York: Doubleday, 1987.

_____. "A Half Century of Ecclesiology." *Theological Studies* 50 (1989), 419-442.

Duquoc, Christian. *Provisional Churches*. Trans. John Bowden. London: SCM Press, 1986.

Fahey, Michael A. "Continuity in the Church amid Structural Changes." *Theological Studies* 35 (1974), 415-440.

_____. "Church." In *Systematic Theology: Roman Catholic Perspectives.* Vol. II, Eds. Francis Schüssler Fiorenza and John P. Galvin. Minneapolis: Fortress Press, 1991, 3-74.

Flannery, Austin P., ed. *Documents of Vatican II.* Grand Rapids, Mich.: Eerdmans, 1975.

Forte, Bruno. *The Church: Icon of the Trinity.* Trans. Robert Paolucci. Boston: St. Paul Books, 1991.

Fuellenbach, John. *The Kingdom of God.* Manilla: Divine Word Publications, 1989.

Ghirlanda, Gianfranco. "Universal Church, Particular Church, and Local Church at the Second Vatican Council and in the New Code of Canon Law." in *Vatican II: Assessment and Perspectives.* Vol. II. Ed. Rene Latourelle. New York: Paulist Press, 1988, 233-271.

Hamer, Jerome. *The Church is a Communion.* Trans. Ronald Matthews. London: Geoffrey Chapman, 1964.

Hastings, Adrian. *Modern Catholicism: Vatican II and After.* New York: Oxford University Press, 1991.

Hertling, Ludwig. *Communio: Church and Papacy in Early Christianity.* Trans. Jared Wicks. Chicago: Loyola University Press, 1972.

Houssiau, Albert. "L'approche théologique de la paroisse." *Revue Théologique de Louvain* 13 (1982), 317-328.

Houtepen, Anton. *People of God: A Plea for the Church.* Trans. John Bowden. London: SCM Press, 1984.

Huels, John. "Parish Life and the New Code." *Concilium* 185 (1986), 64-72.

Janicki, Joseph. "Commentary on Canons 515-552." In *The Code of Canon Law: A Text and Commentary.* Eds. James Coriden et al. New York/Mahwah: Paulist Press, 1985, 415-458.

Kasper, Walter. *Theology and Church.* Trans. Margaret Kohl. London: SCM Press, 1989.

Kloppenburg, Bonaventure. *The Ecclesiology of Vatican II.* Trans. M. O'Connel. Chicago: Franciscan Herald Press, 1970.

Komonchak, Joseph. "The Theological Debate." (1985 Synod) *Concilium* 188 (1986), 53-63.

_____. "The Church: God's Gift and Our Task." *Origins* 16/42 (1987), 735-741.

_____. "L'articulation entre Église locale et Église universelle selon quelques théologiens contemporains." Paper Presented at the *2nd International Colloquium on Catholicity and Local Churches*, Salamanca, April 1-7, 1991.

Küng, Hans. *The Church.* Trans. R. and R. Ockenden. New York: Sheed and Ward, 1967.

Latourelle, René, ed. *Vatican II: Assessment and Perspectives.* 3 Vols. New York: Paulist Press, 1988.

Lanne, Emmanuel. "The Local Church: Its Catholicity and its Apostolicity." *One in Christ* 6 (1970), 288-313.

Legrand, H.-M. "Enjeux théologiques de la valorisation des Eglises locales." *Concilium* 71 (1972), 49-58.

_____. "La réalization de l'église en un lieu." In *Initiation à la pratique de la théologie. Vol. 3.* Eds. B. Laurent and F. Refoulé. Paris: Cerf, 1983.

Le Guillou, Marie-Joseph. "Church: History of Ecclesiology." In *Sacramentum Mundi.* Vol. I. Ed. Karl Rahner. London: Burns and Oates, 1968-1970, 313-317.

Lescrauwaet, J. "De Parochie in de Ecclesiologie van het Tweede Vaticaanse Concilie." In *De Parochie.* Ed. A. Houssiau et al. Brugge: Uitgeverij Tabor, 1988, 37-49.

Lubac, Henri de. *Les églises particulières dans l'Église universelle.* Paris: Aubier Montaigne, 1971.

_____. *Theological Fragments.* Trans. R. H. Balinski. San Francisco: Ignatius Press, 1989.

Lynch, John E. "The Parochial Ministry in the New Code of Canon Law." *The Jurist* 42 (1982), 383-421.

McBrien, Richard P. *Do We Need the Church?* London: Collins Press, 1969.

_____. *Church: The Continuing Quest.* New York: Newman Press, 1970.

_____. *Catholicism.* (Study Edition.) San Francisco: Harper and Row, 1981.

Mersch, Emile. *The Whole Christ: The Historical Development of the Doctrine of the Body of Christ.* Trans. John Kelly. Milwaukee: Bruce, 1938.

Nichols, Aidan. *Yves Congar.* London: Geoffrey Chapman, 1989.

Ochoa, Xaverius, ed. *Index verborum cum documentis Concilii Vaticani Secundi.* Rome: Commentarium pro Religiosis, 1967.

Paul VI. *Ecclesiam Suam. AAS* 56 (1964), 609-659. (Trans.—Boston: St. Paul Books, 1964).

Philips, Gérard. *L'Église et son mystère au IIe Concile du Vatican.* 2 Vols., Paris: Desclée, 1967.

Pius XII. *Mystici Corporis. AAS* 35 (1943), 193-248. (Trans.—London: Catholic Truth Society, 1956).

Pottmeyer, Hermann. "The Church as Mysterium and as Institution." *Concilium* 188 (1986), 99-109.

_____. "A New Phase in the Reception of Vatican II: Twenty Years of Interpretation of the Council." In *The Reception of Vatican II.* Eds. Giuseppe Alberigo et al. Trans. Matthew O'Connell. Washington, D.C.: Catholic University of America, 1987, 27-43.

Powell, John. *The Mystery of the Church.* Milwaukee: Bruce Publishing Company, 1967.

Rahner, Karl. *The Shape of the Church to Come.* Trans. Edward Quinn. New York: Seabury Press, 1974.

_____. *Foundations of Christian Faith.* Trans. W. Dych. London: Darton, Longman and Todd, 1978.

_____. "Basic Theological Interpretation of the Second Vatican Council." *Theological Investigations,* Vol. XX. Trans. Edward Quinn. New York: Crossroad, 1981, 77-89.

Ratzinger, Joseph. *Principles of Catholic Theology.* Trans. M. McCarthy. San Francisco: Ignatius Press, 1987.

_____. "The Ecclesiology of the Second Vatican Council." *Communio* 13 (1988), 239-252.

Rikhof, Herwi. *The Concept of Church.* London: Sheed and Ward, 1981.

Rossano, Piero. "La Chiesa è cattolica." In *Mysterium Salutis IV/I.* Eds. J. Feiner and M. Löhrer. Brescia: Queriniana, 1972, 577-635.

Sanks, T. Howland. "Forms of Ecclesiality: The Analogical Church." *Theological Studies* 49 (1988), 695-708.

Schillebeeckx, Edward. *Christ: The Experience of Jesus as Lord.* Trans. John Bowden. New York: Crossroad, 1981.

_____. *The Church with a Human Face: A New and Expanded Theology of Ministry.* Trans. John Bowden. London: SCM Press, 1985.

_____. *Church: The Human Story of God.* Trans.: John Bowden. London: SCM Press, 1990.

Schmaus, Michael. *Dogma Vol.4: The Church: Its Origin and Structure.* London: Sheed and Ward, 1972.

Segundo, Jean Luis. *The Community Called Church.* Trans. John Drury. Maryknoll, N.Y.: Orbis Books, 1973.

Sharkey, Michael, ed. *International Theological Commission: Texts and Documents (1969-1985).* San Francisco: Ignatius Press, 1989.

Stacpoole, Alberic, ed. *Vatican II: By Those Who Were There.* London: Geoffrey Chapman, 1986.

Sullivan, Francis A. *The Church We Believe In.* New York/Mahwah: Paulist Press, 1988.

_____. *Salvation Outside the Church?* New York/Mahwah: Paulist Press, 1992.

Synod of Bishops (1985). *A Message to the People of God* and *The Final Report.* Washington, D.C.: NCCB, 1986.

Synod of Bishops (1987). "The Synod Propositions." *Origins* 17/29 (1987), 503-509.

Tillard, Jean-Marie. "Final Report of the Last Synod." *Concilium* 188 (1986), 64-77.

_____. *Eglise d'églises.* Paris: Cerf, 1987.

Thornhill, John. *Sign and Promise: A Theology of the Church for a Changing World.* London: Collins, 1988.

Vorgrimler, Herbert. (Ed.) *Commentary on the Documents of Vatican II.* 5 Vols. Trans. L. Adolphus et al. New York: Herder and Herder, 1969.

Winter, Michael. *What Ever Happened to Vatican II?* London: Sheed and Ward, 1985.

Zizioulas, J.D. *Being as Communion: Studies in Personhood and the Church.* Crestwood, N.Y.: St. Vladimir, 1980.

III. PARISH LIFE IN NORTH AMERICA—MODERNITY AND SECULARIZATION—LAY MOVEMENTS AND ASSOCIATIONS

Anderson, W.A. *R.C.I.A.: A Total Parish Process.* Dubuque: W. C. Brown, 1988.

Arinze, Francis. "The Challenge of New Religious Movements." *Origins* 20/46 (April 25, 1991), 748-53.

Balke, Victor H. "The Parish Pastoral Council." *Origins* 16/47 (1987), 821-825.

Baum, Gregory. *The Church in Quebec.* Ottawa, Ont.: Novalis, 1991.

Bausch, William J. *The Christian Parish: Whispers of the Risen Christ.* Notre Dame, In.: Fides/Claretian, 1980.

Bellah, Robert N. et al. *Habits of the Heart: Individualism and Commitment in American Life.* Berkeley: University of California Press, 1985.

Berger, Peter. *The Sacred Canopy.* Garden City, N.Y.: Doubleday, 1967.

Berger, Peter and Richard J. Neuhaus. *To Empower People* Washington, D.C.: American Enterprise Institute, 1977.

Blachnicki, F. et al. *I Movimenti nella Chiesa.* Milano: Jaca Book, 1981.

Boyd, Malcolm. *The Underground Church.* New York: Sheed and Ward, 1968.

Brennan, Patrick J. *Re-imagining the Parish.* New York: Crossroad, 1990.

Byers, David, ed. *The Parish in Transition: Proceedings of a Conference on the American Catholic Parish.* Washington, D.C.: NCCB, 1985, 222-252.

Campbell, Debra, "The Heyday of Catholic Action and the Lay Apostolate (1929-1959)." In *Transforming Parish Ministry.* Ed. Jay Dolan et al. New York: Crossroad, 1990, 222-252.

Castelli, Jim and Joseph Gremillion. *The Emerging Parish: The Notre Dame Study of Catholic Life Since Vatican II.* San Francisco: Harper and Row, 1987.

Champlin, Joseph M. *The Living Parish.* Notre Dame, IN: Ave Maria Press, 1977.

Clark, Stephen B. *Building Christian Communities.* Notre Dame, IN.: Ave Maria Press, 1972.

_____. (ed.) *Patterns of Christian Community.* Ann Arbor, MI.: Servant Books, 1984.

Coleman, John. "Values and Virtues in Advanced Modern Societies." *Concilium* 191 (1987); 3-13.

Commission d'étude sur les laïcs l'Église, *Histoire de l'Église catholique au Québec(1608-1970).* Montreal: Fides, 1971.

Comité de recherche de l'assemblée des évêques du Québec sur les communautés Chrétiennes locales. *Risquer l'avenir.* Montreal: Fides, 1992.

Committee on the Parish. *The Parish: A People, A Mission, A Structure.* Washington, D.C.: NCCB, 1980.

Currier, Richard. *Restructuring the Parish.* Chicago: Argus Press, 1967.

Dolan, Jay P. *The American Catholic Experience: From Colonial Times to the Present.* Garden City, N.Y.: Doubleday, 1985.

_____. *The History of the American Catholic Parish: From 1850 to the Present,* 2 Vols. New York/Mahwah : Paulist Press, 1987.

Dolan, Jay P. and Jeffrey Burns, "The Parish in the American Past." *Parish Ministry* 3/5 (1982), 1-4.

Dianich, Severino. "Le nuove communità e la 'grande chiesa': un problema ecclesiologico." *Scola cattolica* 116 (1988), 512-29.

Dulles, Avery. "Catholicism and American Culture: The Uneasy Dialogue." *America* (Jan. 27, 1990), 54-59.

Dumont, Fernand. "Crise d'une Église, crise d'une société." In *Situation et avenir du Catholicisme Québécois,* Vol II: *entre temple et l'exil.* Eds. Fernand Dumont et al. Ottawa: Leméac, 1982, 3-48.

Farnleiter, Johannes. "Developments in the Lay Apostolate During the Last 20 Years and Challenges Arising for the Laity." *The Laity Today* 32/33 (1989-90), 9-20.

Fichter, Joseph H. "Parochial Realities in America." In *A Sociologist Looks at Religion.* Wilmington, Del.: Michael Glazier, 1988.

Fossion, André. "Faith in a Secularized Society." *Pro Mundi Vita Bulletin* 14 (1990), 17-25.

Gallup, jr., George and Jim Castelli. *The American Catholic People: Their Beliefs, Practices, and Values.* Garden City, N.Y.: Doubleday and Company, 1987.

Geaney, Dennis J. *The Prophetic Parish: A Center for Peace and Justice.* Minneapolis: Winston, 1983.

_____. *Quest for Community: Tomorrow's Parish Today.* Notre Dame, IN: Ave Maria Press, 1987.

Ghirlanda, Gianfranco. "Movements Within the Ecclesial Communion and Their Rightful Autonomy." *The Laity Today: Bulletin of the Pontifical Council for the Laity.* 32-33 (1989-90), 46-71.

Gilkey, Langdon. *Catholicism Confronts Modernity.* New York: Seabury Press, 1975.

Gómez, Felipe. "The Parish: Reality—Problems—Expectations." *East Asian Pastoral Review* 3 (1988), 203-211.

Greeley, Andrew M. *The American Catholic: A Social Portrait.* New York: Basic Books, 1977.

Greeley, Andrew M. et al. *Parish, Priest and People.* Chicago: Thomas More Press, 1981.

Gremillion, J., ed. *The Church and Culture since Vatican II: The Experience of North and Latin America.* University of Notre Dame Press, 1985.

Grichting, Wolfgang L. *Parish Structure and Climate in an Era of Change: A Sociologist's Inquiry*. Washington, D.C.: The Centre for Applied Research in the Apostolate, 1969.

Gustafson, James M. *Treasure in Earthen Vessels*. New York: Harper and Row, 1961.

Hauerwas, Stanley and William H. Willimon. *Resident Aliens: Life in the Christian Colony*. Nashville: Abington Press, 1989.

Herman, Richard R. *A Cultural Approach to Christian Community*. Akron, OH.: Bread of Life, 1991.

Hitchcock, James. *Catholicism and Modernity*. New York: Seabury Press, 1979.

Jacoby, John. "A Parish Renewal Program: Christ Renews His Parish." In *Evangelization Portrait of the Month*. Washington, D.C.: Paulist Catholic Evangelization Center, (n.d.), 11-15.

John Paul II. "The Parish: Family of Families." Discourse to the Hispanic Community in San Antonio, Texas, Sept. 13, 1987. *Origins* 17/17 (1987), 288-289.

Kavanagh, Aidan. *The Shape of Baptism: The Rite of Christian Initiation*. New York: Pueblo, 1978.

Kavanaugh, John F. *Following Christ in a Consumer Society*. Maryknoll, N.Y.: Orbis Books, 1984.

Kelly, G. "The Parish: New Life from Old Roots." *Clergy Review* 64 (1979), 45-59.

Kolvenbach, Peter-Hans. "The Christian Life Community." *Harvest* 24/2 (1991), 21-22.

Larsen, Earnest. *Spiritual Growth: Key to Parish Renewal*. Liguori, Mo.: Liguori Publications, 1978.

Leckey, Dolores R. *Laity Stirring the Church: Prophetic Questions*. Philadelphia: Fortress Press, 1987.

Lemieux, Raymond. "Le catholicisme québécois: une question de culture." *Sociologie et sociétés* 22/2 (1990), 145-164.

Lynch, John. "The Parochial Ministry in the New Code of Canon Law." *The Jurist* XLII (1982), 383-421.

Lyons, Bernard. *Parish Councils: Renewing the Christian Community*. Techny, Ill.: DWP 1967.

May, John. "Parishes in the Laity's Life." *Origins* 17/20 (Oct. 29, 1987), 353-356.

Marcoux, Marcene. *Cursillo: Anatomy of a Movement*. New York: Lambeth Press, 1982.

Martin, Ralph. "Sects Education." *New Covenant* (Oct. 1991), 26-27.

Marty, Martin E., ed. *Death and Birth of the Parish*. St. Louis: Concordia, 1964.

Mathey, Chuck. *Successful CFM Leadership*. Ames: Christian Family Movement, 1988.

McBrien, Richard P. "Catholicism: The American Experience." In *American Catholics.* Ed. Joseph P. Kelly. Wilmington, Del.: Michael Glazier, 1989, 7-25.

McCauley, George. *The God of the Group.* Niles, Ill.: Argus Communications, 1975.

McCready, William. "The Local Parish Community and Religious Socialization." *Chicago Studies* 20/3 (1981), 253-266.

McCudden, John, ed. *The Parish in Crisis.* Techny, IL.: Divine Word Publications, 1967.

McElroy, Robert W. *John Courtney Murray and the Secular Crisis: Foundations for an American Catholic Public Theology.* Doctoral Dissertation. Rome: Pontificia Universitas Gregoriana, 1990.

Murnion, Philip J. "Strategies for Parish Renewal." In *The Parish Project Reader.* Washington, D.C.: NCCB, 1982, 45-54.

_____. "Parish Renewal: State(ments) of the Question." *America* 146 (1982), 14-17.

_____. "The Community Called Parish." *Church* 1/4 (1985), 8-14. Naisbitt, John. *Megatrends.* New York: Warner Books, 1982.

Niebuhr, H. Richard. *Christ and Culture.* New York: Harper and Brothers, 1951.

Ottenweller, Albert. "A Call to Restructure the Parish." *Clergy Report* (April 1976), 10-11.

_____. "Parish Renewal: A Process, Not a Program." *Origins* 8/42 (1979), 672-676.

Palmer, Parker J. *The Company of Strangers.* New York: Crossroad, 1986.

Paré, Ulysse E. "The Catholic Church in Canada." *The Canadian Catholic Review* 4/7 (1986), 247-253.

Parish Project. *Parish Development: Programs and Organizations.* Washington, D.C.: NCCB, 1980.

_____. *The Parish Project Reader: Selected Articles From the Parish Ministry Newsletter 1979-1982.* Washington, D.C.: NCCB, 1982.

_____. *Parish Life in the United States: Final Report to the Bishops of the United States by the Parish Project.* Washington, D.C.: NCCB, 1983.

Peck, M. Scott. *The Different Drum: Community Making and Peace.* New York: Simon and Schuster, 1987.

Philibert, Paul. "Human Development and Sacramental Transformation." *Worship* 65/6 (1991), 522-39.

Pilarczck, Daniel. "Does the Church Flourish in Its Parishes?" *Origins* 16/39 (1987), 681-686.

Poulin, Calvin H. "The Parish in Transition." *East Asian Pastoral Review* 3 (1988), 212-232.

Power, David N. "Households of Faith in the Coming Church." *Worship* 57 (1983), 237-255.

252 \ *Small Christian Communities and the Parish*

Provencher, Normand. "The Family as Domestic Church." *Theology Digest* 30/2 (1982), 149-152.

Ranaghan, Kevin and Dorothy, eds. *As the Spirit Leads Us.* New York: Paulist Press, 1971.

Reilly, John. "The Mission of the Parish." *East Asian Pastoral Review* 3 (1988), 270-301.

Rohr, Richard and Joseph Martos. "Parish Renewal in the 1990s." *Pastoral Life* 40/1 (1991), 2-7.

Scola, Angelo. "Associations and Movements in the Communion and Mission of the Church." *The Laity Today: Bulletin of the Pontifical Council for the Laity.* 32/33 (1989-90), 37-45.

Secretariat for Promoting Christian Unity. *Sects or New Religious Movements.* Rome, May 3, 1986. Trans. NCCB Office of Publishing and Promotion Services, Washington, D.C.

Searle, Mark. "The Notre Dame Study of Catholic Parish Life."*Worship* 60 (1986), 312-333.

Sweetser, Thomas P. *Successful Parishes: How They Meet the Challenge of Change.* Minneapolis: Winston Press, 1983.

_____. "The Parish of the Future: Beyond the Programs." *America* (March 10, 1990), 238-240.

Vanier, Jean. *Community and Growth: Our Pilgrimage Together.* Toronto: Griffen House, 1979.

Walsh, Eugene A. "The Church Makes the Eucharist; The Eucharist Makes the Church." *Church* 2/3 (1986), 24-30.

Ward, Leo R. *Catholic Life, U.S.A.: Contemporary Lay Movements.* St. Louis: B. Herder, 1959.

Whitehead, Evelyn E., ed. *The Parish in Community and Ministry.* New York: Paulist Press, 1978.

Whitehead, Evelyn E. and James D. *Community of Faith: Models and Strategies for Developing Christian Community.* Minneapolis: Winston Press, 1982.

Yuhaus, Cassian, ed. *The Catholic Church and American Culture.* New York/Mahwah: Paulist Press, 1990.

PART TWO: SMALL CHRISTIAN COMMUNITIES

I. SCCs AROUND THE WORLD: EMERGENCE, CHARACTERISTICS, AND ECCLESIOLOGICAL REFLECTION

AMECEA, "1979 Plenary Study Conference: Building Small Christian Communities," and "Conclusions to the 1976 Conference," *African Ecclesial Review* 21/5 (1979), 257-272; and 310-316.

Azevedo, Marcello de Carvalho. "Basic Ecclesial Communities: A Meeting Point of Ecclesiologies." *Theological Studies* 46 (1985), 601-620.

_____. *Basic Ecclesial Communities in Brazil: The Challenge of a New Way of Being Church.* Trans. John Drury. Washington, D.C.: Georgetown University Press, 1987.

Barreiro, Alvaro. *Basic Ecclesial Communities: The Evangelization of the Poor.* Trans. B. Campbell. New York: Orbis Books, 1982.

Birondo, Ruben. "Basic Christian Communities: The Experience of the Philippines." *The Clergy Review* 70 (1985), 249-252.

Boff, Clodovis. "The Nature of Basic Christian Communities." *Concilium* 144 (1981), 53-58.

Boff, Leonardo. "Theological Characteristics of a Grassroots Church." in *The Challenge of Basic Christian Communities.* Eds. Sergio Torres and John Eagleson. Trans John Drury. Maryknoll, N.Y.: Orbis Books, 1981, 124-50.

_____. *Church: Charism and Power.* Trans. John Diercksmeier. New York: Crossroad, 1985.

_____. *Ecclesiogenesis: The Base Communities Reinvent the Church.* Trans. R. Barr. Maryknoll, N.Y.: Orbis Books, 1986.

Bruneau, Thomas C. "Basic Christian Communities in Latin America: Their Nature and Significance (Especially in Brazil)." In *Churches and Politics in Latin America.* Ed. Daniel H. Levine Beverly Hills, Ca.: Sage Publications, 1981, 225-237.

Cadorette, Curt. "Basic Christian Communities: Their Social Role and Missiological Promise." *Missiology* 15 (1987), 17-30.

CELAM. *1968 Medellin Conference—Final Document.* Trans. Washington, D.C.: NCCB, 1970.

_____. *1979 Puebla Conference—Final Document.* Trans. Washington, D.C.: NCCB, 1980.

_____. *1992 Santo Domingo Conference—Final Document.* Trans. Bologna: Dehoniane, 1992.

Clarke, Tony. "Communities for Justice." *The Ecumenist* 19 (1981), 17-25.

Claver, Francisco. "Basic Christian Communities in the Wider Context." *Pastoral Review* 23/2 (1986), 362-368.

Comblin, Joseph. *The Meaning of Mission: Jesus, Christians, and the Wayfaring Church.* Trans. John Drury. Maryknoll, N.Y.: Orbis, 1977.

Congregation for the Doctrine of the Faith. "Instruction on Certain Aspects of the Theology of Liberation." *Origins* (1984), 193-204.

Deelen, Gottfried. "The Church on its Way to the People: Basic Christian Communities in Brazil." *Pro Mundi Vita Bulletin* 81 (1980), 2-18.

Edele, A. "Establishing Basic Christian Communities in Lusaka, Zambia." *Pro Vita Mundi Bulletin* 81 (1980), 21-25.

Fraser, Ian and Margaret. *Wind and Fire—The Spirit Reshapes the Church in Basic Christian Communities.* Dunblane, Scotland: Basic Communities Resource Centre, 1986.

Freire, Paulo. *Pedagogy of the Oppressed.* Trans. M.B. Ramos. New York: Seabury Press, 1970.

Gallo, Jeanne. *Basic Ecclesial Communities: A New Form of Christian Organizational Response to the World Today.* Doctoral Dissertation: Boston University, 1989.

Gichiawa Mwaniki, Francis. *The Small Christian Communities and Human Liberation: With Special Reference to the AMECEA Countries.* Doctoral Dissertation. Rome: Pontificia Universitas Lateranense, 1986.

Goodwin, Lawrence. "The Trouble with Basic Communities." *African Ecclesial Review* 23 (1981), 338-343.

Grootaers, Jan. "Laity in the Field: Polarities and Convergences." *Pro Vita Mundi Bulletin* 110/3 (1987), 2-34.

Guiney, John. "Comparing BCCs in S. America and Africa." *African Ecclesial Review* 30 (1988), 167-180.

Gutiérrez, Gustavo. *A Theology of Liberation.* Trans. C. Inda and J. Eagleson. Maryknoll, N.Y.: Orbis, 1973.

Healey, Joseph. " Basic Christian Communities in Africa and in Latin America." *African Ecclesial Review* 26 (1984), 222-232.

_____. "BCCs in the 1987 Synod of Bishops' Documents." *African Ecclesial Review* 30 (1988), 74-86.

_____. "The Option for Small Christian Communities," *Pro Vita Mundi Bulletin* 12 (1989-90), 11-12.

_____. "Today's New Way of Being Church: Pastoral Implications of the Small Christian Community Model of Church in the World Towards the 21st Century." *African Christian Studies* 7/1 (1991), 63-77.

_____. "Evolving a World Church From the Bottom Up." Background Paper Presented at the *International Consultation on Basic Christian Communities*, University of Notre Dame, IN. Dec. 8-12, 1991, 1-30.

Hearne, Brian. "Priestly Ministry and Christian Community." *African Ecclesial Review* 24 (1982), 221-233.

_____. "Small Christian Communities—Let's Go Ahead!" *African Ecclesial Review* 26 (1984), 262-273.

Hebblethwaite, Margaret. "Base Communities and the Parish." *The Tablet.* 4 Part Series (April 16, 23, 30, and May 7, 1988).

Hetsen, Jac. "The Brazilian CEBs Sixth Assembly." *African Ecclesial Review* 30 (1988), 40-43.

Hewitt, W.E. "Christian Base Communities (CEBs): Structure, Orientation, and Sociopolitical Thrust." *Thought* 63 (1988), 162-175.

Hoeben, Harry. "Basic Christian Communities in Africa." *Pro Mundi Vita Bulletin* 81 (1980), 19-21.

Hoffman, Virginia. *Birthing a Living Church.* New York: Crossroad, 1988.

Holmes-Siedle, James. "Over-view of Small Christian Communities in East Africa." *African Ecclesial Review* 21/5 (1979), 273-285.

International Council for Catechesis. *Adult Catechesis in the Christian Community.* Rome: Libreria Editrice Vaticana, 1990.

Jenkinson, William and Helene O'Sullivan, eds. *Trends in Mission: Toward the Third Millennium.* Maryknoll, N.Y.: Orbis, 1991.

John Paul II. *Catechesi Tradendae. AAS* 71 (1979), 1277-1340. (Trans.—Ottawa: CCCB, 1979).

_____. "Message for Basic Christian Communities." *Origins* 10/9 (1980), 140-141.

_____. *Familiaris Consortio. AAS* 74 (1982), 81-191. (Trans.—Boston: St. Paul Books, 1981).

_____. *Christifideles Laici. AAS* 81 (1989), 393-521. (Trans.—Boston: St. Paul Books, 1989).

_____. *Redemptoris Missio. AAS* 83 (1991), 249-340. (Trans.—Boston: St. Paul Books, 1991).

_____. "Ad Limina Address to the Bishops of Frances' Midi Region," *L'Osservatore Romano* (English Edition, April 15, 1992), pp. 2-3.

Kalilombe, Patrick A. "Building Christian Communities." *Lumen Vitae* 32 (1977), 175-196.

_____. *From Outstations to Small Christian Communities.* Eldoret, Kenya: Gaba Publications, 1984.

Kalonji Ntekesha, A. *Les communautes ecclesiales de base: Foyers d'un Christianisme Africain?* Doctoral Dissertation. Rome: Pontificia Universitas Gregoriana, 1983.

Kelly, James. "The Evolution of Small Christian Communities." *African Ecclesial Review* 33 (1991), 108-120.

Kerkhofs, J. "Basic Communities in the Church." *Pro Mundi Vita Bulletin* 62 (1976), 2-32.

Kiriswa, Benjamin. "Small Christian Communities in a Kenyan Parish." *African Ecclesial Review* 24 (1982), 90-93.

Labayen, Julio X. "Basic Christian Communities." *African Ecclesial Review* 30 (1988), 135-144.

LaPointe, Eugène. *Une expérience pastorale en Afrique australe.* Paris: Editions L'Harmattan, 1985.

Lawrence, Fred. "Basic Christian Community: An Issue of 'Mind and the Mystery of Christ.'" *Lonergan Workshop, Vol. 5.* Ed. Fred Lawrence. Chico, CA.: Scholars Press, 1985, 263-285.

Lobinger, Fritz. *Building Small Christian Communities.* South Africa: Lumko Missiological Institute, 1981.

Losigo Kulu, A. *Perspectives eccesiologiques en Afrique Noire Francophone.* Doctoral Dissertation. Rome: Pontificia Universitas Gregoriana, 1991.

MacEoin, Gary and Nivita Riley. *Puebla: a Church Being Born.* New York: Paulist Press, 1980.

Mandefu, Kambuyi. *L'impact d'un discours anthropothéocentrique sur les Communautés Ecclésiales Vivantes.* Doctoral Dissertation. Rome: Pontificia Facolta Teologica Teresianum, 1990.

Marins, José et al. *Basic Ecclesial Communities: The Church from the Roots.* Philippines: Claretian Publications, 1983.

Marins, José et al. "The Church in Latin America: Basic Christian Communities." in *Trends in Mission.* Eds. W. Jenkinson and H. O'Sullivan. Maryknoll, N.Y.: Orbis Books, 1991, 63-73.

Metz, Johann B. "Base-church and Bourgeois Religion." *Theological Digest* 29/3 (1981), 203-206.

National Conference of Brazilian Bishops Permanent Council. *As Comunidades Eclesiais de Base na Igreja do Brazil.* San Paolo: Paulinas, 1982.

O'Brien, Niall. "Basic Christian Communities and the Parish—A Six-Year Parish Experiment." *Furrow* 35 (1984), 92-102.

O'Halloran, James. *Living Cells: Developing Small Christian Communities.* Dublin: Dominican Publications, 1984.

————. "The Ecclesiology of Small Christian Communities." *The Outlook* 21 (1988), 102-106.

————. *Signs of Hope: Developing Small Christian Communities.* Maryknoll, N.Y.: Orbis Books, 1991.

Okeyo, Vitalis. "Small Christian Communities in Kisii—A New Way of Being Church." *African Ecclesial Review* 23 (1983), 226-229.

Paul VI. *Evangelii Nuntiandi.* AAS 68 (1976), 5-76. (Trans.—Boston: St. Paul Books, 1976).

Perrin Jassy, Marie-France. *Basic Community in the African Churches.* Trans. J. M. Lyons. Maryknoll, N.Y.: Orbis, 1973.

Regan, David. *Church for Liberation: A Pastoral Portrait of the Church in Brazil.* Dublin: Dominican Publications, 1987.

Ruether, Rosemary. "Basic Communities: Renewal at the Roots." *Christianity and Crisis* 41/14 (1981), 234-37.

Sanks, T. Howland, and Brian H. Smith. "Liberation Ecclesiology." *Theological Studies* 38 (1977), 3-38.

Schaull, Richard. *Heralds of a New Reformation.* Maryknoll, N.Y.: Orbis Books, 1984.

————. "The Christian Base Communities and the Ecclesia Reformata Semper Reformanda." *The Princeton Seminary Bulletin* 12 (1991), 201-213.

Torres, Sergio and John Eagleson, eds. *The Challenge of Basic Christian Communities.* Trans. John Drury. Maryknoll, N.Y.: Orbis Books, 1981.

Twinomugisha, Silverio. *Ecclesiological Meaning of Small ChristianCommunities in Uganda Today.* Doctoral Dissertation. Rome: Pontificia Universitas Urbaniana, 1991.

Ugeux, Bernard. *Les petites communautés Chrétiennes: Une alternative aux paroisses?* Paris: Cerf, 1988.

Unknown. "Basic Christian Communities in Europe." *Pro Mundi Vita Bulletin* 81 (1980), 30-38.

Valera, Edmundo. "Theology of Struggle: The Philippines' Ecclesial Experience." *New Theology Review* 5/2 (1992), 62-83.

Winter, Michael. *Blueprint for a Working Church: A Study in New Pastoral Structures.* St. Meinrad, In.: Abbey Press, 1973.

II. NORTH AMERICAN PARISH-BASED SCCs: EMERGENCE, CHARACTERISTICS, AND ECCLESIOLOGICAL REFLECTION

Baldwin, Robert F. "Think Small." *New Covenant* (Nov. 1991), 7-12.

Baranowski, Arthur R. *Creating Small Faith Communities.* Cincinnati: St. Anthony Messenger Press, 1988.

_____. *Pastoring the Pastors.* Cincinatti: St. Anthony Messenger Press, 1988.

_____. *Praying Alone and Together.* Cincinatti: St. Anthony Messenger Press, 1988.

_____. "Small Christian Communities and the Parish." *Church* 5/4 (1989), 38-40.

Blueher, Rosemary. "Creating Our Future: A Prophetic Way of Being Church." *Gifts* (Summer 1990), 1-8.

_____. "A Response to a Paradigm Shift: The North American Forum for Small Christian Communities." *PACE* 21 (1991), 115-118.

_____. "Shared Leadership as Experienced in Small Christian Communities." *The Catholic World* (July/August 1991), 161-65.

Brady, Patricia C. *Has Anything Really Changed? A Study: The Diocese of Victoria since Vatican II.* Winfield, B.C.: Wood Lake Books, 1986.

Buena Vista. "Mission Statement." *Today's Parish.* (Sept. 1990), 16.

_____. *The Buena Vista Resource Book.* Arvada, CO.: Buena Vista, 1991.

_____. *Newsletter* (1987-Present). Arvada, Colorado Caroluzza, Thomas. *Parish Catechumenate: Pastors, Presiders and Preachers.* Chicago: Liturgy Training Publications, 1988.

Cho, Paul Yonggi. *Successful Home Cell Groups.* Plainfield, N.J.: Logos International, 1981.

Coleman, Lyman and Marty Scales. *Serendipity Training Manual for Groups.* Littleton, Co.: Serendipity Publications, 1988.

Collins, Raymond F. "Small Groups: An Experience of Church." *Louvain Studies* 13 (1988), 109-136.

Collins, Robert W. *The American Church at the Crossroads: Towards Imaging a New Paradigm of Local Church in the United States.* Licentiate Dissertation. Rome: Pontificia Universitas Gregoriana, 1989.

Comité de recherche de l'assemblée des Éveques du Québec sur les communautés chrétiennes locales, *Risquer L'Avenir.* Montreal: Éditions Fides, 1992.

Cooney, Tom. "Parish Cells." *Intercom* (Dec. 1990), 14-15.

Deck, Allan F. *Hispanic Ministry in the United States: Pastoral-Theological Research.* Doctoral Dissertation. Rome: Pontificia Universitas Gregoriana, 1988.

_____. *The Second Wave: Hispanic Ministry and the Evangelization of Cultures.* New York/Mahwah: Paulist Press, 1989.

Diocèse de Saint-Jean-de-Quebec. *Les petits groupes et le projet communautaire dans l'église.* Montreal: Éditions Fides, 1980.

Eivers, Michael J. and A. Perry Vitale. *St. Boniface Church Parish Cell System: Leaders' Training Manual.* Pembroke Pines, Fla.: St. Boniface Catholic Church, 1991 (Revised edition).

Fitzpatrick, Bishop John J. *Base Communities of Faith.* Diocese of Brownsville, Texas: Pastoral Letter, May 6, 1990.

Gaillardetz, Richard. "Base Communities: Where Does the Parish Fit in?" *Today's Parish* (Jan. 1990), 11-13.

Ghezzi, Bert. "A Parish with Pizzazz." *Charisma and Christian Life* (Oct. 1989), 80-83.

Hartford Diocese Pastoral Dept. for Small Christian Communities. *Guidebook.* Bloomfield, CT., 1989.

Hennelly, Alfred. "Grassroots Communities: A New Model of Church?" In *Tracing the Spirit: Communities, Social Action, and Theological Reflection.* Ed. James Hug. New York: Paulist Press, 1983, 60-82.

Hurley, Archbishop Dennis. *Address to the International RENEW Convocation.* Raleigh, June 1989.

International Consultation on Basic Christian Communities. *Final Statement.* Institute for Pastoral and Social Ministry -University of Notre Dame, Dec. 8-12, 1991.

Ivory, Thomas P. *Conversion and Community: A Catechumenal Model for Total Parish Formation.* New York/Mahwah: Paulist Press, 1988.

Kelly, James. "Does the RENEW Program Really Renew?" *America* (March 7, 1987), 197-199.

Kilian, David, "How to Develop Basic Christian Communities in Your Parish or Diocese." In *Handbook for Developing Basic Christian Communities.* Ed. National Federation of Priests' Councils. Chicago: NFPC, 1979, 14-17.

Kleissler, Thomas A., Margo A. LeBert and Mary C. McGuinness. *Small Christian Communities: A Vision of Hope.* New York/Mahwah: Paulist Press, 1991.

_____. *Resources for Small Christian Communities.* New York/Mahwah: Paulist Press, 1991.

Lee, Bernard. "The Eucharist and Intentional Christian Communities." *Alternative Futures for Worship. Vol. 3,* Ed. B. Lee. Collegeville, MN.: The Liturgical Press, 1987, 11-15.

Lee, Bernard and Michael Cowan. *Dangerous Memories: House Churches and Our American Story.* Kansas City: Sheed and Ward, 1986.

Maney, Thomas. *Basic Communities: A Practical Guide for Renewing Neighborhood Churches.* Minneapolis: Winston Press, 1984.

Mayer, Henry C. "A Close Up of RENEW." *Pastoral Life* 36/8 (1987), 12-27.

Milwaukee Diocese Office of Adult and Family Ministry. *Living the Vision: A Handbook on Small Groups.* Milwaukee, 1990.

Monette, Maurice L. *RENEW Small Group Leader's Workbook.* New York/Mahwah: Paulist Press, 1990.

National Alliance of Parishes Restructuring into Communities. *Newsletter (1988-Present).* Troy, Michigan.

National Federation of Priests' Councils. *Handbook for Developing Basic Christian Communities.* Chicago: NFPC, 1979.

_____. *Basic Christian Communities: The United States Experience.* Chicago: NFPC, 1983.

National Office of RENEW. *RENEW: An Overview.* Ramsey, N.J.: Paulist Press, 1988.

_____. *Seven Questions about RENEW.* Ramsey, N.J.: Paulist Press, 1984.

NCCB. *The Hispanic Presence: Challenge and Commitment.* Pastoral Letter on Hispanic Ministry. Washington, D.C.: NCCB, Nov. 12, 1983.

_____. *National Pastoral Plan for Hispanic Ministry.* Washington, D.C.: NCCB, 1987.

NCCB Committee on Doctrine. "The RENEW Process: Strengths and Areas for Improvement." *Origins* 16/30 (1987), 547-549.

Newell, William. "The Reflection Groups." In *Tracing the Spirit: Communities, Social Action, and Theological Reflection.* Ed. James Hug. New York: Paulist Press, 1983, 38-59.

North American Forum for Small Christian Communities. *Mission Statement.* Crookston, MN.: NAFSCC, 1988.

_____. *Theological Reflection on Small Christian Communities.* Crookston, MN.: NAFSCC, 1989.

_____. *Newsletter (1988-Present).* Waterdown, Ontario.

O'Brien, William. *Small Christian Communities: Canada 1991.* Waterdown, Ont.: Canadian Office of RENEW, 1991.

Pravera, Kate. "The United States: Realities and Responses." *Christianity and Crisis* 41\14 (1981), 251-255.

Quebec Bishops. *Towards a More Fraternal and Communal Church. 1987* Pastoral Letter.

Quintaville, Bev. *Year End Report (July 1990—July 1991).* Archdiocese of Saint Paul-Minneapolis, Office of Evangelization, Dept. of Small Faith Communities.

Reid, Clyde. *Groups Alive—Church Alive: The Effective Use of Small Groups in the Local Church.* New York: Harper and Row, 1969.

Secretariat for Hispanic Affairs. *Proceedings of the II Encuentro Nacional Hispano de Pastoral.* Washington, D.C.: NCCB, 1978.

_____. *Basic Ecclesial Communities: An Experience in the United States.* Ligouri, Mo.: NCCB, 1980.

_____. *Guidelines for Establishing Basic Christian Communities in the United States.* Ligouri, Mo.: NCCB, 1981.

_____. *Prophetic Voices: The Document on the Process of the III Encuentro Nacional Hispano de Pastoral.* Washington, D.C.: NCCB, 1986.

_____. [Draft] *Guidelines for Small Church-Based Communities.* Washington, D.C.: NCCB, 1991.

Systematic Integral New Evangelization (SINE) Team. *People of God.* Rockford, Illinois: SINE Publications, 1990.

_____. *What does SINE Really Mean?* Rockford, Illinois: SINE Publications, 1990.

Texas Bishops. *Mission Texas: A Pastoral Letter on Evangelization.* March, 1989.

Timlin, Bishop James. "The Welcoming Church: A Pastoral Vision." *Origins* 20/36 (1991), 596-600.

Tomonto, Bob and Irene. "Basic Christian Communities: The Christian Family Movement Model." In *Basic Christian Communities: The United States Experience.* Ed. National Federation of Priests' Councils. Chicago: NFPC, 1983, 42-43.

Westley, R. "Base Communities in the United States." *Concilium* 9 (1975), 35-42.